D0596960

LOADED DICE

LOADED
DICE
The True Story of a Casino Cheat

JOHN SOARES

TAYLOR PUBLISHING COMPANY
DALLAS, TEXAS

Copyright © 1985 by Taylor Publishing Company

Library of Congress Cataloging in Publication Data

Soares, John.
    Loaded dice.

    1. Soares, John. 2. Gamblers — Nevada — Biography.
3. Gambling — Nevada — Las Vegas.   I. Title.
HV6721.L3S63 1985   364.1'72'0924 [B]   85-8160
ISBN 0-87833-460-2

Printed in the United States of America

First Edition   1 2 3 4 5 6 7 8 9 0

ACKNOWLEDGMENTS

I want to thank Judy Hoffman, Debi Coleman, Stuart Fink, Rudy Navarro, Gus Nichol, Harry Crow, Lake Headley, Nick Goodman, David Jones, Bob Johnson, Charlie McNealy, Jimmy DeFord, Charles Zed, Ethan, Micah and Lea Lewis, Terri Hoffman, John Joseph Soares, Carol Navarro, J. B. and his wife Charmaine, Tiffany, Diana and Sam Osborne, Jim Gosdin, Richard Hedrick, Mark Munoz, Bob Frese, Kevin Howe, Bill Hoover, Bill and Mary Beth Wells, Jeff Cordrey, Norman and Nelda Lockhard, and especially Debi Soares and my children Billy, John, Jr., Laura Lee and Fred.

I am especially grateful to my brother, Richard Soares, for his determination in getting me to tell my story. Without his support and understanding, my years in Las Vegas and in casinos around the world may have been nothing more than a sucker's bet.

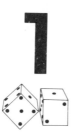

The crew came in three cars. It was best this way. It would attract too much attention if we all arrived in one car, and it could be disastrous later, should a hasty exit become necessary.

I rode this early September night with Glen Grayson, the heart and soul of our crew. The boss, if you will. Glen had hand-selected the seven members of the crew, as carefully and with as much consideration as a heart-transplant surgeon assembling his operating team. I don't recall other crew members ever arguing with him. It wasn't just his size — a rugged six feet four inches and 275 pounds — that discouraged debate, but the fact that, where our "business" was concerned, he was *always* right. No one wants to start an argument with an individual who can beat him physically *and* mentally.

It was 9:30 p.m. in heat-choked Las Vegas, and the oppressive desert air threatened to suffocate anyone foolish enough to stand out in it for long. The heat of southern Nevada seems to emanate from hell itself, and so would the fate that awaited us if we made the slightest slipup. We were headed for the Desert Inn, owned by the Cleveland mob (Howard Hughes had not yet moved in and exercised a cleansing effect). And the Boys from Ohio, a particularly virulent strain of the Syndicate, would not take kindly to what we had in mind: we intended to help ourselves to $20,000 of their money, a healthy amount of loot in the mid-1960s.

"Who are these two new people?" I said to Glen Grayson. It was cool in his Cadillac, the air-conditioner functioning as smoothly as the crew always had. Glen had just turned left from Charleston onto the Strip — Las Vegas Boulevard — and it would be only a one-mile straight run to the Desert Inn.

"Teddy and Lenny?" He glanced at me sideways. "They're okay."

"I don't like it," I said. "What if there's a screwup?" The Desert Inn goons wouldn't hesitate a second before burying us in the vast Nevada sandscape. They would break our legs first, though. As a lesson to others.

"Big Daddy knows what he's doing," Glen said, huffily. A lot of people called him Big Daddy and he liked the name. And no one who knew him would deny that this very clever, very audacious man knew what he was doing. Still, I was more nervous than usual. We could be killed if we got caught, and it seemed to me that two extra people joining the crew greatly increased the chances of that unhappy ending.

But there was no arguing with Glen. This was the first time in more than a year that I'd even questioned him. I looked now at his massive body, his unbelievably large and strong hands (many people could palm a playing card, Glen could palm a whole deck), and all I could manage was a sigh. I looked out the window at the neon lights of the Strip, Street of Dreams, and watched the Sahara go past.

"You met Teddy and Lenny," Glen Grayson said, his voice soft and conversational. Rather than get angry, he'd decided to use his considerable persuasive powers. He wanted to clear the way before the crew went into the Desert Inn. Our move would be as tensely executed as crossing a field of land mines. "What were your impressions of them?"

"I only met them for a few minutes. Not much more than a handshake. I get the idea they have money."

"Money and smarts. I'll tell you."

As we drove past the Riviera (owned by the Chicago mob), then the class of the Strip, Glen told me about Teddy Lewin. A friend of long standing, Teddy owned parts of casinos in London, Tokyo, Madrid, Portugal, Guatemala, and Ghana. Years before, Teddy had retained Glen to bankrupt a competitor by winning large amounts of money at craps. Glen had done it with such ease, and so impressed Teddy Lewin, that the casino owner went out of his way to cultivate a relationship. And for his part, as Glen pointed out, Teddy was a good man to know. He could point us toward some big scores, and if what it took was taking him along with us on one of our casino raids, that was a small enough price to pay.

"What if he messes up?" I wanted to know. "What if he panics?"

"He'll be okay," Glen said, showing what for him was remarkable restraint in submitting to having his judgment questioned. Glen told me that Teddy Lewin, now about sixty, had been a much-decorated World War II hero. He'd spent three and a half years in a Japanese prison camp and had survived the Bataan Death March. But more telling even than his own survival, his cool head, daring, and ingenuity were credited with helping others survive.

The mob or the Japanese, I mused. *I'm not sure which would be more dangerous.*

The Strip, unreal, bright as daylight, was strangely deserted for 9:40 p.m. on a Saturday. A few tourists ambled from one casino to the next, discussing what had gone wrong and how they would correct their mistakes. I knew it wouldn't happen. Something would occur to bring them to their knees again. What they were doing wasn't gambling, a word that means chance is involved. Chance didn't have anything to do with it. In every game in Nevada, the odds are tilted to guarantee the casino's success.

The streets wouldn't be empty for long. The 8:00 p.m. dinner shows would be letting out, and people would pour into the casinos. The crowds would be our cover. We intended to blend in with them, let them swallow us up, make us invisible.

"If Lewin is rich," I said, "why does he want to come with us?"

"Why do you?"

"The money," I said honestly.

"It's more than that," Glen said.

"It's the money with me," I said heatedly.

Glen Grayson smiled. This legendary casino cheat seemed at peace with himself. We went by the Old Frontier (now the New Frontier) and the Silver Slipper with its glittering Cinderella shoe. I wasn't really noticing. I'd begun to force my mind to focus on what lay ahead, to channel it into a sort of tunnel vision so clear and precisely directed that a mistake would be impossible. It wasn't unlike the concentration required of a knife thrower, I think, where the slightest error could mean the most terrible consequence. But more than tunnel vision: When we stepped inside the Desert Inn, my senses would need to be super-alert. I would have to call on extra-sensitive antennae to detect anything even vaguely amiss. This latter I couldn't force. I had to count on it happening when we set foot on enemy territory. It usually did.

Glen began talking about Lenny Hall, the other addition to our operation. I had met him before, and remembered him as being medium height and stocky with curly black hair. A big-time diamond dealer in Los Angeles, he was another who would be in on the play for sheer excitement. I figured it had to be the excitement for both Teddy and Lenny, the nerve-tingling thrill of the scam. Certainly neither had any compelling financial reason to be tagging along with us. All I could do was hope they didn't treat it as a lark. Bigshots or not, the Cleveland mob would treat them democratically, the same as anyone caught cheating.

I got out of the car in the Desert Inn parking lot and headed inside. Glen Grayson remained behind. There was no way he dared come in with me. Every casino in Nevada, each of whom he'd cheated countless times, knew his face, and he would have been surrounded by security personnel moments after entering. A disguise just wasn't practical. I could have gotten away with a disguise, had it been necessary, but not Glen, a large bear of a man. He liked nothing better than outwitting the wise guys who ran the casinos, but now he had done it so often, gone to the well so frequently, that he was reduced to masterminding the play, having to be satisfied with the vicarious enjoyment of knowing the crew he had selected and trained was doing the work for him. I thought about Glen as I made my advance foray into the Desert Inn: Even the most jaded observer would have to concede that our boss had had quite a run.

Born in 1920, Glen began his hustling career in Fort Worth, Texas, as a greenhorn youngster with dirt still behind his ears. He hustled his grammar-school friends out of their lunch money and his high-school buddies out of their date money. At age nine he was an acknowledged pool shark, and he could pitch a penny so accurately — or so I'm told, and I believe it — it would land on top of the one he had already thrown.

While in high school, Glen was a respected figure around legitimate poker games, games against men three and four times his age, and when the state of Texas outlawed the poker games Glen quit high school and moved to Chicago. He went from Cowtown to the City of Big Shoulders. Both were tough places in the 1930s.

In Chicago Glen met Jackie Gillitzer, now a member of our crew, and the two remained friends all their lives. They began cheating the slot machines in private clubs, using a small battery-powered drill and a fine wire to set the reels. It was primitive but very effective.

In 1945, when he was twenty-five years old, Glen moved on to Las Vegas and became a dealer. Before long he turned to hustling the casinos that once employed him.

Glen soon knew everyone in the gambling business and became familiar to insiders throughout Nevada by his nickname, King of the Crossroaders. A crossroader is so called because in Old West days the inns, where gambling flourished, were located at busy intersections — crossroads — where the hustlers gathered.

The people who knew and worked with Glen admired his ability to win the money. There wasn't a casino game he couldn't cheat. Even those who did not like him acknowledged his versatility and cunning. He could do it all, never dogged it, and was always there when it was time to work.

As I was leaving the car to head into the Desert Inn, Glen told me to "be careful," a warning he seldom felt was needed. Except for the unwelcome newcomers, Teddy and Lenny, I'd thought this would be just like all the other times when we simply went in, got the money, and strolled out. That "be careful" told me I'd really have to be on my toes. A "be careful" from Glen was the equivalent of five bell-ringing alarms from anyone else, and I wondered specifically what he feared.

I went into the Desert Inn from the side, or south, entrance, and the feeling took hold of me again. Every sense I possessed seemed suddenly alert, like a rabbit's in a field full of foxes. I wore no jewelry or flashy clothes, nothing to call attention to myself. My job on this initial venture into the casino was to get a look at the security guards, crap dealers, cocktail waitresses, pit bosses, floormen — anyone the crew might have encountered before, either in this casino or another one. I also wanted to see if there were any other crossroaders at work. It's not that we feared they would turn snitch on us, or in some manner give us away; we just didn't want anyone watching us and seeing what we were doing. We had a very special play we didn't want to share with anyone.

There were two or three sheriff's detectives I especially wanted to be certain were somewhere else. They had seen us win money several times before, and although they couldn't *prove* we were cheating, they *knew* we were. Win often enough, and the Boys from Cleveland, tipped off by a detective, wouldn't feel they needed proof.

I walked casually past the banks of slot machines played by little old ladies with the gray, walleyed look of exotic fish startled in the deepest part of the ocean. The machines themselves — no group was ever more rightly dubbed "bandits" — were filling with coins, rising and proliferating, like the magic mill that lies at the bottom of the sea, forever grinding salt. Occasionally I'd be tempted to tap one of the ladies on the shoulder, stop her furious arm movements for just a moment, and show her how *we* won jackpots. *Every time.* But the urge never lasted very long. I had the impression that if I ever did stop one of them, she would whirl on me and slug me with her handbag.

I walked past the cashier's cage and onto the main casino floor, mentally recording faces. The casino itself was like any other, just fancier and smelling of more money than the ones downtown or those in the outpost towns. As always, the setting seemed frozen in space, as if the games had been going on forever, and even the smoke formations above the tables looked stable, solid, permanent. The gray players and the smoky room and the carefully manicured green felt tables blended together in a manner that suggested they had been there for a very long time.

There were five crap tables in the Desert Inn, and I had to choose the one where we'd make our play. What I mainly looked at were the dealers. Were they bright or dull? Dull was definitely preferred. Did thay care about their jobs, the gung-ho ever-eagle-eyed types, or were they just bored and drawing a paycheck? What would be best of all for our crew would be a high roller from the East waving a fistful of hundred-dollar bills at another table, screaming Texas-type yells as he flung the dice, jumping up and down whenever he won. Such an individual inevitably attracts the shift boss, floormen, and maybe even a casino manager, all of whom love to see a loud, reckless sort such as this, but fear he may get hot and interrupt the steady flow of winnings to which they've become accustomed. With the more experienced and keenest of the casino's personnel thus occupied, the crew's job would be considerably easier and safer.

No play had yet begun at three of the five crap tables, and the action was thin at the other two. The dinner shows weren't quite over. I knew, however, that all five tables would soon be packed, this being a Saturday night, Las Vegas's busiest. I let my eyes flicker from one group of dealers to another, and right away I could tell what table we wanted to play.

I looked for the group of dealers that was least well-dressed. I'd learned from Glen that when you found these, you'd inevitably find other attributes favorable to a crossroader. Like a lack of attention to detail. A tendency toward banter rather than seriousness. An inclination to look at pretty girls, of which Las Vegas has many. Crap dealers who are something less than professional frequently crane their necks to follow the shrieks of a hot player at another table, rather than tending to their own business, or you can catch them trying to hear the show taking place in the lounge.

Usually four casino employees tend a crap table: the stickman (calls out the numbers, rakes the dice back and forth, and handles all the hard-way bets); the boxman (guards against the dealers making a mistake or trying to steal money); and two dealers (pay and collect bets). At the table I chose for our crew's play, the stickman fit his job title. He was tall, thin, nervous, and young. I thought his youth might work in our favor. Generally an older casino employee has been around, knows all the moves, and has learned to be suspicious when the situation calls for it. Of course, this rule of thumb does not always hold true. There are some very bright young people, and some older employees even the bosses who hired them consider lunkheads. But this young stickman looked ready to fly out of his skin he was so tense.

The two dealers wouldn't pose a problem, either. One was young and suntanned, a beach boy with a firm jaw who ogled the cocktail waitresses and misunderstood the smiles they were paid to wear. The other dealer, middle-aged, was as pale as the beach boy was tanned, and his recognizable hollow eyes suggested that he spent most of his non-working time gambling his paycheck at other casinos. Many gaming employees do precisely this, never seeming to learn from the unending series of examples they witness that you can't beat the odds.

The boxman might pose a problem, but nothing we couldn't handle. He was perhaps sixty, gray-haired, with the tired, bored eyes of someone who has seen too much. The boxman gets to sit down during the job, and often has earned this concession through years of faithful service to his employer. His chief duty is to make sure the dealers and stickman don't rob the house blind. Many boxmen are alcoholics who spend their free time betting football, baseball, and basketball games, and few ever leave an estate large enough to bury themselves. The boxman we would face tonight, I trusted, had plenty of personal concerns with which to occupy himself and would be going all-out just to keep his eyes on his fellow employees. Certainly he wouldn't be prepared for the devastating assault we had planned, probably the best grab-the-money act ever to perform on the Strip.

Glen Grayson didn't think it was possible for us to be caught cheating, and I agreed. Casinos might suspect we were cheating, but they couldn't prove it. A Harry Houdini might even know how we did it, but he wouldn't be able to see it happen.

I retraced my steps back through the casino and out to the south parking lot. Waiting with Glen, as I knew they would be, were our crew: Barry Churchman, age 45, ten years of experience working for casinos and thus completely at home in the surroundings, a man with larceny in his heart; 38-year-old, six-foot Don Allison, impossible to panic, a handsome cowboy from Reno who usually wore a cowhide jacket, boots, jeans, and a cowboy hat, yet his own mother couldn't pick him out of a crowd if he chose to become a part of it; Rollie Malone, 22, more massive even than Glen Grayson (Rollie was an outstanding college football tackle), a ding-y, flaky, good-natured kid no one would ever suspect of cheating; Jackie Gillitzer, five feet five inches and slender, Glen's old friend from the days in Chicago, a man who had spent his entire life in one gambling scam or another and had never been caught; and finally Jan Deerwood, 35, ex-prostitute, an icy blonde with an average face but absolutely great body, a woman with awesome presence of mind under pressure and enormous courage.

The seven of us (only six would go back inside) huddled in that still-steaming parking lot, and I talked to Glen. I told him what table I'd chosen.

"Has the show broken yet?" he asked.

"No. A couple more minutes."

"What's it look like in there?"

"Good. A lazy crew on number three crap table."

"You didn't see that big fat floorman?"

"He's not there."

"Good. We couldn't play on him. Did you check the craps?"

"Yes."

"What craps are down?"

"Sand-finished three-quarters-inch dice."

"Okay." Glen went to his car, sat down, and opened his suitcase that had sliding doors. Inside were dice that matched those used in almost every casino in Nevada. He removed a single die and handed it to Rollie.

"You'd better be getting inside," he said to all of us. "Get into position. I'll call Teddy and Lenny."

The six of us entered the Desert Inn from different doors, at different times, and approached the target table from different angles. It would have been folly to arrive as the cohesive gang we actually were. The dinner show had let out and the big casino hummed and buzzed with activity.

By pre-plan I reached the table first, establishing a position directly to the stickman's right. Rollie came second, just several moments later, wearing a sport jacket two or three sizes too big, which meant it resembled a tent, and set himself up at the end of the crap table, right at the center. Under the huge sport jacket he wore a loud Hawaiian print shirt, and on his face was plastered a silly grin that shouted to the world, I Don't Have a Single Ounce of Sense.

Jackie Gillitzer arrived next, looking like a jockey or a former bantamweight fighter, and he had to use his sharp elbows to station himself at my right side. Jackie always made me nervous. He had darting, shifty eyes, reminded people of Peter Lorre, and always seemed to be edgy, trembling and perspiring. If I'd been working for a casino, I'd have watched him like a hawk. Maybe Jackie's secret in never getting caught was that he looked so guilty nobody believed he could be.

Jan Deerwood pranced in, dressed stylishly but not in a manner to attract attention. Usually she was so covered with jewels she resembled a gypsy. Jan was a genuine head-turner, and on occasion we used that quality to advantage on the tables. Tonight, standing behind Jackie Gillitzer and me, her role would be less glamorous, but still utterly essential.

None of us spoke to the other, of course. Each had a separate part, one we had rehearsed and played in real life until it was second nature to us, and each had complete confidence in the other.

Barry Churchman followed a moment after Jan, squeezing in at the end of the table to get next to the bulky Rollie. Churchman might have been a life-insurance salesman on vacation, a bit puzzled by all the hubbub but eager to taste the evil ways of Las Vegas. Behind what appeared to be a bland-as-vanilla-ice-cream Midwestern face was a cobra coiled to strike.

As planned — *everything* was by plan — Don Allison sauntered in, taking up the position on the stickman's left. This quiet cowboy's eyes were almost hidden from view beneath the brim of his big hat, but I knew he was seeing everything. He could have been anything from a confident, moneybags oilman to a mild, polite department-store clerk. No one would have suspected the truth: that Don was one of the most brilliant crossroaders ever to challenge the omniscient casinos and come out on top.

All six of us were in place. Ready to go. Champing at the bit to hand the Desert Inn a first-round $20,000 knockout punch that would leave the casino's management puzzled and stunned, shaking their heads in wonderment for months. Emotions strung tight as piano wire, there wasn't a blessed thing we could do but *wait.*

Damn Glen, I thought. *Absolute insanity to bring those two rich screwups into this.*

Teddy and Lenny, our *bettors* for God's sake, hadn't made an appearance, and there we were, six cheaters, standing around with our hands in our pockets shuffling our feet. I felt like a fool, and worse, now the stickman was emptying the bowl of dice in front of Jackie Gillitzer, and he was going to have to throw them. Jackie fumbled a couple of dollars out of his pocket, laid them on the "come" line, where they were immediately replaced by casino checks (chips), and fired the dice over the stickman's right arm before he even had a chance to put the other dice back in the bowl. I glanced over at Jackie and, as always, he looked like he'd done something dishonest.

"Ten's the point," intoned the stickman, a bit disoriented by the speed and suddenness of Jackie's move.

Seven yourself out, I prayed to myself, and after a few more rolls Jackie did just that.

The bowl of empty dice was emptied in front of me.

Where the hell are those two?

Quick as lightning with my left hand I sent the dice hurtling to the far end of the table. Again the stickman was still collecting the cubes.

"Six! Six is the point!"

Again, I prayed for that seven, and after several rolls the prayer was answered.

I could relax for a while. The dice would be passed around the table to perhaps fifteen other shooters before they were returned to me. I let myself go limp for a moment, there was no sense getting so tense. I soaked up a bit of the big gambling house's atmosphere. It was very loud and smoky, and the noisy dinner show patrons, now unleashed, applied themselves with gusto to the real purpose of their being in Las Vegas. I could hear the whirrrr of the slots behind me, catch snatches of the show in the lounge, occasionally even discern the crisp click-click-click of the ball on the roulette wheel. Loudest of all, necessarily so to be heard above the tumult, the cries of the stickmen at neighboring tables: "Seven! A winner!" The noises of a casino were never more clear to me than when I was trying to cheat one. I think fear gives clarity to the senses.

At our table were several women in expensive fur coats, though the Desert Inn maintained an ideal temperature control. And there were several well-dressed men, experiencing the beginning of what would become copious perspiration, sporting gaudy gold rings. A few of the men puffed fat cigars and drank beer. On the ledge beneath the rail of the table sat the highballs of their ladies. All drinks were free, of course. Casino management didn't mind if you got roaring drunk.

Where are those two?

The dice had gone halfway around the table. We could have had the money and been on our way to the motel room for the pleasant task of counting it. I was angry with Glen, and a bit bewildered, also. Was this what he had hinted at when he said, "Be careful?" Normally Glen himself was the most careful of men, he had to be, as befitted someone who had earned the title King of the Crossroaders. He wouldn't have made it to "vassal" had he regularly taken chances like this. Every moment that ticked by increased the likelihood that someone out of a best-forgotten past would recognize one of us or, more likely, that some diligent floorman was recording our presence for future reference. It was always best — Glen had preached this endlessly — to get in and out quickly.

There was nothing to do but hang on. I leaned back to stretch and yawn and suddenly was jolted out of my lethargy by a stampede of people, cries and shouts. A moving mass was coming down an aisle, resembling pictures I'd seen of Muhammad Ali approaching the ring, surrounded by his entourage, admirers reaching out to touch his robe or pat his back.

I squinted my eyes and tried to peer through the smoke to sort out the commotion. Out of the lights and the haze and the crowd came Teddy Lewin, puffing a cigarette and smiling, and a step or two behind, equally at ease amid the confusion, was Lenny Hall.

Teddy Lewin was every inch the celebrity. He wore a blue silk suit, white shirt, and tie. He looked like a proud patrician with his white mane of hair, and he stood so erect he seemed taller than his six feet. What took me aback, however, were the *types* of people who rushed toward him. These included shift bosses (at this time, these individuals often owned a point or two in the casino), floormen, and even the casino manager. To these hardened gentlemen, who would have remained unimpressed by the entrance of European royalty or a high-up U.S. senator, clearly Teddy Lewin was a citizen of substance. The casino manager especially, a man who like the Lodges of Boston purportedly speaks only to God, couldn't find words to express to Teddy how welcome he was. I couldn't even make an intelligent guess why the Cleveland mob was so enamored of this man. And he intended to cheat them.

The commotion was such that players at other tables stopped what they were doing to stare, the ultimate compliment. Ordinarily a flash flood could sweep through the casino and not interrupt the action. "Rather bet than screw" is a phrase used to describe many gambling regulars.

I immediately began weighing the effect of Teddy Lewin's unexpected celebrity on our action. His popularity might either help or hinder us, and since I didn't feel we needed any help, hindrance loomed the larger possibility. It was clear the casino bigshots would stay to watch Teddy play, ostensibly to cheer him on and with their presence demonstrate they wished him well. This would be quite an acting job. Casino bosses are constitutionally incapable of hoping a player does well, even if that player is a close blood relative. But they will pretend that's what they want.

On the plus side of all this commotion, because the Desert Inn elite would be watching Teddy, they wouldn't be watching the crew, from where the real action would be coming. But still, I felt they could observe us under a microscope and not know what we were doing to them.

On the minus ledger, the mere presence of floormen and the casino manager, especially the latter, made our job more risky.

Today, perhaps, a casino manager might be a businessman, more skilled in the arts of bookkeeping, employee and customer relations, and turning a legitimate profit than in gambling. He might, in fact, not know the difference between a roulette wheel and a daily-double wheel. Not so in the mid-1960s. The casino manager of that time most likely had cut his teeth on high-stakes dice games in the back rooms of Cleveland or Chicago or New York City. Futhermore, he had thirty or forty more years of experience dealing with wise guys and had the nose of a bloodhound when it came to sniffing out something amiss. He wouldn't know what we were doing, but he might suspect something, and he wouldn't need more than good healthy suspicion to become very unpleasant.

But the man was all smiles now, his arm around Teddy's shoulders. They had reached the table, Lenny Hall right behind Teddy maneuvering for an up-close position. They were to my right and across the table from me, right where Glen had told them to be, and I thought for a moment this might turn out okay after all.

Teddy reached into his pocket and pulled out a fat roll of hundred-dollar bills. Five thousand dollars, I estimated. More than he'd need. Lenny Hall had a similar amount clutched in his hand. We were ready to go, as soon as the dice worked themselves around to Jackie Gillitzer.

Fortunately, there were still people who wanted to shake Teddy Lewin's hand, so the game resumed without his having to wager. I put a few dollars out on the come line — I'd never be called on to risk more than this — and studied Teddy Lewin. His face was as white as his hair and he looked almost sickly in the smoky, unhealthy casino light. He did not look like a man with many years ahead of him. I wondered if this had anything to do with his willingness to take a risk for money he didn't need, or if he figured there wasn't any risk, what with his being so cozy with the Desert Inn's management. I guessed Glen had been right: Teddy wanted excitement, a thrill. I suppose after the Bataan Death March most endeavors would seem as tame as needlework.

The stickman was pushing the bowl of dice towards Jackie. My stomach fluttered, my fingers tingled. No matter how sure I was of the play — and we had worked it hundreds of times successfully, our crew an irresistible, permanent parasite on the body of the

Nevada gambling industry — no matter how certain I was, I realized there would always be acute nervousness. Especially at this moment, the moment to begin.

"Money plays!" Teddy Lewin announced, spreading five $100 bills (the maximum bet allowed by the house) on the "field" portion of the table. Lenny Hall made the same bet. I caught a glimpse of the casino manager, looking paternal, or like a genuinely concerned big brother, a friendly smile on his swarthy face. He had every right to be smiling. The field bet is a sucker's play, the odds stacked lopsidedly in the house's favor.

Smooth as silk Jackie deftly picked up two dice from the bowl that had been emptied in front of him and sent one of them zipping at eighty miles per hour over the stickman's right arm to the end of the table. At exactly the same instant, proving practice makes perfect, Rollie Malone in his oversized sports jacket was leaning far over the table and placing with his left hand a two-dollar bet on the field, while with his right hand, concealed from view by the bulky jacket and his left arm, he set the die Glen had given him down with the six showing.

"Nine!" the stickman announced. "Your point is nine, shooter! A field roll!"

Jackie had thrown a three. Combined with the six Rollie Malone had placed on the table, it added up to nine and a winner for those who had bet on the field, namely Teddy and Lenny.

The "field" numbers are two, three, four, nine, ten, eleven, and twelve. The two and twelve pay two-to-one odds; the other numbers pay even money. Thus, with the nine turning up, Teddy and Lenny were each ahead $500, $1000 between them.

The casino manager patted Teddy Lewin's back. The CM's smile was confident and, if possible, broader than before. His only worry was that Teddy and Lenny might bet something more sensible than the field. There are sixteen possible ways the field numbers can come up, while there are twenty ways the house numbers (five, six, seven, eight) can appear. It takes no mathematical genius to see that the casino will come out on top over the long haul.

The house advantage is twenty to sixteen, a killer spread, but unknown to the Desert Inn we had turned those odds massively and decisively in our favor. In fact, we had a better than two-to-one advantage. The only losing numbers Jackie Gillitzer (or myself) could throw were one and two, because any other number — three, four, five, six — combined with the six Rollie could be counted upon to lay down added to nine or higher.

The die Jackie *had not thrown* was surreptitiously passed back to the comely Jan Deerwood, who, while bets were being paid, walked it down the table to Rollie. Teddy and Lenny again each bet $500 on the field. And again — whoosh — Jackie fired that single die to the back wall, just as fumble-fingered Rollie was laying his two dollars, *and* the second die, out on the felt.

"Twelve!" hollered the stickman. "Craps! Twelve, in the field! Good field bet! Pay the field!"

Damn right it was a good field bet. I clenched my left fist, once, twice. I wanted to be loose if Jackie sevened-out.

Together Teddy and Lenny were $3,000 ahead. The casino manager, sixty years old but still sharp as a new tack, was smiling at Teddy and offering encouraging words. I figured I knew what was going on in his head. He was thinking this might all be for the best. Let them get a little ahead. Offer them hope. Sooner or later the unchangeability of the odds would grind those hopes to dust.

Again that single die hurtled to the end of the table.

"Ten! A field roll! Your point is still nine, shooter!"

And again, faster than any eye could follow.

"Eleven! A field roll! The point is still nine!"

Whoooooosh.

"Twelve! Craps! Twelve, in the field! Pay the field!"

I resisted a momentary urge to glance around the table at my friends. The briefest eye contact had to be avoided; nothing could be allowed to associate one of us with the other. Besides, I was perfectly aware of what each was doing: Rollie, reinforcing his image as a flake, a clumsy blunderer always late getting his bet down; Barry Churchman, next to Rollie, providing "shade" — a diversion, perhaps asking for change just as the die was hurled; Cowboy Don Allison, as alert as the Secret Service guarding LBJ after John Kennedy had been gunned down, seeing everything from beneath the wide brim of his hat, ready with a preassigned signal to brush us out of the casino at the first sign of trouble; Jan Deerwood, the messenger, walking from the shooter to Rollie and back again; and beady-eyed Jackie Gillitzer, Glen's old friend, firing the die with the jerky suddenness of a man caught in the midst of a seizure.

We were $7,000 ahead. We'd been in action less than ten minutes. It was so easy, so beautiful, and absolutely undetectable. We were a magic act, all of us, and Glen Grayson's genius had presented us a virtual license to steal.

But not quite. If the house got even the slightest bit suspicious we could be in deep trouble. Fortunately, Teddy Lewin's presence seemed to work in our favor, despite all that experienced mob talent watching. The casino manager and floormen were paying so much attention to Teddy that they were ignoring everyone else, including the ones who had already robbed them of $7,000 and intended to take $13,000 more. The CM's smile, to his credit, was still there, though it now seemed locked in place. The dealers, the stickman, and the boxman, chosen especially for their apparent lack of alertness, followed the lead of their bosses and centered their attention on the two high rollers playing the field. We had *never* gone this long before.

I hoped Jackie would roll us right up to the $20,000 we'd agreed we would win, without ever sevening-out or hitting his point and having to start again. I knew the others wished for the same result. Get in and get out, quickly, that's what we believed in. Not a one of us wanted to play the daredevil.

Jackie usually played a different role from the one he was cast in tonight. On most occasions I was the one who handled the dice. Friends said I was the best they'd seen with cards and dice, though I was really just a very proficient mechanic. This night we had decided to use two shooters because we anticipated correctly that the action would be extra-heavy at the tables, and we didn't want to have to stand around shuffling our feet waiting an interminable length of time for the dice to come back around to a single player. As it was, there was a good chance Jackie and I could win the designated $20,000 without the dice ever getting past us.

Regardless, Glen had put me in charge of the crew whenever he wasn't present, which was almost every time we set foot in a casino. It was my job to brush us out when I thought the play had gone on long enough, and also to signal when and when not to bet. If Don Allison flashed a warning that it was time to leave, I was free to ignore it, though I couldn't imagine a situation when I would. I had complete faith in the cowboy's judgment, and in that of the others, also.

Teddy and Lenny had their usual $500 each on the field numbers, and I thought it would have been a simple matter now to introduce a couple of other bettors, their wives perhaps, to ride the coattails of their unusual "hot streak." Often this is precisely what we did: get a streak started, and have additional bettors ready to jump in on it. It made for less time in the casino, which, as I've said, was a top priority.

I had two dollars riding on the come line, and with nothing better to do I perfunctorily urged Jackie to hit the nine. Of course, it didn't matter unless he threw a seven or eight.

He hit ten, plus-$8,000; eleven, plus-$9,000; ten again, plus-$10,000, halfway there. On many occasions it would have been time to root for a seven, have Jackie say "Damn, I wish I could have caught that niner," and one by one drift away from the table and melt into the casino crowd. But $10,000 would rarely be enough for us in a single night; we'd regroup at several other casinos and let them share in the losses. Tonight, however, Glen had insisted it would only be the Desert Inn. A favor to Teddy and Lenny, which he must have been convinced would pay big dividends later.

Jackie rolled us up to plus-$17,000 before he threw an eight, minus-$1,000, and the Desert Inn management was visibly anxious. The CM no longer had his arm draped over Teddy's shoulder, his smile icy. Something was awry. Fishy. He could smell it, he could feel it in his bones. People who have been intimately involved with something for decades develop what I can only call a sixth sense. They can be utterly sure something is wrong, even if they can't tell what it is.

Trying to appear disinterested, I watched the CM. He muttered something to Teddy, then whispered into the ear of one of the floormen. The floorman began to prowl the length of the table and back, eyes flickering to one face after another, as if he could read larceny in one of them. Well, maybe he could. The shifty Jackie Gillitzer looked like he was committing a crime when he ordered a cup of coffee.

But the floorman and the casino manager had a problem. No one except the trusted Teddy and his friend Lenny were betting heavily, and those two were considered above reproach. When any bettor gets hot, throwing a lot of numbers (meaning he holds the dice a long time), an astute bettor would likely ride his streak. Good gamblers will tell you that's the thing to do. At our table, however, a common mistake was being made: people felt Jackie was "due" to cool off and, if anything, were wagering more cautiously than usual.

If it looks like a duck, walks like a duck, etc., is the way I believe I would have reasoned, but then I wasn't in the casino manager's shoes. Teddy and Lenny were the only big winners. Something was wrong, the CM was *sure* of that, as sure as most people are that the sun is coming up in the morning. Ergo, look to Teddy and Lenny. As I've mentioned, I don't know what bond existed between Teddy and the Cleveland mob; but whatever it was, in the CM's mind it obviously precluded the possibility of his cheating them.

Not that it would have helped to study Teddy's and Lenny's actions. All they did was lay their money on the table. What should have aroused suspicion was the *way* they bet: the maximum in the field. Teddy Lewin owned casinos. If anyone knew this was a loser's bet, he did.

Big, elaborate gambling casinos, so profitable they might as well have printing presses, are hard to picture in the role of the underdog, but against us they were. They could have had a dozen eyes on Jackie Gillitzer, Jan Deerwood, and Rollie Malone, and still wouldn't have figured out what we were doing. No matter how large the audience, it doesn't increase the chances of the magician's methods being exposed.

Jackie still had the dice in his hand — only a seven would have passed them along to me — and *zing* went one of them to the end of the table. A five. Total: eleven. We had $3,000 to go. The CM had joined the floorman, each pacing like a tiger and just as dangerous.

Zip. A four. Two thousand dollars to go.

"Don't throw the dice so hard," the floorman growled at Jackie.

"Go yell at somebody else," Jackie whined. He was perfect. A gambler hates to be interrupted in the midst of play.

"You can knock somebody's eye out throwing that hard."

I thought even the most naive bettor at the table knew the floorman's concern was not over safety.

Jackie, as if in a pique, threw the die even harder. Four. Total: ten. Just $1,000 to go. With luck, only three more throws.

"Keep your hands up," the floorman said to Rollie.

"Me? Are you talking to me, sir?"

"Keep those hands up!"

The floorman was steaming mad, and the CM seemed to be trying to stare a hole through Rollie's head. But he had no doubt what that sixth sense told him. Rollie looked like a big, shambling, out-of-shape college football player. Good-natured jokers like this might, as a lark, try to put something over on the casinos.

They'd be found out right away, jostled a little bit, maybe cuffed about once or twice, and told to be on their way. But they didn't get away with it. Not to the tune of $19,000, which I was certain the CM had counted as meticulously as I had.

It can't be the big kid at the end of the table, the CM's mind must have been telling him. *Then again, maybe it is.*

It shouldn't have gone this long, I knew. Normally we were in and out without an eyebrow being raised. Only later, when they realized we'd tagged them for a lot of money, would questions arise. Once again I mentally cursed Glen. He'd risked our necks to impress two rich guys. It was bad business to carry it so long the bosses started questioning.

Jackie fired the die and it came up five. We had the $20,000.

"I told you to keep your hands up!" the floorman said threateningly.

"I was just placing a bet." Rollie feigned suprise at the harshness of the floorman's tone.

Two more rolls, I thought. *Just let us get through two more rolls.*

"I'm warning you, fatso, keep your hands up!"

Rollie looked hurt. The CM studied him like an eagle. He must have been wondering if this buffoonish-looking college kid in the sports shirt and baggy jacket could really be the cause of this, and if so, what possible connection there could be with Teddy Lewin and Lenny Hall. The CM shrugged. *This can't be happening,* I imagined him thinking, *not in my place.*

Jackie closed it out with a six. At two-to-one we were $22,000 ahead.

"I warned you, you tub of lard, about . . ."

"Let it be," I could see the CM say. It just couldn't be that clumsy kid, and the CM didn't want an awkward scene in front of all those customers. In front of *Teddy Lewin*, for God's sake.

So it was over, I thought, and breathed a sigh of relief I hoped no one noticed. I thought I'd give Glen a good piece of my mind, really stand up to him and tell him it was rotten to put us in danger like this. Well, maybe I'd tell him.

Jackie had the dice in his hand. Rollie couldn't resist. He held his hands up in the air, palms out. "Does this make you happy?" he wanted to know.

Jackie fired both dice, and seldom have I seen a more beautiful seven.

"Damn!" he cursed. "All that time, and I come up a loser."

Lenny and Teddy wore all-good-things-must-end smiles as they watched the dealer rake in their $500 field bets. When I saw this I wanted to hug them.

A moment later I wanted to strangle them.

I'd already brushed the crew out, rubbing my right sleeve with my left hand, the signal that in an orderly but seemingly random fashion we should disperse, meeting in an hour in Glen's motel room to split the money. The stickman was emptying the bowls of dice in front of me — it was my turn, now that Jackie had sevened-out. I was about to wave the dice away, and lead the exodus from the Desert Inn. Then I saw something I couldn't believe.

Lenny and Teddy had $500 bets down on the table, on the field, wore eager grins on their faces, and looked to all the world as if they were set to go on forever.

Damn fools, I thought. *Damn greedy fools.*

At first I was more shocked than angry. I was simply stunned that anything of this sort could happen. We had taken an enormous chance, literally put our lives on the line, right under the noses of the Cleveland mob, and through skill and courage had not only survived but triumphed. We'd done what most gamblers don't even dare dream, and now two rich guys — no, two rich idiots — wanted to place us in no-return jeopardy. I blinked a couple of times, risked a look at them, and when that elicited no response I rubbed my right sleeve as nonchalantly as I could. The beach-boy dealer, his eyes temporarily diverted from the lovely, scantily clad cocktail waitresses drawn to our table not so much by Teddy and Lenny's winning streak but by the presence of the casino brass, noticed the motion of my left hand, but nothing registered in his eyes. Still, it wasn't prudent to make any gesture that might seem out of the ordinary, especially with the CM and that floorman already on the prowl.

Glen had told Lenny and Teddy what the brush-out signal would be. I'd been there when he'd explained it. Still, I thought, that didn't absolve him of blame. They were his friends, and he had a responsibility to be a better judge of them.

"Do you want to take your roll?" the stickman asked me. The dice were splayed out on the table in front of me.

Jackie was on my right, Jan behind us, and both had sized up the situation. It struck me as remarkable that the man who had put together such a crew could be so deficient in the selection of friends. Regardless, I had to make a decision.

What Teddy and Lenny wanted to do now was *gamble*, something we never did. We scoffed at gambling and gamblers, holding them in the lowest esteem. We knew they stood virtually no chance against the immutable odds weighted in the casino's favor, and even if the odds were overcome for a short period, almost every casino at this time employed very talented people — mechanics — who could bring the hottest streak to a dead halt.

But Teddy and Lenny wanted to gamble. The fact that Teddy usually stood at the opposite end of the casino spectrum didn't matter. Casino employees, even managers and owners, get bitten by the same gambling bug, or whatever it is, that transforms otherwise normal people into maniacs. I figured I knew exactly what was going on in Teddy's mind. He reasoned that we were playing with "their" money and could shoot the moon without danger of a loss.

It was insanity. The money had once been theirs. It was now ours. We had it and we could lose it. It made me even angrier that what Teddy and Lenny intended to do involved money that wasn't entirely theirs. The crew, even Glen, always split our winnings into equal shares. What Lenny and Teddy were betting was mostly the crew's cash.

"I've had enough for tonight," I said, and headed back through the casino, lights popping in my eyes and inside my head. I knew the other crew members would soon depart also.

"It go okay?" Glen asked, when I reached him in the parking lot. He was behind the wheel of his Cadillac, would have appeared to be dozing if I hadn't known better.

I told him the unvarnished truth. I said that at this very moment his friends Teddy and Lenny were losing our money. I said I might have been able to salvage the situation, but the risk wasn't worth it. Finally, in a manner I'd never talked to Glen before, I added that I thought it irresponsible of him to saddle the crew with dead weight, people we didn't need — more than irresponsible, they were dangerous.

"You did the right thing," Glen said.

"What?"

"Getting out of there. It was the right thing."

I sat next to Glen in the Cadillac as he headed downtown, towards the motel. He didn't say anything, and his teeth were locked so tight I though his jaw might freeze in place. But except for that there was no sign he was angry. Solemn is the word to describe his mood.

Without so much as an "I'll see you" he left me off at the motel, and I let myself in and waited for the others. Jan and Jackie arrived first, followed by Rollie, Barry, and Don. I'd never seen my friends with such conflicting emotions.

Everyone was hot about Teddy and Lenny, especially since the consensus was that we wouldn't see a nickel from our efforts. But there was an odd elation in the room, also. It wasn't winning the $20,000 — we usually won more than that in an evening — but *how* we had done it: in one place, all at once, and from some of the sharpest-eyed hoodlums in Vegas.

Rollie had his usual quart of Chivas Regal, and the thought of the money we'd probably never see didn't deter him from enjoying it. Glen, whom he very much wanted to emulate, drank Chivas Regal, and that was a strong enough reason for Rollie. The rest of us rarely drank, maybe a glass or two of wine every six months or so, but whatever Rollie did was all right with us as long as he performed at the table.

There was nothing to do but wait. We figured Glen had gone to meet Lenny and Teddy at their hotel room, and there was no telling what would come out of that meeting. So we talked about our plans for the week (we only worked on weekends) and laughed out loud when Don recalled the look on that CM's face. He'd known for certain something was wrong. He just couldn't tell what.

When Glen arrived he simply walked in and laid $21,000 on the bed, and began counting it for everyone to see. Barry Churchman let out a yelp of delight, but no one dared ask Glen if Lenny and Teddy had had to cough it up themselves, or if a shaft of reason had penetrated their skulls and they had left the casino on their own accord. I guess it didn't matter, and Glen never told us. He kept out shares for Teddy and Lenny (each of us received a little over $2,000), then poured himself a full glass of Chivas Regal.

"To the best crew in the world!" he said, and drained the glass in one long swallow. It was quite a compliment, coming from Glen.

"To the best crew in the world!" we all repeated, as if with a single voice.

Jackie Gillitzer leaned over to me and, under his breath, whispered, "Did it ever occur to you that Glen did this on purpose? A test. A test under fire to see just how good we really are."

2

The year 1959 was difficult for donut-shop owners in the San Joaquin Valley of California. I know. I opened a one-man shop on the outskirts of Visalia, hardly the action spot of America, in reality a small town in central California midway between Los Angeles and San Francisco. Visalia was a good place for me. My goals were solid, if modest, and I wasn't looking for excitement.

As a child in Oakland I had dreamed the usual dreams of a young American boy. I wanted to be a policeman, then a fireman, then an FBI agent, then a bemedalled general, maybe I could even be President of the United States. But by the time I left grade school I knew none of those things were for me.

Harry Truman was president during my senior year at Visalia High School (1948), and I remember my mother listening to radio programs like "Inner Sanctum," "The Jack Benny Show," and "Fibber McGee and Molly." I don't remember anyone in Visalia having a TV at this time. Fun was dancing to a local band each Saturday night at the Visalia Ballroom, and a really big time was driving to Fresno, forty-three miles away, to hear Tex Beneke. Just recently, in January, 1985, I read a survey that sought to name the best and worst places in America to live. Fresno was voted the absolute worst. Visalia, I suppose, was too small to qualify for the award. As a youngster I never knew Visalia wasn't an "in" place.

My dad, whose last twenty working years were spent as a truck driver, and my mom, an accountant, were as different as could be. Dad had advice for everybody: He was sure he had life figured out. He told me once, jokingly, "I have three words that if you memorize them, you'll never be broke: 'Stick 'em up.' " Actually, he was a very hard worker whose main advice for me was to get a college education so I wouldn't have to work as hard as he did. Mom also worked hard — a full-time job plus all the duties that went into making a home — and very much enjoyed good music. We always had lots of albums around. Mom's favorite was Mario Lanza; Dad leaned to Spike Jones. My mother was gentle and cultured — she had once appeared in a Broadway play — and had a college degree, while Dad, a fighter who once knocked out the middleweight champion of California, never got past the sixth grade. What my parents had in common was a desire to see me succeed in a worthwhile and conventional way.

I did apply myself and save my money, and several years after graduating from high school I realized a small portion of the American Dream: I bought that donut shop, made a down payment on a little house with a white picket fence, and married my high-school sweetheart. She had been the head cheerleader at Visalia High School.

The dream seemed to be working. The donut shop produced a small but steady income, and we had two healthy, active boys: Billy, born in 1953, and John, born in 1956. But then in 1959 the donuts began to accumulate on the shelves and the bills mounted and Peggy began to lose faith in the dream. She was 27; I was 29.

"This donut shop is killing us," she said. "You don't know how to run a business."

Peggy was right. I gave away more donuts than I sold, and there was a growing list of customers who bought only on credit.

"Maybe if we just hang on a little longer," I said doubtfully.

It was what Peggy wanted to hear. She wanted me to stick with the business, and even expand the operation. I thought I should deep-six it and get a job. Earlier I'd bought a truck and hired a driver, which did increase sales, but the profits from these were more than wiped out by the additional expenses. I'd borrowed money from my parents to keep going, and it didn't appear this would ever be paid back.

"I'm tired of just hanging on," Peggy said. She was worked up now, confused and frustrated by our inability to make ends meet. And I felt like a heel. I'd wanted better for her than this.

Looking at Peggy, I felt like the worst sort of failure. She was blonde and pretty, still wore ponytails, and everybody in Visalia knew and liked her. She might, I thought, still be that fresh, good-looking cheerleader who loved to ski on mountaintops.

"I want more out of life," Peggy said, "than a run-down house and a paint-peeled picket fence and a shop full of stale donuts."

Well, so did I, but I didn't know what to do. A job seemed like the best idea, but how could I be sure? I *was* sure that what was wrong with the donut shop was its location, far out on the edge of town. It was hardly a place people would drive to just to buy donuts.

"I'll try hard," I said. "I'm no quitter." That was true enough. As both an amateur and a professional fighter, I'd taken pride in not quitting. Maybe sometimes I should have. But I think that's the way a lot of us were in the 1950s. I'm not saying it was better — just different. Marriage, for example, was more of a lifetime commitment. When you got married it really was for better or for worse. You stayed with things.

A few weeks after that talk with Peggy — I remember precisely, it was December 12, 1959 — an event occurred that altered forever my American dream. Sully Kelly came by to see me. Sully was an ex-classmate from Visalia High School, best remembered for pinpoint spitball throwing and miserable, failing grades. Sully was flashing a fistful of hundred-dollar bills. I had never seen a hundred-dollar bill.

"How's the Donut King?" Sully Kelly asked.

"Not so good," I said.

"Why don't you sell this dump and move to Las Vegas? I can get you a job dealing craps at the Thunderbird. You can make an easy six or seven hundred dollars a week."

"I don't know how to deal craps."

"You can learn."

"Six hundred dollars a week?"

"Maybe more."

I'd never realized anyone could make that much money working in a casino, and I was enthusiastic. I told Sully I'd talk it over with Peggy. It would be difficult for her to argue against the move if Sully was on the level and if he could guarantee that job in Las Vegas.

Peggy and I talked. She didn't like the idea. The donut shop fit more into her perception of how a middle-class family should earn its living. Also, she was an only child and didn't want to move that far away from her parents. Our home, modest as it was, represented a triumph for us, and there were things to be said for the atmosphere in which our boys were being raised.

It was, of course, a lot easier to own a house in the 1950s than it is now. Our home cost $7,000 ($700 down) and the mortgage interest rate was six percent. I think the payments were $60 a month. A shrewd real-estate investor could have made a fortune in those days. I hear the average-priced home in California is now close to $100,000.

We had a circle of twelve to fifteen friends, mostly chums from high school, and we'd go to their homes for dinner, or they'd come to ours. Once a week we went dancing, and Sunday afternoons there were picnics in Moony's Grove, between Tulare and Visalia, where it was almost a ritual for people from both towns to gather. Life in Visalia was more what you'd imagine it would be in a small Iowa farm town than the conception many people have of laid-back, swinging Californians lolling on beaches and shattering moral codes.

"Besides," Peggy argued, when we talked about our moving to Las Vegas, "you don't have to go there to get a job and make money. You can do that right here in Visalia."

But I knew a regular job wouldn't pay as much. Not if Sully Kelly was telling the truth. "We could live like kings on six hundred dollars a week," I said.

"You'd be making a mistake," Peggy said.

I hated to go against her, but I didn't want to pass up a major opportunity, either. It was clear the out-of-the-way donut shop was never going to make it, nor would a regular job likely allow us to do any more than tread water. The big money Sully Kelly talked about had put stars in my head, as Peggy pointed out, and in the end I called him and said I was interested in his proposition.

"You're using your head," Sully said.

Sully had been in Las Vegas since 1950, and I fervently hoped he knew what he was talking about. In high school he'd been known as a "hell-raiser," which only meant that he drank beer. He'd been expelled from school once for stealing a case of beer off the back of a brewery truck. All of this was small potatoes, I figured.

Sully gave me his address in Las Vegas and three and a half weeks later — early January, 1960 — I left Visalia. Peggy and my little boys stood in the yard and waved good-bye. The boys cried. Peggy was frustrated that I was going away against her wishes and her face seemed carved in stone. She didn't want me to leave, but it wasn't decided whether she'd join me once I was established. The unsettling possibility that our marriage was over played havoc with any peace of mind I might have had, but I rationalized that when she saw how well I was doing, how I was building a nest egg for our children's future, she would see I had made the right choice.

The drive to Las Vegas took five hours. I went south to Bakersfield, thinking every mile of the way that I was crazy and should turn around and go home, but in Bakersfield I turned east and started up over the snow-capped Tehachapi Mountains. Travelling over the mountains was breathtaking — cattle grazing on the slopes, big stately evergreen trees as far as the eye could see. Coming down the mountain was entering a different world. From the lush greenery of the high elevations I descended into the barren wastes of the Mojave desert. My spirits, which had risen going up the mountain, descended into a whirlpool of doubts as I came down.

Now it was just a race across the desert. The road was not flat, since the blacktop had been poured over sand dunes, and if you went fast enough you could become airborne. There was no speed limit in Nevada at this time, and driving over 100 mph was not unusual. After Wells Corner, Barstow, Baker — hot, dry, desolate, sand-blasted sleepy little towns — I was in Nevada. Only sixty miles now to Vegas. I wondered what waited for me there.

Lights. I was just amazed by the lights of this city that never closed down. I drove along the Strip, which resembled a carnival midway, neck craning left, then right, as bedazzled by the surface glitter as a child seeing Disneyland for the first time. It was a miracle I didn't crack up the car. Las Vegas has more neon lights than Broadway, more, I believe, than anywhere else in the world. I cruised the Strip, where the high rollers played, and then downtown, more a blue-collar milieu, where working people felt more at home. It was almost like daylight in this town, though it was night when I arrived. I'd show Peggy, I thought, caught up in the glamor of the place. I'd make a good life for us here.

Las Vegas at the beginning of the 1960s was still very much a frontier town, and the population was not nearly so large as it is now. You expected to see dust devils flurry up in the streets. Most of the men wore cowboy hats and western boots and Levis. Las Vegas is more sophisticated today and has lost much of its Old West flavor. A certain corporate sameness is taking over from the gamblers and mobsters who were so prominent when I first arrived.

I found Sully Kelly's house in a suburb. For some reason I had never thought of Las Vegas as having suburbs — or even houses,

for that matter. Sully shook my hand and patted my back —
"Good to see you, John" — and insisted I stay with him and his
wife until I got on my feet. He said he had left the Thunderbird
and was now dealing craps at the Silver Slipper. He said he had
an easy job for me.

"What kind of job?" I asked.

"Most dealers in Las Vegas steal money from the houses,"
Sully said, as matter-of-factly as he might talk about the weather.
"The way they do it is simple. They wear a 'sub' to work. That's a
piece of material sewn inside your pants. It looks like a big sock.
If a dealer steals five-dollar chips and slides them into his sub, he
can walk out of the pit when he goes on break with close to five
hundred dollars. By the end of an eight-hour shift, a dealer can
have two or three thousand dollars."

"Where do I come in?" I couldn't imagine how this was leading to any kind of legitimate job.

"The dealer needs a clean-up man," Sully said. "Someone to
take the money off him. All you have to do is meet me in the
men's room during my coffee breaks. I'll pass the take to you
under a partition between stalls and you can cash it in at another
casino." At this time, chips were exactly like money in Vegas.
You could buy meals or a car or a new house with them. Each
casino honored the chips of the other casinos.

I let what Sully had said roll around in my head. I'd be going
from middle-class entrepreneur to crook in a single decisive step.
Sully was telling me how it was common practice among dealers
in Las Vegas, but this wasn't what mattered to me. I'd never really
done anything that smacked of dishonesty, and alarm bells went
off in my head.

"I don't know," I said. "I came out here looking for a job."

"This is a job. And everybody does it."

"I don't."

"I mean, the dealers."

"Well, it's not what I had in mind."

"Wise up, John. The casinos are just clip joints. You have no
idea what goes on in the casinos. The dealers are just taking
money that's already been taken from someone else, and I'll tell
you, that person could damn well less afford to lose it than a
casino."

"I'd rather just take that job you talked about."

"All in good time. You can't just walk in here and get a job."

This wasn't the tune he'd been singing when he'd talked to me in Visalia, but getting into a fight with him wasn't going to help. I was already here, and I didn't want to turn back. At least not so abruptly. I began thinking that stealing from casinos, themselves hardly paragons of morality, could not be classified as a heinous crime. At this point I wasn't even rationalizing; I was trying to persuade myself it was really okay. I needed to prove to Peggy and myself that I could be successful, and although there were many things I would never do, this didn't seem to be one of them. In fact, it seemed far less undesirable than turning around and heading back to Visalia, looking like a fool. The truth is, Sully didn't convince me; I convinced myself. I decided I liked the idea, although I hated the possibility of getting caught. I was brand new in Las Vegas and wanted to begin my career on the right foot.

"You get ten percent of what I take," Sully said.

Ten percent of $2,000, and I assumed he worked five days a week ($10,000), would be $1,000 a week. But I was still worried about getting caught. Even people from Visalia had heard that cheats ended up with their legs broken, or worse.

"Look at this place," Sully said.

It was nice, all right. Expensive furniture and drapes. Two cars in the driveway. A pool in the backyard. Sully's wife, who he said made the best subs in Las Vegas, was fashionably dressed.

"I'm not pressuring you," Sully said. "But it might be a couple of months before I can get you on as a dealer. You're going to need money for yourself and your family."

That's what I'd been thinking, and he had me over a barrel. I bit my lower lip and stared out the window. My temper flared for a moment, and I glared at him. He was a real sweetheart. He had come to Visalia and promised me a job in Las Vegas, and there never was a job. He was simply looking for a clean-up man, someone whose face was not known in the casinos, a *sucker*. My muscles tensed. I wanted to break his jaw, but I was in a bad position. I was tapped out. I didn't want to go back to Visalia a loser.

"All right," I said. "I'll do it for a little while."

"You won't regret it."

"Right. But if you don't help me get a job dealing, *you're* going to regret it."

"Not to worry."

Sully Kelly wore his sub to work every night. Silver dollars were still in use in 1960, and when Sully walked out of the pit for a coffee break he sometimes had as many as eighty in his sub. It was a lot of weight, and it was comical to watch him try to walk normally. Sully would go to the men's room and go into an empty stall, I would take an adjacent stall, and he would pass the silver underneath to me. During an eight-hour shift he would hand me nearly $800. He did this every night he worked, and the count would be much higher if he stole five-dollar or twenty-dollar chips (called checks in Las Vegas). These were the denominations used by Eastern high rollers. Little old ladies played with silver dollars.

Once, with Sully sitting in one stall on a toilet stool, me in the stall next to him, we fumbled a handoff — maybe because he was nervous or drunk — and the noise was deafening. Fifteen silver dollars crashed to the tile floor and began clattering about, rolling every which way in crazy circles, the sound loud and incriminating. Luckily, no one else was in the restroom to hear.

My idle time was spent at local banks, cashing in silver dollars (how I wish I'd saved them), or at the casinos, cashing in five-dollar and twenty-five-dollar checks. The checks, as I've said, were money in Las Vegas.

My average take was $80 a day, which was good, though certainly not the amount Sully had bubbled about at the outset. I sent Peggy $250 a week. This welcome and rather substantial sum (for 1960) made her think my decision might have been a most prudent one, though of course I didn't tell her *how* I obtained the money. I missed my family and I didn't like being a thief, nor did I like having to rely on Sully Kelly. He was a drunk and a compulsive gambler besides. Most of the money he stole was spent on booze or at the craps tables in other joints.

One night I was at the Silver Slipper waiting to clean-up Sully. He was ready to leave the pit on his coffee break, but he had so many silver dollars in his sub he could hardly walk. To leave the pit he had to step over a rope. He got one leg over, but he couldn't lift the other one, the one with the loaded sub. He was drunk. He grunted and strained against the weight of so many silver dollars. When he finally got his leg high enough to clear the rope, the sub tore apart and three hundred dollars, in silver and checks, poured down his leg and rolled across the floor.

Sully knew he was in deep trouble and he ran for his life. Shoving customers aside, bowling over others, arms and legs pumping up and down like a sprinter headed for the tape, he managed to make it out the door, and I picked him up in my car and drove him home. An hour passed before he conquered the shakes.

There was no chance of ever working for the Silver Slipper again, but Sully didn't pull up stakes. His wife's grandfather was an important landowner in Las Vegas and could fix things. Sully could always find work. He got a new sub and a new job and was soon back doing his thing.

Sully Kelly was a first-class nut. He stole more in Nevada than any other dealer who ever worked a casino. He had been stealing in Nevada long before I arrived; in fact, he started as soon as he got there. Sully couldn't have existed on $1,500 a month salary. What kept him going was the $800 or $900 he stole each day. Nonetheless, the casinos never lost money on Sully. He poured every cent of it back into drinking and gambling. Although some of the bosses had to get wise to him after a while, and though they despised an employee who stole (worse, one who got caught), they seemed to love Sully. The money he took never left town. It all wound up back in the casino counting rooms.

Sully called me one night and asked if I would meet him at Pegleg, a bar where dealers hung out. He had been drinking a lot, was close to but not staggering drunk, and he was burning mad when I arrived. A crap dealer named Frenchy had seen Sully going to his sub and put the finger on him, and Sully had lost still another job. Sully wanted me to go with him and put some knots on Frenchy's head, and I agreed because Sully was an employer, of sorts.

We drove to the snitch's house and rapped on his door. Frenchy was in the living room with a girlfriend. He looked out the window, saw Sully, and refused to open up. Sully got even hotter. We got into the car and drove around until we found a construction site. There was a large stack of new red bricks, and we stopped and gathered up ten of them. Then we drove back to Frenchy's house and parked in the driveway. Sully wound up and heaved a brick through the large bay window in the front of Frenchy's house. Frenchy and his girlfriend were sitting on a couch watching television and she let out a terrifying scream. She wasn't hit, she was just frightened. When she stopped screaming, I hurled another brick. Frenchy had already dived for cover. There was no longer any glass in the bay window, and my brick sailed cleanly into the living room, hitting the television set and causing it to explode.

Frenchy got the message. He never again put the finger on Sully, although he continued to snitch on other people. Once a rat, always a rat, goes conventional Las Vegas wisdom, and sometimes it applies.

Throwing bricks through Frenchy's bay window gave me pause to wonder in what direction I was headed. At the time it had seemed the right thing to do, and I didn't spend a lot of time considering my actions afterward. But it bothered me some. It showed how far removed I was from that donut-shop owner of a year before. Perhaps I didn't do a lot of self-examination because there was so much to see and learn. And maybe I didn't want to self-examine. Las Vegas was getting in my blood.

One thing I learned was that few people ever left Nevada with stolen money. Most of the thieves, like Sully, blew it back into the casinos, shooting craps, playing "21," or any other game available. Sully himself would bet on anything, including which of two raindrops sliding down a car's windshield would get to the bottom first. Still, Sully had a certain amount of luck, namely his wife's grandfather, and he was always able to find another job. Also, owners of the joints changed frequently, and the casinos were not nearly as sophisticated as they are now.

Sully never made good on his promise to get me a job, but it didn't matter. I met a guy named Harry Hershey who was a shift boss at the Mint, and we hit it off from the start. This was February, 1961, and he put me to work as a break-in dealer on the roulette wheel. I stood next to the croupier and stacked and sorted the various denominations of chips. It worked like this: after the croupier spun the ball and the ball dropped off the rail and finally settled on a number, he called out the number, placed a marker on it, and raked in the losing checks while paying the winning ones. All during this procedure I was maintaining order among the multicolored chips arriving from all sides. A certain speed and dexterity was required; a fumble-fingered break-in dealer could make a mess of a table.

I racked colors for two months. When I was confident the job would be permanent and that promotions were likely, I asked Harry Hershey for a few days off to drive to Visalia and pick up my family. We had been separated for more than a year.

"Sure," said Harry. "If you need more time, just call and tell me."

The trip to Visalia caught Peggy by surprise. She had been

making it with my friend, the guy who had been best man at our wedding. The affair, Peggy tearfully admitted, had been going on long before I left for Las Vegas. Peggy and I had a terrific fight.

Peggy didn't want to leave her lover, nor did she want a divorce. I thought I was still in love with her. Well, these things happen, I told myself, and the thing to do is forgive and forget and go on with the marriage. I finally persuaded her to move to Las Vegas and give it another try.

We sold the donut shop and the little house with the white picket fence (for $7,000, just what we paid for it — I think our equity was $800) and stacked our belongings into a trailer. We were not ten miles out of Visalia when a wheel fell off the trailer and we had to hire a moving company. It seemed like an ominous beginning.

We set up housekeeping in Charleston Heights, a middle-income neighborhood, and the next day — it was in June, 1961 — I reported for work. I was greeted with the news that I no longer had a job.

While I had been in Visalia, the manager of the Mint had seen a customer buy a stack of chips with a hundred-dollar bill. When they took the money box, located under the table, to the count room the hundred-dollar bill wasn't there. The guy working the wheel had stolen it, and everyone on the day shift was fired. That was the law of the casinos.

Getting fired by the Mint was the first mark against me in Las Vegas. It would not be the last. What happened was unfair — I had not even been in Nevada when the hundred dollars was stolen — but the pessimistic Peggy was certain she could sense impending disaster. She was right, though that occurence was still some months in the future.

"John," Peggy said, "what's going to become of us?" Our furniture hadn't even been arranged in our new home, and already I was out of work.

"We'll be okay," I said. There was no way I could be sure of this, but I was trying to lift the gloom hanging over both of us.

"We should have stayed in Visalia. At least we had friends there."

"Things will work out, Peggy. You'll see."

Harry Hershey had a friend at the Royal Nevada named Jake Killoran. Harry told Jake I had been bum-beefed and asked him to take me on. Jake needed a "21" dealer and I was hired to deal cards.

Jake Killoran was a legend in Las Vegas. He would bend over backward to help someone who was down and out, but it was a big mistake to cross him. Jake Killoran ran his business with an iron fist, and if you did a good job he took care of you.

I picked up a lot of scuttlebutt working at the Royal Nevada. According to one rumor there were three cops in Las Vegas, in the sheriff's department, who hired themselves out as hit men, and whenever they hit some luckless slob, the newspapers covered it as a Mafia killing.

Anyway, I worked the Royal Nevada for nearly a year, until March, 1962. One day a schoolteacher from California came into the casino. He was losing his money at my table, and I tried to talk him into quitting. This was not a way to win job security. The casinos wanted to grab every buck they could. Just as I was finishing my shift the schoolteacher bet his last dollar and lost. I reached into the rack and handed him a twenty-five-dollar chip and told him to go home.

One of the bosses in the craps pit saw me give the teacher the twenty-five dollars. He told my boss and I was fired. It was the second mark against me in Las Vegas.

I'd just felt sorry for the guy. He looked like he had problems, which was not unusual, many people at the tables have problems. I probably should have let someone else deal with him. A pit boss would always give a busted player enough money to get home on. At that time, three dollars would fill a gas tank. If a player was from a long way away and had blown enough money, he might even get airfare. However, my dismissal taught me that the casino's arbitrary benevolence was reserved for bosses only, it didn't trickle down to dealers.

After the Royal Nevada incident, I bounced around town working one joint and then another. It wasn't any way to raise a family, and just putting food on the table was a day-to-day proposition filled with suspense. And there was more trouble with Peggy. She assured me she had stopped seeing her lover from Visalia, but something was going on, and I soon found out what: she had a new boyfriend.

Once again we had a confrontation. We talked about her affair and about my seeming inability to provide any sort of secure environment for raising children. I thought a divorce might be best — I convinced myself I somehow could support my boys better if I weren't married — but Peggy wanted to keep the family together. I think she was concerned about what her folks would say. Also, in the support area, I suppose I was better than nothing. Peggy promised to break up with her new boyfriend, which she did, dropping him and, as I later learned, taking up with another.

I began to gamble and stay out late. I knew I was hurting my little boys but I did not seem to be able to control myself. It regressed to a point where I couldn't get a job anywhere in town. Desperation set in. My sons weren't eating properly and Peggy was dating another man. My life was a sorry mess, or so I thought. I didn't realize it was going to get a lot worse.

Happy Heagan was a craps dealer at the Stardust who spent his spare time running around town robbing beer joints and supermarkets. One afternoon Harry stopped by our house in Charleston Heights. He said his partner was out of town and he needed someone to drive while he took off a finance company.

"You're crazy," I said.

"Things have been rough for you," he said. "Do this one little job for me and it's worth two grand in your pocket."

"I'm not interested."

"It will be easy. The cops are too busy collecting their take from the casinos. They don't bother with petty stuff like robberies."

"I don't want to be involved."

"We have to do a lot of things we don't like."

This was true enough. I walked over to a window and watched my boys playing in the backyard. Their clothes were ragged. There was no food in the refrigerator. They would eat hot dogs again tonight, *if* I could boost a package from the supermarket. Two thousand dollars would go a long way toward solving my problems. With that amount of money I could go to Reno, get a job, and start over. Maybe the marriage could still be patched up, and I could support my family in a rational fashion. I told myself I wouldn't repeat my mistakes.

"It's a piece of cake," said Harry Heagen. "Believe me. It's a piece of cake."

I knew even at the time that what I was going to say was a mistake. It was stupid and it was wrong. But the words came out of my mouth anyway. "All right. I'll do it this one time. Don't ever ask me again."

"I know you need the money," said Happy Heagen.

We got into my car and I drove him to a loan company on East Charleston. Happy ran in and got the money. He came out as fast as he went in and I drove him twenty blocks away.

"Stop the car," he said.

I pulled over to the curb, and he handed me $2,000. Then he climbed out and walked away. I drove to a supermarket and bought several large cartons of food for my kids. It was time to celebrate.

Two hours later the police knocked on my door. There were two of them, both big men, and they weren't very polite. Happy Heagen had been arrested, and he'd told the cops I was his driver. I was quickly convicted of armed robbery and sentenced to five years at the state prison in Carson City.

3

High on a hill outside of Carson City, Nevada, sits a medieval fortress of solid granite blocks, gray in color. It is imposing and frightening. I saw the gun towers on the walls and what little courage I possessed slipped into my socks.

The judge had said five years but I wasn't sure I could last five hours. I thought of stabbings and gang fights, of being locked up with sex-crazed vicious animals, of sadistic guards who took pleasure in doling out pain and torture. I considered myself a family man — ten years of marriage and two children hadn't prepared me for this real-life nightmare — and I thought seriously it might be best if I were simply killed quickly and spared the misery. *Five years.* In my mind the days and months stretched into eternity.

I imagined I'd have to fight, but that wasn't what bothered me. As an amateur in high school I'd fought Eddie Machen, later a contender for the heavyweight championship. I also fought Olympic champion Johnny Davis, and the number one lightweight contender in the world, Johnny Gonzales. Some people thought I had the chance of a promising career as a professional. Actually, my record as a pro was a respectable 12-2. I was never knocked out, but I saw guys who could hit so hard they could kill you, and I never regretted my decision to quit fighting.

No, I wasn't afraid to fight. What I was afraid of was five or six people coming at me with knives, or even just one, slipping up from behind. I certainly didn't want it known I'd been a fighter. I guessed this would attract more assailants than it would warn off, like in the Old West, where we're told a fast gun never got a moment's rest.

Worst of all was the shame I felt. I knew how disappointed my father was, and hurting him was a betrayal of the many years he'd given me. Those three words said jokingly, "Stick 'em up," now echoed in my mind with bitter irony. I had to fight back tears every time I thought of my mom and dad, and also when I thought of what was going to happen to me.

If I was *lucky* it would be two and a half years before I saw my sons again. Peggy would never allow them to visit me. She said it would be bad for them to see their father in prison. She claimed the experience might damage them for years to come. Well, I thought it was just as bad for them to have a mother whose sex life was more important than her children's welfare. But my bitterness, I knew, wasn't entirely justified. Peggy hadn't forced me to go along on that insane, low-type loan-company stickup.

I knew my life would be vastly different if I ever did survive Carson City. The chances were nil that Peggy would have waited for me, which was just as well, but I wondered if legally I'd even be able to see my sons. Any rights to visitation could be taken away while I was locked up.

The guard who processed me in told me bits and pieces about the place, and I found out the rest firsthand. For many years, a man named Joe Falano had been warden at Carson City. He knew how to get along with the men, and he was highly thought of by both his staff and the inmates. This old maximum security prison had housed both men and women, and the warden's wife was in charge of the women's section. The well-being of the inmates always came first with her, and she was popular with everyone. Then the political opposition took control of the state and Mr. and Mrs. Falano were ousted from their jobs. It was a severe setback for the Nevada penal system.

It didn't take long for me to learn that the Carson City prison was different from any other prison on the planet. The bullpen in the prison was a casino! Crap tables, "21" tables, and poker tables were everywhere. There was a window where inmates could bet on any horse race in the country, and another window for ball games and other sporting events. The gambling flourished around the clock, just like on the outside. If your whole life was betting, the Carson City prison wasn't a bad place.

Big Jim was the head con, which is an important position, second only to the warden in power. The head con maintains an arbitrary order, keeping gangs from killing one another, settling disputes, deciding who gets what job, etc. The head con, in exchange, can make a lot of money in the myriad of illegal activities that flourish in a prison. I doubt if a modern penitentiary could exist at all without the Big Jims of the world. There simply could never be enough guards to keep everything functional.

Big Jim was forty years old, six feet two inches, 230 pounds, had a thick black beard and was tougher than anybody. Big Jim was a natural leader: he had a powerful personality and plenty of money. He was doing life for stabbing a Western Union operator to death in Carson City. He had been in town drinking and gambling and went busted. He wired home to New York City for money, and four times he checked with that Western Union operator to see if it had arrived. It hadn't. So he took a screwdriver and stuck it in the woman's chest. Big Jim was an impatient man.

The moment I arrived at the prison, I was sent to the screen cell. The cell was cramped, like solitary confinement, and I was not allowed out for any reason — no showers, no exercise, nothing. I was not being discriminated against. All new inmates were quarantined until a medical check assured against tuberculosis and venereal diseases. The medical check took three to four days, since blood samples had to be drawn and sent to Reno in a mail truck.

Five days passed and I was still in the screen cell. Before I'd entered prison I'd thought I wouldn't mind spending the entire five years by myself — it would be preferable to the trouble that awaited out in the population — but it didn't take long to realize why solitary confinement is a *punishment*. I thought, after five days, that I was quickly going crazy. I began to suspect someone had it in for me.

"What's the delay?" I asked a guard.

He said he would check my records, but he didn't hurry. And I suspected he did not speed up when I complained about the length of time being taken. Finally, two days later, he told me the glass tube used to transport my blood sample to Reno had been broken. They took another sample and I got another two weeks in the screen cell with nothing to do but make myself sick thinking about my father and my children.

Three weeks, I learned, is a long time in solitary, especially for a newcomer. I was convinced I was going crazy, and I made up my mind to break out. It was impulsive and totally irrational: I had no idea where I would go once I was outside the cell. But it didn't matter. Cages were built for dangerous animals and I was in a cage. And the stark reality that *no one cared* contributed to the hopelessness.

Each morning and evening a convict, escorted by a guard, delivered meals to my cell. He would return thirty minutes later to pick up the tray. I stole a spoon from the tray, filed it down to a fine, sharp edge, and waited for my chance.

One night, after the convict had picked up my tray, I followed him out into the corridor. I was going to grab the guard and hold him hostage. Then maybe they would listen to me, I thought. But the guard saw me coming.

"Roll up your gear," he said. "You're going out into the population tonight."

It never bothered the guard that I was outside my cell. I guess he knew I wasn't going anywhere.

Once I got out into the population, I noticed most of the inmates were neatly dressed. Some of them were actually clotheshorses. It was just part of the system. For five dollars a month an inmate could have his clothes cleaned and pressed, and if a convict wasn't sharply attired it was because he didn't have the money, or was a cheapskate, a miser. As I understated earlier, this was a different kind of prison.

Work crews lined up every day in the prison yard for a count, no matter what the weather was. There were always ten lines of men, twelve men in each line. Somehow the count was never right the first time, nor the second time, nor the third. The guards would smile and say they just wanted to make certain everyone was present and accounted for, when they knew full well the first count was accurate. I think they enjoyed watching us stand in the cold and shiver. Carson City was freezing in the winter.

I was assigned to a dormitory with thirty-nine other men, and luck was with me. I got the last bunk next to the wall. It was comfortable and afforded a minimal amount of privacy.

Then I got unlucky. An Italian homosexual was moved in next to me. His name was Victor, but he preferred to be called Vicki. He had thick black hair all over his body, and wore jeans so tight they nearly choked him. He was repulsive to me, as hairy as an ape, but he considered himself a beauty queen.

All the prisoners referred to Vicki as "she," which he didn't seem to mind, and were happy when he chose me as the recipient of his affections. Vicki would shave his legs, cross them primly, and blow kisses in my direction. He was serving life for murder, which lent him a certain prestige among the inmates, and his insistence on privacy in the john was always respected.

Vicki tried to put the make on me every night. "Fuck off, Vicki," I would tell him.

"But I love you."

"When I look at you," I said unkindly, "I want to vomit."

"I know you don't mean that. I know you care about me too."

"I hate you, Vicki. Go bother somebody else."

"You're the only man I'll ever love."

"Drop dead, Vicki."

"You'll learn to love me. I know you will."

No matter how hard I tried, I couldn't insult or discourage Vicki. After a time I learned to tolerate him. After more time I could even joke with him. He wasn't a bad guy.

Vicki would tell me each morning how he had lain awake the entire night waiting for me to get an erection while I slept. He said how much he admired me. He would get up every morning before the rest of the men to wash and shave and make himself immaculate. When Vicki took a piss, he never stood at the urinal; he always squatted on the stool like a woman. But Vicki was good to me. He got a job in the laundry and began to take care of my clothes, and every night there were freshly-pressed sheets on my bed.

A month after I was transferred into the population, I landed a job in the barber shop. I knew nothing at all about cutting hair.

Ned Coleman was my first customer. It was almost providential, certainly the most important single chance meeting I've ever had. Ned was six feet tall and very thin, with a narrow, intelligent face. He was sixty years old, soft-spoken, a neat dresser, and one of the few people of his generation who smoked marijuana. If a person used grass during the 1930s or 1940s, people thought he was frying his brain, because of the mellow, laid-back, happy effect usually derived from smoking. Ned didn't care what people thought. He was satisfied with who he was and what he knew. And Ned knew more about gambling than anyone else who ever lived.

During the late 1920s and early 1930s Ned Coleman operated illegal casinos, "sneak joints," in California — San Jose, South San Francisco, Palm Springs, Beverly Hills, and Thousand Oaks. Wilbur Clark of the Desert Inn, Johnny Hughes of the Sahara, and Carl Cohen of the Sands were just a few of the men Ned broke into the gambling business. He taught them how to deal craps and "21," and when the gambling boom began in Nevada they set up business there and became tycoons. Ned remained in California and missed his opportunity to become rich, but he was a generous, easygoing man without a trace of bitterness or regret.

Ned told me about the history of Las Vegas, a city officially founded on May 15, 1905, when the San Pedro, Los Angeles & Salt Lake Railroad Company sold plots of land to eager homesteaders. In this dusty, godforsaken nowhere, the railroad thought it was putting one over on the citizenry, but some of those plots of land would come to be worth millions of dollars. Gambling had been going on in the area of Las Vegas (which means "The Meadows") for hundreds of years (the Paiute Indians played a version of craps, betting horses and sometimes their wives), and it was semi-legal until 1910 when it was banned by the Nevada State Legislature. The ban was lifted early in the Great Depression.

Las Vegas was settled in the first place because it was about halfway between Los Angeles and Salt Lake City, and had an abundant water supply. The gold rush 49ers had swept across Las Vegas to California, passing right over the Comstock Lode on their way. A few years later the Mormons tried to make the desert bloom, but the desert was too tough even for those hardy souls. Gamblers made Nevada what it is today.

Ned Coleman even knew the history of gambling, which goes back almost as far as man himself. And as long as there have been gamblers, there have been the men — the crossroaders — who dared to take the edge away from the house. George Washington was a gambler, and the Duke of Wellington, Caligula, Disraeli, the soldiers who marched in the Crusades with Richard the Lionhearted (that may be why he lost to Saladin), the Roman Emperor Augustus, and U.S. President Warren G. Harding. Aristotle wrote a scholarly essay on how to cheat at dice. Other gamblers included Henry IV (he cheated), Claudius, and Nero.

Mario Puzo, author of *The Godfather, Inside Las Vegas*, and *The Sicilian*, wrote that King Henry VIII of England was not only a tough guy with women but a reckless gambler. He lost the famous Jesus Bells, the greatest in England, which hung in the tower of St. Paul's Church. The guy who won them, a Sir Miles Partridge, made the mistake of collecting his bet. Those same bells rang in his ears when he was hanged a few years later for a "criminal offense."

Puzo also proposed an interesting way of reducing the federal deficit. He estimated that if gambling were legalized in the United States, the amount wagered each year would be one trillion dollars. If the government took just ten percent of that, the yearly total would be *one hundred billion* dollars!

Anyway, Ned Coleman and I hit it off right from the beginning. I couldn't imagine anyone not being fascinated by his stories, and for some reason he took to me also. I loved to hear him talk about his gambling days. He knew all the moves. I was surprised when he said he was doing ten years to life for killing a man.

"What are you in for?" Ned asked. We were in the prison barber shop.

"Armed robbery."

"That's dumb."

I smiled and he knew I agreed with him.

"You married?" he asked.

"I was. My wife's getting a divorce."

"Any kids?"

"Two boys. Eight and five years old."

"That's nice. Did you ever do any gambling?"

"I stacked colors at the Mint. And I dealt '21' for a year at the Royal Nevada. But *gambling* gambling, not much. I went out once in a while to get away from my wife."

"It can hook you just the same. Get you down and beat you till you're dead. I've seen guys who'd bet instead of eat. Anyway, how much time are you doing?"

"Two to five years."

"First offense?"

"Yes."

"Hell, if you don't screw up, you'll be out of here in twenty months."

"You really think I could get out that soon?"

"Sure. If you keep your nose clean and don't cause any problems, you'll get an early release."

During the next few months Ned Coleman and I became good friends. He was a source of guidance, a confidante, and I really didn't want to get close to anyone else. I figured the best way to survive in prison was to mind my own business, stay away from people, and hope they stayed away from me. I wasn't unfriendly. I just didn't encourage relationships. Then came the day, it was in the prison barber shop again, when, as Ned put it, "I'm going to prepare you for the rest of your life."

"I'm going to teach you everything I know about cards," he said. "When I'm through, you'll be the best card hustler in the world. Bar none. What do you say to that?"

"When do we start?"

"As soon as we arrange with Big Jim to make us cellmates."

"I've got no bargaining power with Big Jim."

"Don't worry about it. He's a friend."

We shook hands on the deal, and in three days were cellmates. I figured there was nothing to lose. I had failed with the donut shop, struck out as a legitimate dealer, ended up in prison, and was being sued for divorce by my wife. My life had hardly been an uninterrupted climb up the ladder of success.

The first time Ned Coleman dealt a "deuce" on me — dealing the second card from the top — I couldn't believe my eyes.

"I'll never be able to do that," I said.

"Yes, you will."

Ned was patient, infinitely so. He could be tough when he didn't think I was concentrating, but usually he was as kind as a father teaching his son how to ride his first two-wheeler. Ned began by demonstrating the proper way to hold a deck: lightly, in the palm of the hand, feathered between the forefinger and thumb. In the beginning, when I tried to deal seconds, I pulled out four or five cards at a time. My hands felt thick, slablike, and awkward. Ned's hands were delicate, smooth, dexterous.

I practiced daily, two hours in the morning, two hours in the evening. Learning to deal seconds is nerve-racking, frustrating, very difficult to master. But mastering it was a necessity. Woe is what befalls an inept mechanic, and Ned delivered this message over and over. He also told me that I wasn't going to be just a good mechanic, but the best who ever held a deck of cards. He said I was his "project."

To deal seconds the top card is moved a fraction of an inch, just enough so your thumb can catch the edge of the second card and slide it out of the deck. After weeks of instruction and practice, in December, 1962, Ned decided it was time to test me.

I was bad. Ned could call every hand I dealt.

"Keep at it," he encouraged. "You're getting there."

Ned would be kind and supportive at times when I thought he had every reason to get hot. But his anger showed at the slightest sign of carelessness. And his anger seemed almost profound. He knew everything there was to know about dealing cards, and it genuinely pained him when I made a bonehead move. His thin body would tense, and I could actually see pain in his eyes and hear it in his voice.

Ned knew that practice — long, unrelenting doses of it — is far more important than natural dexterity. I increased my practice time from four to six hours a day, my skill and confidence gradually increased, and eventually I became a master mechanic. In fact, I became so good at dealing seconds that not even Ned could tell when I was moving.

"I know I'm being hustled," Ned told me one day. "But I can't see it." His eyes seemed to twinkle with delight. I took what he said as high praise, coming as it did from the man who had taught many of Las Vegas' gambling pioneers.

"It's one thing," Ned cautioned, "to be able to sit with me and do it. It's quite another matter when the pressure is on, when a lot of people are standing around observing closely, and when the money is on the table. But I think you'll be all right."

Ned's confidence would turn out to be well-placed. In years to come I would develop a reputation for icy calm, for being able to keep my wits under extreme pressure. But until I was put to the test, all Ned could do was guess.

Ned taught me how to deal the punch (a way of marking cards by wearing a ring with a sharp protrusion); edgework (marking the sides of cards with a piece of emery board attached to a ring); bend (crimping high cards one way, low cards the other); sorts (shaving cards so high cards can be identified); daub (marking cards with a dye, usually hidden in a fake shirt button); and numerous other ways to cheat at "21" and poker.

The daub was a method favored by many crossroaders. You purchase a dye made with beeswax and secrete it in a shirt button. While practicing, it should be painted heavily on the card. As the practice continues, you apply the dye lightly and ever more lightly. The time will come when only the crossroader will be able to spot the dye. It will be invisible to everyone else. Red dye is applied to red cards, blue to blue. Incredibly, the beeswax dye is purchasable in gaming supply stores open to the public, and its only purpose, so far as I know, is to enable a person to cheat at cards.

When Ned wasn't teaching, he was telling me stories about his past. He told me why he was in prison.

"I was the casino manager at the Senator Hotel right here in Carson City. One day an agent from the Nevada Gaming Commission caught my pit boss using loaded dice at his table. He was doing it on his own. I never gave a man permission to cheat the players.

"The agent confronted the hotel owner with the evidence. 'I know nothing about it,' he said. 'Ned Coleman manages my gambling operation. If there's cheating going on, he knows about it, and he's the man you want to talk with.'

"I told the agent I hadn't known about the cheating. It was the truth. But they held a hearing, didn't buy my story, and I was barred for life from gambling in Nevada. I appealed the decision, but the appeal was denied. Gambling was my whole life, and in an instant they took it away from me.

"I went to the hotel owner and asked him to use his influence with the Gaming Commission. He laughed at me and told me to get lost. He acted like I was slime, said I was no good and had gotten what was coming to me. I couldn't believe this man was talking to me this way. I had a good reputation among casino operators, had done a great deal helping people get started in Nevada gambling, had spent a lifetime learning the business, and now this man was putting an end to my career. Hatred swelled up in me as I left the Senator.

"I had a few drinks down the street, and as the evening passed I became more enraged. I decided he shouldn't get away with doing this to me. I went home, got my .22 rifle out of the closet, went back to the Senator, and sat in the alley waiting for Mr. Big Shot to come out.

"I waited all night in that alley. He left just about at dawn, and I emptied the gun into him. It was Christmas Day. The next day I was arrested and charged with first-degree murder. It was a bum rap. It should have been called self-defense.

"I retained the best criminal lawyer in northern Nevada, and he did a superior job. He persuaded the jury to call it second-degree murder, which saved me from the gas chamber. His job wasn't easy. I had used a .22-caliber rifle, and when the coroner examined the body he found eight bullet holes."

Ned had been one of the great crossroaders, had made his living beating them at any game they could invent. And he set up his own games in California, in Beverly Hills and Palm Springs, where famous entertainers eager for action never stood a chance against him. After decades of living (very well) on his wits, he had gone legitimate by accepting the job at the Senator Hotel, whose owner thought, rightly, that no one would ever cheat him while Ned was around.

Prison, I guess, has been a rite of passage for many people. And meeting Ned Coleman was certainly a key in my life. I would never be the same. I never doubted that one day I would use what Ned was teaching me. I believe I was lured by both the money and the adventure. Ned talked about fortunes that the great crossroaders made, about the thrill of matching wits against the casinos, about the pleasures of being beholden to no one. I was thoroughly captivated, though almost solely by the money aspect. Money — everywhere, but especially in Las Vegas — has a great deal to do with whether life is worthwhile. Never having had any, but seeing what it could bring, made me determined not to be broke again.

Of course, nowhere else could I probably have met anyone like Ned Coleman. You can't look his sort up in a phone book, nor would you recognize his occupation if you saw him practicing it. He was the best at what he did because no one could prove he was doing it. Because Ned was in prison, and because he really didn't think he would ever get out, he chose to pass his knowledge along to someone, who happened to be me.

As I've tried to make clear, most of my free time in prison was spent learning (prison really *is* a school for criminals) a myriad of moves useful to a mechanic from a teacher who knew them all. But no matter how busy I kept myself, it was impossible not to become acquainted with other inmates. Atlas was the inmate who ran the coffee shop, a place next door to the commissary where we could buy donuts, hot cocoa, milkshakes, breakfast rolls, and soup. The warden had asked me to run the shop, but I declined — this type of work reminded me of Visalia. Atlas was a huge man who weighed 250 pounds. He had a black belt in judo, had spent six years in the Marines, and was a homosexual who also enjoyed blowing kisses at people. He looked ridiculous wearing baby-blue eyeliner and pale pink lipstick, but he was a big healthly guy, a very tough character. He had beaten someone to death with his bare hands.

The prison had a dance band. It was the pet project of the captain of the guards, a moody man named Orville Jackson. He could be friendly for a few days, then turn on you for no reason and order you thrown into the hole. Orville's wife was named Ivie. Orvie and Ivie. Several years after I left Carson City, I learned Captain Jackson had died of a brain tumor. That explained the strange behavior, I guess.

Nearly everyone in northern Nevada knew the prison band as the "Boys in Blue." There were five men in the band, and Orville Jackson accompanied it wherever it went. His unpredictable behavior, which I thought might be intentional to keep prisoners worried and off balance, assured that no one overly enjoyed the trips outside the walls.

Abe was the band's pianist. He was a black man from Las Vegas who was doing ten years for possession of drug-store stuff — uppers, downers, nothing more serious. He'd had a rare taste of coke, but nobody ever found out about that. Abe was short, stocky, and talented. He resembled Count Basie, had a good personality, and was pleasant to be around. He never griped, which is a favorite pastime in prison, even though he'd gotten a long sentence for taking pills that most truck drivers use every day they're on the road. Abe had countless funny stories about famous people he knew and had played with. He'd performed with several name bands, including Duke Ellington and Oscar Peterson, mostly rhythm and blues, and was an exceptional musician.

Tex, a cattle rustler, was the band's violinist. He looked like a cowboy — with his weather-beaten face a person might have thought he'd been born on the range. Tex could play country and western, rock, even classical music. No one could do "Orange Blossom Special" better than Tex, and not only was he a skilled violinist but he was a talented painter. He did portraits of many of the men in prison. I still have the one he did of me.

The rhythm guitarist was a legitimate cowboy named Cal. The Bunco Squad had picked him up for defrauding an innkeeper. This is a serious crime in Nevada (what Tex did was dodge out of paying a bill), which gives a good indication of the power of hotels in this gambling state. Tex got five years, perhaps as a warning to others who might consider attempting this horrible crime.

Don, a car thief, was the vocalist. He often talked about his wealthy parents, who evidently hadn't been able to keep him out of jail. Actually, authorities weren't reluctant to put someone away. Federal money was linked to the number of prisoners being kept incarcerated, and scuttlebutt had it that Nevada politicians wanted the jails packed because of the payments available to the state. I liked Don, but he had a terrible voice and was always off key, sounding as if he were in pain. Captain

Jackson liked him, however, and made him the singing star of the "Boys in Blue."

Abe, the pianist, came to my barber shop every morning for a shave. He would sit and talk for hours about the gigs he had played around the country. Anyone would have enjoyed listening to him, and I was no exception. One morning Abe told me that the drummer had recently been paroled and the band needed a replacement.

"I want in," I said.

The job paid $100 a month, which was twice what I pulled down for cutting hair, and it got you away from the depressing prison atmosphere, if only for short periods. I'd been thinking about getting out of prison since the moment I'd gotten in. It seemed to me that being in the prison band might hasten the day of permanent departure. By getting out with the public I believed I could show I was no menace to society, that I was a good fellow who'd made one terrible mistake which wouldn't be repeated. What I would do when I got out wasn't resolved. There wasn't any legitimate job training at the prison, unless you call making license plates job training. Ned Coleman said I was becoming a great mechanic, which would put me in a top income bracket, but just *how* this would work he hadn't yet explained, and I didn't ask. Also, the extra money from being in the band would cover my commissary needs and I could send Peggy $50 a month to help feed and clothe the boys. Above everything else I wanted to see and help my sons.

"Can you play?" Abe asked.

"I taught Gene Krupa everything he knows."

"Are you sure you can play?"

"Of course I am."

I was lying through my front teeth. I didn't know the first thing about drums.

"Don't bullshit me," Abe said. "If I take you in, you'll have to audition for the Captain. You know what he's like. If you can't play he's going to be real hot."

"Give me a chance, Abe. If you'll show me a few moves with the sticks, I can fake the rest."

Abe agreed to help, and I practiced like a fiend for two days. Getting away from the prison once in a while seemed like a high goal to shoot for, a veritable Mount Everest as far as I was concerned. It would make life livable, I thought, if only for brief intervals. Practicing each night for hours with Ned Coleman was better than solitary confinement, and something might come out of it in the future, but actually *getting out from behind the walls.* . . well, during those two days with Abe, the idea became an obsession.

On the day of my audition Abe had fixed it for the other guys in the band to make so much noise that Orville Jackson couldn't tell if I was beating the snare drum or not. Evidently the Captain liked what he heard: I got the job. Even Ned Coleman congratulated me. He thought having a diversion from my "true calling" would be refreshing and might serve to hone my skills more sharply. "It can't be all work, boy," he said when I told him about my new job. Increasingly he had been praising my progress, and praise was not something that came easily from this man's mouth.

The prison at Carson City was built in the 1860s, and was constructed of granite blocks. The authorities had at some time or another ordered holes cut into the granite. It was a diabolical project: for disciplinary reasons, the holes (called caves) were large enough to stuff a man into. One of these forbidding caves was large enough to hold two men, so Abe and I sat in there several hours each day. He played blues on a guitar, and I gave him a little rhythm on the drums. The music was western because the band played mostly at rodeos and barbecues and the majority of the audiences were ranchers and their families. The food was outstanding at the barbecues and all of us looked forward to them.

Soon after I joined the band, the American Legion asked us to make an appearance. The Carson City Legion hall was packed, the dance floor was jammed, and everyone was having a good time. Captain Jackson was in his usual position, sitting on stage with the band. Suddenly he got an idea.

"Get up there and sing a song," he said to me.

"I don't know how to sing, Captain." I was lucky I hadn't been exposed for a fraud on the drums.

"Get your ass up there and sing. If you don't, you won't be with the band after tonight."

I walked up to the microphone and did the only song I knew, "Tennessee Waltz." As I started to sing, everyone stopped dancing. They stood for a moment watching and listening to me, and when I finished there was no one left on the dance floor. Most of them had gone to the bar, and it took thirty minutes to convince them I wouldn't sing again. Jackson knew he had made a mistake.

Another early appearance during my stint with the band was at an annual affair in Gerlach, Nevada, in the northern part of the state. It was typical of what we did. The band put up a big tent and strung up lights in the prairie. A steer was barbecued, there was dancing on the dirt, a lot of it square dancing, and everyone had a good time. Residents in many small towns loved the Boys in Blue.

Except for patients at the mental hospital (there an old Indian woman with no teeth would smile and wave at me, saying I was her one true love), the band was not allowed to talk to any of the citizens while we were out on a playing date. If someone requested a song, they were referred to the Captain.

A pretty young girl came up to me one night in Fallon, Nevada, while we were on a break. She looked about sixteen years old.

"You play very well."

She obviously didn't have an ear for music. "I can't talk with you," I said.

"Oh."

"I'm sorry."

"Could I write to you?"

I thought it would be good to get mail. Except for my father, no one seemed to care that I was in prison. I gave the girl my address.

The second letter I received from her ended my musical career. There was a sergeant at the prison who didn't like me. In fact, he didn't like anyone. He was a stickler for rules and regulations, they were the only things he knew, and his job was checking the incoming mail. He saw the girl's name and her return address and got hot. The girl's parents were friends of his, and he knew the only way I could have met her was at a dance. He took the letter to Orville Jackson and I was fired from the band.

It was for the best. A guy named Jack Farmer had just come into the prison. Jack had been convicted of a petty drug charge similar to Abe's, and he was a jazz drummer who wanted to join the band. His picture had been in *Down Beat* magazine, and he was rated the seventh best drummer in the country. His talent would add a lot to the group. Since I couldn't *quit* the band (you could only get out if Orville Jackson let you), the sole way Jack Farmer could realize his ambition was for the Captain to fire me.

I guess the most controversial character I met in Carson City was Joe Conforte. Joe was serving a year for extortion. He was five feet seven inches tall, weighed 180 pounds, was olive-skinned and balding and always smoked a cigar. Joe is of course well-known as the proprietor of the Mustang Ranch, fifteen miles east of Reno, a group of house trailers (and one brick building where you could get drinks) ringed by a cyclone fence topped with barbed wire. The Mustang Ranch was really a single house of prostitution. Twenty or thirty girls worked there at any given time, making Joe a rich man. Later heavyweight contender Oscar Bonavena was gunned down at Mustang Ranch. Conforte is currently trying to sell his "ranch." Asking price: $25 million.

While Joe Conforte was in the slammer, his wife ran the business. She knew how to handle the girls, and she made a ton of money for Joe.

Life in prison was not terribly uncomfortable for Joe. He had piles of money and was able to buy almost anything he wanted. He smoked dollar Havana cigars, ate steak, and for five dollars a week had his meals served to him.

Conforte came into the prison as a regular tough guy. He hired four young hoods as bodyguards. One day Joe was in the bullpen relaxing at a card table that he did not realize was the exclusive domain of a huge Indian named Turk.

"Would you please move?" Turk said. "I'm going to start my game."

"Go play somewhere else," Joe suggested.

Turk was one of the toughest guys in the joint. He weighed nearly three hundred pounds. Joe did not know there was a tribe of Indians in the prison, and they all stuck together.

"You've got thirty seconds to move," said Turk.

Joe nodded to his four goons. "Throw this son of a bitch out of here," he said.

Twelve Indians stood up and Conforte's bodyguards ran out the door. Turk jerked Joe up off the table and beat on him pretty good, and after this Conforte became a nice guy. On the Fourth of July, 1963, there was a celebration in the yard for all the prisoners, and Joe bought lemonade and hot dogs for everyone. The Warden furnished watermelons. By the time Joe left prison he had won the respect of nearly everyone, although there were a few who were envious of his money. Joe provided financial assistance to quite a few men after they were released from prison, especially those who were down-and-out.

The Indians also had plenty of money. It was a long-overdue

gift from Uncle Sam, partial payment for the vast tracts of land the Government had stolen from them. The Indians also enjoyed steak nearly every night, although they said they would have preferred buffalo meat had it been available. Most of the Indians in the prison were doing time for killing another Indian on a reservation.

The women's section of the prison was located above the infirmary and was small compared to ours. Joe Conforte, always the businessman, concocted a scheme that endeared him to prisoners and officials alike. Conforte knew there were no facilities for women at the local jail in Carson City, so he had some of his girls from Reno come to town and get busted for prostitution. They were sent out to the fortress, usually for thirty days. Big Jim okayed the scheme, and Joe was able to open a whorehouse right inside the prison walls. The price was reasonable, and most men were able to afford at least one lay a week. Many inmates *and* prison administrators benefited from Conforte's ingenuity and Big Jim's benevolence. Of course, Big Jim cut himself in for a good percentage of the profits.

Gambling and prostitution were the chief forms of entertainment at the prison, just as they were outside the walls. For additional diversion, boxing matches were held once a month, and the heavyweight champion was a homosexual. "The world's turned upside down in this joint," an inmate remarked to me. He had been raised to believe that homosexuals were limp-wristed, delicate, frail, and cowardly. The opposite was true at Carson City. Homosexuals were among the biggest and toughest guys in the prison. People might laugh whenever they saw the heavyweight champion swish across the yard, but no one messed with Sally. He could be real mean if someone made him mad.

An inmate I'd gotten to know who was a boxing fan persuaded me to come out of retirement for one fight. The prison's middleweight champion was an unpopular individual who'd been champion of the ship he'd been aboard while in the U.S. Navy. By this time I thought, why not? I caught the man early with a hard right hand and he spent the remainder of the four rounds backpedaling. It was an easy win.

The victory was a popular one, and other inmates urged me to become a regular on the monthly fight extravaganza. I replied with a quick and emphatic no. Many of the bouts were bloodbaths, and a person could be permanently injured. Besides, I was happy spending my time with Ned Coleman, who assured me I was a natural as a mechanic. Even if I could manage to avoid serious injury in one of those fights, I didn't want to risk hurting my hands.

One of the saddest things I saw in prison was what happened to Animal Braun. Animal came to Carson City because he grabbed a handful of silver dollars off a "21" table at the Silver Slipper in Las Vegas. The coins didn't belong to him. Animal was in the Slipper having a good time, doing some drinking and gambling, and went busted. The pit boss refused him credit, so Animal grabbed the silver dollars and ran out the door. The police were called and they arrested Animal for theft. The judge laughed when he heard the charges. He laughed so hard he sentenced Animal to *five years* in the state prison at Carson City.

Animal was angry when he heard the sentence, and extremely bitter by the time he arrived at the joint. He cursed the guards and they threw him into one of the caves. It was winter, and the guards stripped him naked before they put him in the cave.

There was no bed in the cave, only a dirt floor and a steel-barred door that let in the cold air. That night when the guards brought Animal his dinner and slid it through the bars, he grabbed hold of it and threw it back at them, splattering one of the guards with lukewarm stew. The guard got a garden hose and doused Animal with ice-cold water. Inmates all over the prison could hear Animal screaming and cursing defiantly.

Every time Animal got noisy, the guard doused him again with freezing water. Animal was forced to stand the entire night and he almost froze to death. He had icicles hanging from his eyebrows. At eight o'clock in the morning when they took Animal Braun to the hospital, he was very sick. His hands and feet were frozen and he had pneumonia. He was in the hospital for two months. When he joined the prison population he was minus one big toe, amputated because of gangrene.

Animal Braun was a big, hard-headed kid, six feet four inches tall and 240 pounds. He had a good sense of humor and when he wasn't in the caves (though he usually was) he entertained the inmates and kept them laughing. Animal had a long list of curse words which he used freely to describe the guards and their relatives.

Everyone in the joint knew when Animal went into the caves. As soon as the guards hit him with cold water, he would scream and holler and curse his tormentors. The guards would laugh when Animal roared, and continue to douse him with the freezing water. But Animal had courage. He never begged them to show him mercy.

Animal swore he would never serve his five-year sentence. He vowed to escape. Then the infection in his foot returned, and this time the doctors amputated it just above the knee. Animal was escaping from the joint in pieces.

Animal was no longer the big, light-hearted, noisy kid who had entered the prison eight months earlier. Now he limped around on crutches. He no longer cursed or shouted or told jokes. He hardly talked to anyone. He shrank before our eyes, lost more than a hundred pounds, became old and haggard. I asked him how he was getting along.

"Not too good," he said. "The medics keep treating me for tuberculosis. I've told them it's gangrene."

"Why don't you file a lawsuit? Maybe you can get some action."

"It won't do me any good," he said. "I'm dying."

I saw Animal two days later on my way to work. He looked terrible. That afternoon he limped into the showers and lay down and died.

4

Big Jim approached me in the yard one day in August, 1963, when I'd been in prison just over a year. The big, bearded head con got straight to the point, and I literally could not believe what I was hearing.

"The Warden's looking for someone to work at the Governor's mansion," he said. "The Warden doesn't want a killer, and neither does the Governor. Are you interested in the job?"

"Who wouldn't be?" I said. I didn't care what kind of job it was. I would wash dishes, hump heavy furniture, clean toilet bowls, anything to get outside the walls once a day.

The job turned out to be a snap. My duties were to answer the telephone and serve meals. If a party was scheduled, I stayed late and served drinks. Big Jim had tabbed me for the job for several reasons: the Governor had a twelve-year-old daughter and did not want someone working at the mansion who had been convicted of a violent crime. Big Jim trusted me and knew I was not a petty thief. Also he was fascinated by the way Ned Coleman had taught me to handle a deck of cards. He figured it might be a talent he could later employ, so it made sense for him to have me in his debt. In addition, my looks worked in my favor. I had very dark hair and clean features — some people even said I was handsome — and all my life I had kept trim by working out.

There were six hundred prisoners at Carson City, and I was envied by all of them. Indeed, the job's benefits were beyond my wildest hopes. A *chauffeur* drove me to work every morning. When it was time to return, usually about 9:00 p.m., I would call for a driver. I ate my meals at the mansion — there was a night-and-day difference between this food and the gruel served in the prison — and friends and relatives were able to visit me.

My father spent an entire afternoon with me in comfort, rather than the few minutes he would have been allowed in the prison visiting room. Several times I wrote to Peggy and told her she could now bring my boys to visit. She never answered the letters.

I was introduced to the Governor and his family on my first day at the mansion. He seemed to me an honorable man, a rare breed in the arena of Nevada politics. He was about five feet nine inches tall, perhaps forty years old, slim, with black hair and a ready smile. He treated everyone with respect, like human beings, and during the time I worked for him I never heard him discredited in any way. This was unusual indeed in the sewer world of Nevada politics, where fixes and shady deals were the rule, not the occasional exception.

The Governor's Mansion, located on the west side of Carson City, was a large two-story white colonial home. The entrance was banked by massive columns, and a big wooden veranda wrapped around the front and sides. The mansion had a huge formal dining room with a long table for entertaining dignitaries, as well as a smaller dining room for the family's private use. The Governor's office, including his library, was on the second floor, which was reached by a spectacular staircase. Perhaps the second most impressive room in the house (after the formal dining room) was the drawing room, which featured a baby grand piano, magnificent crystal chandeliers, and expensive draperies and tapestries.

To my surprise, the Governor and I soon became close friends. He trusted me. A few times he asked my opinion on an issue, and seemed sincerely interested in my reply. The Governor introduced me to state senators, the Attorney General, Supreme Court justices, and other dignitaries. Some of them thought I was the Governor's confidential assistant, and we did nothing to discourage their thinking. It was our own private joke.

"Would you like to attend the inaugural ball?" the Governor's wife asked me when that event was upcoming.

"I'd love to," I said. "But I don't have anything to wear."

"You and my husband are the same size." Actually, I was an inch taller at five feet ten. "Why don't you go upstairs and select something appropriate?"

I chose a tuxedo, and it was almost a perfect fit. In fact, I thought his clothes looked better on me than on him. I came down the spiral staircase, feeling like a star making an entrance, and the Governor's wife looked up and saw me dressed in her husband's tuxedo.

"John!" she said. "You can't wear that. That's what my husband's planning to wear!"

I was embarrassed, but was put somewhat at ease when she laughed and waved the incident away. I went back upstairs and selected a dark blue, pin-striped suit with a white-on-white shirt, and stood before a mirror for a while admiring myself. I hadn't worn nice clothes for a long time, and I looked sharp. I was ready for the ball.

At exactly 7:00 p.m. the limousine pulled up in front of the mansion. I started to get into the front seat, next to the driver, but the Governor stopped me.

"Sit back here with us," he said.

He also insisted I sit with him and his wife in their box at the ball, and people wondered who the "movie star" was that the Governor had invited for the occasion. It was impossible not to be aware of the curiosity. I could read it in people's eyes. Women smiled and glanced sideways, flirting and whispering. I'd never been the object of such attention.

The Governor was having a great time. He introduced me to people as his confidential assistant, *his closest advisor*. Politicians and newsmen engaged me in political discussions, which I sidestepped with a straight face, the way a real advisor would have. A reporter asked me to define the Governor's position on a proposal put forward by a consumer group.

"The Chief Executive," I said, "is giving the matter his usual careful consideration."

A politician wanted to know if the Governor sided with the majority or the minority on a key legislative issue.

"The Chief Executive is giving the matter his usual careful consideration."

Actually, the Governor was doing everything he could to keep from breaking up with laughter. I had never seen anyone so often put a handkerchief over his mouth.

Another politician wanted to know if the Governor supported the President's position on nuclear testing.

"The Chief Executive is giving . . . ."

"How did you learn to talk like that?" the Governor asked when we were on the way back to the mansion.

"From watching your *real* advisors on television," I said.

With that, all of us cracked up laughing.

It was 11:30 p.m. when we returned to the mansion. A small group of close personal friends had been invited to a private party, so we pulled the drapes, locked the doors, and had a good time. The Governor revealed my true identity to his friends, and everyone enjoyed a good laugh. The party broke up at 5:00 a.m., and I was beat. I had to work that day. One of the guests at the party was Superintendent of the Nevada Highway Patrol.

"I'll drive you to the prison," he said.

"You might get in trouble," I said.

"I don't think so," he said with a half-drunken smile.

The State had just provided the Superintendent with a brand-new Chrysler with radial tires. It was souped-up and he was eager to show what it could do. The prison was just three miles from the mansion, but the Superintendent decided to take the long route. He screeched off in the direction of a town twenty-five miles away.

It was a straight stretch of highway, as are all roads in Nevada. The Superintendent pushed the car to its limit. The speedometer needle hovered at 120 m.p.h., and if it was his intention to scare me, he succeeded. I sat in the death seat realizing there was one fortunate aspect of the trip: at 120 m.p.h. it would not last long.

When we finally approached the prison the Superintendent was traveling so fast he had to lock the wheels to keep from roaring through the fence, which the guard on Tower Number One did not like. The guard almost went berserk when he saw *me* in the car.

"Why in hell didn't you call for a guard to pick you up?"

"Because I offered to drive him back," said the Superintendent.

"You don't have the authority," said the guard.

He knew it was a mistake as soon as the words were out of his mouth. Technically, the Superintendent of the Nevada Highway Patrol might not have such authority, but in any showdown between him and a lowly prison guard, the outcome of that struggle could never be in doubt.

What really bothered the guard, all the guards, was that the Governor liked me and gave me special privileges. It seemed to them that I, a convicted robber, was living a better life than they were.

One Sunday afternoon the governor was in the main reception

room with a U.S. Senator, and I had just served them drinks.

"I'm having a party this evening," the Governor said. "Do you know a good cocktail pianist?"

"Yes, sir. A guy named Abe at the prison. He's one of the best in the country."

"What's he in for?"

"Minor use of drugs."

"Telephone the prison and have him sent over."

I went out to the hallway and called the joint. The sergeant who hated me, the one who had me thrown off the band, answered the phone.

"Sarge," I said, "send Abe over to the mansion."

I held the phone receiver away from my ear and waited for the explosion.

"Who the hell do you think you're talking to? You don't call here and give orders."

"They're not my orders. They're the Governor's."

"Well, hotshot, you tell the Governor I don't do a thing unless he tells me personally."

"Hold on," I said.

It was a great opportunity for revenge, and I couldn't resist it. I walked into the main reception room.

"Governor," I said, "the sergeant on duty at the prison told you to go to hell."

He jumped out of his chair, strode into the hallway, and snatched up the telephone. "Sergeant," he said, "this is the Governor. If Abe isn't here in thirty minutes, you're fired."

Fifteen minutes later a station wagon from the prison pulled up in front of the mansion. Inside was Abe, a wide smile on his face. I greeted him at the door.

"How did you manage this?" he asked.

I told him about the sergeant, and Abe laughed all the way into the kitchen. Mable, the cook at the mansion, had food for us. Mable was a big black woman, and though I couldn't judge her exact age, she was somewhere between fifty and sixty-five. The first day we met, she had laid down her ground rules.

"If you want to call me 'nigger' in a joking way," she said, "that's all right. If you call me 'nigger' and mean it, I'll take a butcher knife and cut your throat."

"Mabel," I said, "I don't play that shit. I just want to do my time and get out." She understood what I meant.

Later that evening Abe played rhythm-and-blues piano and drank whiskey all night. Abe was super. It seemed impossible to make a request he couldn't play.

The following early morning the Superintendent of the Highway Patrol, the same guy driving the same 120 m.p.h. route, took us back to the prison. Abe thought it was great fun. Both he and the Superintendent were drunk, and this time the guard in Tower Number One pretended not to notice anything amiss when we skidded to a stop. I was grateful for this, since I was sober and would have had to bear the brunt of the abuse.

I do not drink, and didn't back then. Not drinking was a major reason I survived and prospered so long in the dangerous profession I adopted after release from prison.

The next morning Abe told me again how grateful he was to me for getting him the gig. He said he wanted more, especially since he had been dropped from the band.

"What happened?" I said.

"I got my hands on some grass. Orville found out and dumped me."

Abe had grown accustomed to the gigs, had come to rely on them to maintain his sanity. The deadly dull grind of prison life could break the defenses of the strongest individual. Without those trips outside the walls he was afraid he would go crazy. I had seen it happen to inmates less sensitive than Abe.

I told Abe it would be a while before the Governor had another party, but that I would talk to Big Jim for him. "Maybe he can get you a job driving the prison garbage truck," I said. "At least you'll get outside once a day."

"You're doing me a big favor," Abe said.

It turned out I was arranging for his funeral.

Big Jim fixed Abe up with the job. Abe and Willy, another black man, drove the garbage truck to the dump each day, a ten-mile round trip. On one occasion, on the way to the dump, they saw a white girl hitchhiking. They pulled over and offered her a ride, and she jumped in beside them.

When they got to the dump the girl took off her clothes and the three of them had a time. Everyone was satisfied. Then they emptied the truck and started back to town.

Abe figured it would be unwise to drive too far with the girl in the truck, so they let her out along the highway, not far from Carson City. A highway patrolman saw her get out, stopped, picked her up, and asked what she was doing in a prison truck.

The girl panicked. She had been skipping school regularly and was afraid she would be sent to a juvenile home. She told the patrolman she had been walking to school and the two black men stopped and forced her into the truck. She told the patrolman they drove her to the garbage dump and raped her.

Abe and Willy were arrested by Carson City authorities and charged with kidnapping and rape. They were housed in the county jail while they awaited trial. Both men admitted to having sex with the girl, but denied having kidnapped and raped her.

The good citizens of Carson City went wild. Inside the prison we heard ugly rumors that castrations and lynchings were planned. The presiding judge ordered an immediate trial, which was a swift, no-nonsense affair where justice took a bad mugging. Abe and Willy got off with imprisonment for the rest of their natural lives. It was the most expensive sex either of them would ever have.

Abe and Willy were returned to the fortress to serve their sentences. At least they were safer in the prison than in the county jail.

Abe couldn't accept the thought of being locked up for the rest of his life. He loved music and good times too much.

Abe grabbed a guard's gun and ran across the yard firing at the towers. The guards returned the fire and cut Abe's sentence short, which was what he intended.

Things would have been different had Abe possessed a modicum of patience. The captain of the guards knew the girl and her parents, and he also knew her reputation. Under pressure he pulled the truth out of her. She admitted lying.

The convictions were overturned, posthumously for Abe. The confession did help Willy, but it came too late for my friend. The world lost a damn good pianist.

Prison life went on as usual. The economic system was modeled on the system outside the walls: wealth was acquired, and with it favors were bought. Big Jim and Joe Conforte were aristocrats, the ruling class, who accumulated large reserves of capital. Big Jim made his fortune from gambling, Conforte from prostitution.

Joe Conforte came up to me one day in the yard. "Do you get along okay with the Governor?" he asked.

"Sure," I said. "We're friends. Why do you want to know?"

"Will you take a message to him?"

"What is it?"

"I understand his family is in Europe for six weeks."

"That's right."

"Give him this message. Tell him I'll send some girls over."

"What kind of girls?"

"Working girls."

I started to laugh.

"I'm serious," said Joe Conforte.

"Okay," I said. "I'll deliver your message."

The next morning I approached the Governor while he was eating breakfast. I asked him if he knew of Joe Conforte.

"I've heard of him. Why do you ask?"

"Well," I said, rubbing my hands together anxiously, "Conforte said to tell you if you needed any girls, he'd send them over right away."

The Governor had been sipping coffee, but when I gave him Conforte's message he nearly swallowed the cup. I couldn't help it: I began laughing, and I laughed until my sides hurt.

"Tell Conforte," the Governor said, "that I appreciate his offer. But no thanks."

And then the Governor began to laugh.

That night Joe asked if I'd delivered his message.

"Yes," I answered. "But he said to tell you he's very busy right now."

"That's okay," Joe said magnanimously. "Just tell him to get in touch whenever he wants girls sent over."

My time in prison was drawing to a close, and I was amazed I'd survived it so well. Minding my own business had helped, and not trying to make too many friends among the inmate population. My own problems were enough; sharing those of others would have made matters that much worse. What I mainly felt was that I was going to make it through the ordeal, not the smallest of accomplishments, and that once on the outside I'd find the success that so far had eluded me.

The day before I left Carson City I had a long talk with my mentor, Ned Coleman. Ned had written a glowing letter of recommendation for me to a casino manager in Las Vegas who was an old friend of his.

"Any hotel in Las Vegas," Ned said, "will be happy to give you a hundred dollars a day just to be on the payroll. I've never seen anyone use a deck of cards better than you. And I've seen the best. You'll only have to work when someone is winning a lot of money. The pit boss will call you in to stop the hot hand."

"Well, I want to thank you, Ned."

"Always good to see someone learn a trade in prison."

I promised Ned I would take care of him, that he had it coming. He had taught me how to use the cards and how to whack out on the craps. He had been a friend and counselor when I needed one, and as long as I had money Ned would never want for anything. We embraced and patted each other on the back.

I also had a talk with the Governor. He had a different vision of my future from that which Ned held. He said I should spend six months in California, making sure to live an exemplary life, and then write him a letter asking for my civil rights to be restored. The Governor assured me he would sign the necessary papers. He then suggested I return to Nevada and run for a minor political office. He said I could count on his support.

I suppose this was one of the forks a person encounters in his journey through life. Turn right, and one thing will happen. Turn left, and it will be something altogether different. There really was never any doubt in my mind which direction I was headed.

My stay in prison had shaped me differently from most of the other men. For one thing, I'd actually improved my social graces. I had become more sophisticated. Ned said I reminded him of a diplomat. A common practice among inmates, perhaps their favorite pastime, is to sit around and talk about the big scores they're going to pull off when they get out: a kidnapping, maybe, or hitting on some isolated farmhouse whose owner, they've heard, keeps a fortune stuffed in his mattress. I was doing the same thing in a way, sitting quietly each night in my cell with Ned, but there was a difference. While many prisoners talked about the violence they were willing to unleash if necessary, really bone-chilling stuff, we concentrated on how it must be avoided at almost any cost.

"Guns and knives are for losers," Ned emphasized. "You can make a lot more money without them."

One thing I did learn in common with all the inmates: I didn't like prison. And I would do everything I could to avoid coming back. Of course, everyone in the joint thought he was a smart guy and could avoid the mistakes of the past.

I was thirty-four years old when I left prison.

When I stepped outside the walls I was dreaming of all the money I was going to make. The prospects were exciting and seemingly unlimited. I would have a pocket full of hundred-dollar bills, an expensive car, a fabulous wardrobe, and life in a first-class hotel with all the amenities. My sons would worship me, and I would give them everything they previously had done without. Peggy would be sorry she divorced me. She would come crawling back when she discovered how well-off I was.

5

My father was waiting for me outside the prison. He had been almost my sole contact with my past while I'd been in prison. First off we went to the mansion. I wanted to say good-bye to the first family, who had been so kind to me.

It was the same air I'd breathed every day since I'd been locked up, but somehow it was cleaner and sweeter. I took it deep into my lungs, then stretched my muscles to the limit, as a man might when he awakens from sleep. The desert sky was a bright blue, and the sunlight glistened, as if it knew precisely how to match my mood. When the car pulled away from the gates, I craned my neck backwards to see what I was leaving, to record the scene in my mind so I would never forget.

I felt relief that the long-awaited day had arrived, and a certain negative sense of accomplishment. It hadn't seemed possible when I'd entered prison that I could survive it, but I had, and there were even a few good memories.

We had coffee at the Governor's mansion and visited for thirty minutes. Then the Governor shook my hand, patted me on the back, and wished me luck. His wife and daughter actually cried. It made me sad to leave them too, but I was overjoyed to be out of prison and free again. Perhaps I'd see them again, I thought, though it was impossible to imagine the circumstances.

I was on my way to Las Vegas!

"Do you want to drive?" my dad asked.

I sat behind the wheel of his new car and felt good. On the way to Las Vegas I kept the speedometer needle near 80 m.p.h. It had been a long time since I'd seen my sons. Being apart from them was by far the worst part of prison, and I missed them very much. Anticipating being with them made both my blood and the car run fast.

My dad knew of my plans, and predictably thought I was making a mistake. He believed I should do what the Governor had suggested, and used words like "crazy" and "boneheaded" to describe what I had in mind. He just wanted the best for me, and he was never reluctant to tell me what that was. I nodded my head a lot as he talked, but my mind was made up. I wanted to make money, and figured that what Ned Coleman had taught me was almost as valuable as a printing machine.

We hauled into town at 3:00 p.m. on that April, 1964, evening, and Las Vegas was the same spectacular sight I remembered. Bright lights, sidewalks packed, billboards advertising glamorous shows and big-time entertainment. During the day Las Vegas could be anything but a spectacular sight. It could be hot, dusty, dry, an almost depressing desert settlement baking under a brutal, unmerciful sun. But at night it was really something.

We went directly to Bill Kuchenbecker's apartment. Bill was a friend and former boxer who had attended Visalia High School with Peggy and me. He lived across the street from the Riviera, where I had helped him get a job dealing "21." Kuchenbecker was someone I knew I could count on. I called him on the lobby phone.

"Come on up," he said. He sounded happy to hear from me. I had wondered how friends would react to my having been in prison.

"I've got my father with me."

"Bring him up."

Bill was waiting at the door, a short, friendly man with pale skin that bespoke of too many hours in smoky, artificially-lit casinos. We shook hands, exchanged a few preliminaries, and I got right to the point.

"Bill," I said, "I need to ask a favor."

"What is it?"

"Do you know where Peggy and her new husband live?"

"Yes."

"Would you drive there and pick up my sons and bring them back here? It's been a long time since I've seen them."

"Why can't you do it?"

"Peggy and I aren't friends. Also, I don't want to see her until I'm on solid ground and can show some success."

"I understand. You make yourselves comfortable, and I'll be back in thirty minutes."

The telephone rang fifteen minutes later. It was Peggy.

"Why did you send Bill over to get the kids?" she asked. "Couldn't you come yourself?"

"I don't want to see you," I said, "and I don't think you want to see me. I do want to see my sons. That's mostly what's kept me going."

"I think you've got something up your sleeve."

"What?"

"I think you're planning to kidnap them."

"Peggy, you're crazy."

"Well, that's what I think."

"Do you? I just got out of the state pen. What I did to get sent there was stupid, but if you had any brains you'd know I did it to put food on the table for you and the boys. Do you think I'm going to kidnap them so I can get sent back to Carson City for ten or fifteen *more* years?"

"All right," she said. "Bill can bring them over to see you, but I want them back in time for supper."

"They'll be back."

It was beautiful and wonderful and more when I saw my boys, Billy and Johnny.

I was sitting by the pool when I saw the car pull up in the parking lot with the boys. I could read Billy's lips through the car window as he shouted, "There's Dad!" Their eyes were big as saucers and they could hardly wait for the car to come to a halt. They jumped out and ran as fast as they could into my arms.

Tears came to my eyes as we all hugged together, an embrace warmer than anything the Nevada sun could produce. I was in paradise, and was forced to concede that Peggy must not have tried to turn them against me.

I had had absolutely no contact with the boys for the eighteen long months I had been gone, and I was euphoric at the way they clung to me. We couldn't get enough of each other. Their appearance had not changed a lot except they had both grown noticeably taller.

Bill gave us passes to his swimming pool. With money I had won playing cards in the joint I bought bathing suits for the boys and myself, and we swam and played away the afternoon. In the water I threw them up into the air, they turned somersaults, and we had a real workout. The crowning achievement of the afternoon was when I taught them how to dive in head first. At ten and seven they already knew how to swim quite well, but it was a joy for me to witness their elation and feeling of conquest when they finally overcame their fears and mastered a dive (in their own frog-like style).

As I reveled in my time with Billy and Johnny, I couldn't help but think of how different things could have been over the past year and a half. I wished I could have lived with these two little boys, rather than with cons, many with hearts as cold as the granite walls that housed them.

Darkness came sooner than we wanted. After we showered and dressed, Bill and my father went with us for a good dinner at the Riviera to cap off a super day. I deliberately kept them past the agreed-upon hour, partly wanting to break Peggy's chops a little bit but mainly because I was having such a good time. Bill finally drove the children back to their mother, and my father, grumbling still that I was making a mistake, departed for some gambling and a later trip to San Francisco.

"Have you got a place to stay?" Bill Kuchenbecker asked when he was back in the apartment.

"No."

"You've got one now. I have an extra bedroom, and you're welcome to it until you're on your feet."

"Are you sure?"

"You got me a good job out here. I owe you."

"You don't owe me anything."

"I *want* you to stay."

In the morning I walked across the street to the Riviera and filled out a work application, and on the strength of Ned Coleman's recommendation I was offered a job. "You'll need a Sheriff's Card," the casino manager said.

I went to the Sheriff's office, and the deputy on duty refused to give me a card because I was an ex-convict. My mind worked fast. I had wasted too much time in prison, and I felt a strong need to do some fast catchng up. The only solution I could think of was distasteful — I disliked resorting to drastic measures — but I needed that job at the Riviera. I *really* needed it. So I called the Governor in Carson City and told him what had happened.

"I'll put a man on it immediately," he said.

Within twenty-four hours an official of the Nevada Gaming Control Board called me at Bill's apartment. "Can you come to my office right away?" he asked.

I was there in twenty minutes. I imagine he just wanted to see if I had horns and a tail, because after a short meeting he told me to expect a call from the Sheriff's office the next morning at nine. The call came on schedule and I was there in fifteen minutes.

I was greeted by the Sheriff himself, who arranged personally for me to get my card. "If you have trouble again," he said, "get in touch with me at once."

My job at the Riviera was a snap. The money was good, my fellow workers were cordial, and the hours agreeable. I worked the swing shift from 4:00 p.m. to midnight, and never actually worked more than thirty minutes at a time. Occasionally I was called to work an hour or so on the graveyard shift, midnight to 8:00 a.m., but never later than two in the morning.

When I was called onto the graveyard shift, it was to use my skills as a mechanic to stop a hot streak. When the casino manager had gotten the letter of recommendation from Ned Coleman, he had suspected I was more than just a person in need of work.

"Ned teach you how to deal?" he asked.

"Yes. And some other things."

"Show me."

We went into an office and I dealt for him. His face was impassive as I made my moves with the cards, and I couldn't tell what he thought. I dealt for about an hour.

"What do you think?" I said.

"You know what I think."

"No, I don't."

"Ned Coleman taught you, didn't he? Spent a lot of time with you?"

"Yes."

"Then don't be a wise guy and ask me what I think. You know. You're as good as I've ever seen with cards."

My job when I was called to the graveyard shift was to second-card a sucker a few times and suddenly his streak would be over. I still deeply regret allowing rich casinos to use me this way against people who already face long odds, and I'm ashamed of what I did. But at the time I was simply happy I was doing so well.

The casinos eventually installed shoes, or boxes, on the "21" tables. Shoes could hold four or eight decks of cards, and it was almost impossible for a player, a counter, to memorize that many. Previously card counting had been a not uncommon method a dedicated and mathematically brilliant player could employ to switch the odds in *his* favor. There are still a few gamblers — bridge champions mostly — who can count through four or five decks of cards, their brain power in this limited area truly prodigious, and usually when casinos discover them they are barred from playing. These players are not even cheats. They play by the house rules, but they are barred nonetheless. Their "crime" is that through concentration that borders on the unbelievable they take away the casino's sacred edge.

In any case, life was just as easy as Ned Coleman had said it would be. I kept my promise and never forgot him. I sent him money every month to let him know I was grateful. He loved fine handkerchiefs, and I mailed him a box whenever I found his brand.

When I was dealing, women of every age, shape, and color would come up to me and stuff notes into my coat pocket. They wanted me to know where they were staying for the weekend, and all of them had one thing in common — the search for a good time. Most were secretaries from Los Angeles, but some were married women from Beverly Hills whose husbands were away attending business meetings or conventions. Playing the stud did not bother me. It was good for my ego after the divorce and the time at Carson City.

One woman stood out above all the others I met while working at the Riviera. Her name was Delores. She was thirty-five, quite attractive, classy, educated, and very rich. Delores gave me fifteen hundred dollars to spend with her every time she was in Las Vegas, which was often. Her husband was a prominent Beverly Hills physician, loaded with loot, and Delores didn't mind having a good time with it, even though she had a healthy nest egg of her own. She was lonely and lovely and knew how to make me feel bigger than I actually was. Several times on my days off I flew to Los Angeles to be with her. Delores would pick me up at the airport in her Mercedes and drive me to her beach house at Malibu. She introduced me to art galleries and good food, but mostly our days were spent relaxing on the soft, sandy beach, and our nights making love in the cool California evening air.

We went to Tracton's restaurant on LaCienega, and for candlelight dinners at the Mediterranean and Captain's Table. Occasionally there were parties attended by Hollywood celebrities, or opening nights at theaters, which were just beginning to come to prominence in Los Angeles. These were times of ease and relaxation, and there was plenty of money for anything we wanted to do.

Delores always insisted on paying for everything, and on the Los Angeles jaunts I couldn't blot the phrase "kept man" from my mind. I didn't like what that implied. I'd taken care of myself since I'd been a teenager, but I went along because she wanted it that way. It just wouldn't have been possible to live in such luxury on what I was earning.

One warm desert afternoon I was sitting at the pool of the apartment house where I'd rented a unit, sipping an iced tea and reading the *Las Vegas Sun*. On the front page was a picture of the Governor and his wife, who were visiting the city and staying at the Thunderbird Hotel. I went upstairs, dressed, caught a cab, and rode over to the Thunderbird. The desk clerk was an acquaintance — he gave me their suite number — and I took the elevator up and rang their doorbell. I'd expected to be stopped by security, but there was none.

"Who is it?" the first lady asked.

"It's me."

"Who is me?"

"Your former top confidential assistant from Carson City."

She opened the door, her face broadened into a big, happy smile. She hugged me.

"Come in," she said. "What are you doing here?"

"Have you forgotten? I'm dealing '21' at the Riviera."

"Of course. It's good to see you. How are you?"

"I'm fine. How are you and the Governor?"

"We're both doing well."

I looked around and noticed the door to an adjacent room was closed. I figured the Governor was probably behind it.

He was, and heard us talking. "Who is it, honey?" he shouted.

"Your confidential assistant from Carson City," she said. He came out in his bathrobe, smiling, and shook my hand. "You look great," he said. "Prosperous, I might add. What are you up to?"

"He's a '21' dealer at the Riviera," his wife answered.

"Now I know where I can make a fortune," the Governor said.

He was joking, but I could easily have passed a bundle off to him had he asked.

"You're having dinner with us tonight," the Governor said. "I won't take no for an answer."

"I have to be at work in an hour and a half," I said.

"Your boss won't mind if you're a few minutes late," the Governor said.

We had a magnificent meal at the Thunderbird. I was introduced to the owner and a few other Las Vegas bigshots. I couldn't help but compare my present situation to what it had been not long before at Carson City.

"I'm sorry," I said finally, "but I really do have to run along. Why don't you stop by the Riviera later in the evening?" It would be good to see them again, but more important, I knew if I introduced them to my boss it would take some of the heat off for being late.

"We'll come by and see how you're doing," the Governor said.

My boss, a predictable sort, was angry when I got to the Riviera. "Where the hell have you been?" he said. "You been drinking?" Getting drunk was a problem congenital to many who worked the casinos.

"I don't drink," I said.

"Well, where were you?"

"I was having dinner with the Governor and his wife."

"Right. And I balled the Queen of England last night. Look, I don't mind if you're a few minutes late, but more than an hour is beyond what I allow anyone."

"I'm not lying to you. I had dinner with the Governor. He and his wife are stopping by later."

My boss didn't believe me and walked away angry. At 10:30 p.m., the Governor and his wife walked into the casino, causing a great stir, and came directly to my table. I called my boss over and introduced him. Before the state's first family departed, I said in a loud voice, meant for the ears of my boss: "I want to thank you again, Governor, for having me to dinner."

"It was our pleasure, John," the Governor said. "Next time the dinner is on you."

I continued as a streak-breaker at the Riviera, but increasingly my talents were called on less and less. One incident I remember very clearly. My regular boss was off for the night. He was the one who called me in when someone was denting the house's bankroll, and his replacement had no idea of my real purpose in the joint. Regardless, most bosses in Nevada are superstitious, and one of their superstitions is that a break-in, or new, dealer (which the substitute thought I was) is invariably lucky. This particular night a player was on a roll. Although the house limit was $500, he was circumventing the rule by playing four separate hands at once, while his girlfriend was playing three more. In effect, every hand dealt was worth $3,500, and the players were red hot. They were perhaps $40,000 ahead, and the new boss was nervous. He called me in, counting on the so-called luck of the break-in dealer.

It took me virtually no time at all to get some $20,000 back, and I would have gotten it all if the brother of the casino manager hadn't shown up. "Isn't that a break-in dealer?" he asked the substitute boss. Obviously, the brother wasn't aware of what was going on either.

"Yes," said the boss. "And he's gotten hot, just like I thought he would. New dealers are always lucky."

"Are you crazy? A lot of money is being bet at that table."

"That's why I'm using the break-in man. He's lucky."

"You believe those old wives' tales? My God! Look, get him out of there before he screws up bad."

"But he's hot."

"Get him out or I'm going to be hot!"

And so it went in Glitter Gulch. Many times the left hand didn't know what the right hand was doing. What a boss was mainly concerned with was showing a profit during his shift. The big bosses got very upset if a shift came out in the red. I left the table, the CM's brother glaring at me, and hoped the poor slob who'd been on the hot streak won every cent the Riviera had.

The year 1964 turned into 1965. Lyndon Johnson became president on his own merits, and the Vietnam War heated up. It was a time of great change in the nation. Las Vegas began changing rapidly, also, mostly for the better. My talents as a streak-breaker became less needed at the Riviera. Cheating the players was not the priority it had been, and such was the case all over town, as big image-conscious coporations began buying into the casinos. The laws of probability ensured them a big profit without the hanky-panky, though of course there were still plenty of joints you could frequent if you got your kicks by being cheated.

"How would you like to be a regular '21' dealer?" my boss asked. "The salary is not as good, but it's a job."

"Do I have a choice?"

"There's always unemployment."

"I'll deal '21'."

Working regularly was an education. As a streak-breaker I'd been a celebrity of sorts to those who knew my true function, admired, resented, viewed with awe, a loner with a special talent who had little to do with the daily action on the floor. As a full-time dealer, hanging out with the other dealers and just keeping my eyes open, I came to understand how the casinos had cheated the players and how it still continued in some of the joints.

The approach was insidious. Before each shift, the dealers assembled in their dressing room, and as a matter of routine were familiarized with mug shots of known hustlers and cheaters. The casino manager would remind the dealers that the casinos did not tolerate cheating the players, but this policy underwent a sea change once the dealers started their shift. The lecture was delivered simply for cosmetic purposes, for protection should a scandal arise, as insurance that plenty of testimony that the casinos were on the up-and-up would be available if required.

If a player held the dice for a long period of time, thirty minutes or more throwing lots of numbers, the boss would get hot and start calling the stickman names, not loud enough for the players to hear, but the other dealers would know. The floorman would ease up to the dealer and whisper in his ear: "What's the matter? Can't you cool this guy off?" As I've said, floormen were very superstitious, and very suspicious, and would blame a dealer for losing the house's money. If he lost often enough, he was fired.

Often a boxman, to stem the abuse he was taking from his bosses, would substitute flat dice into the game, and the player would soon be out of action. Flat dice have sanded edges, and their roll favors certain numbers. If the bets were heavy on the back line — those players betting *against* the shooter — sanded dice were switched into the game. The sanded dice favored the shooter and wiped out those betting against him. If the bets were heavy on the front line — those players betting *with* the shooter — loaded dice were switched into the game, destroying the shooter and his backers.

Many dealers cheated because they could not afford to come up short at the end of their shifts. The bosses counted what was in the rack before each shift, and those chips, plus the cash in the money box, were counted again at the end of the shift. If the latter total was less than the former, the dealers were berated by their superiors and sometimes threatened with loss of their jobs. Each dealer in Nevada knew there were a thousand people waiting to take his place.

Superstition wasn't the only mental problem suffered by many casino bosses. Because the odds were fixed in the house's favor, a number of bosses thought the house should never lose. They seemed unable to comprehend that a player could beat the odds for a short period, maybe even for a whole shift, and that temporary losses were inevitable. I've known dealers who were suspected of cheating simply because they came up short one time.

Shortchanging the players was the simplest method to stay ahead of the game and assure that the house made money and the dealer kept his job. Shortchanging on the crap tables was accomplished by cupping one or two chips on every exchange. The dealer held the chips in the palm of each hand, and the unsuspecting sucker, caught up in the excitement of placing the winning bets, never noticed what was being done to him. His stacks were kept *even* by the dealer, and the sucker assumed the amount was correct. It is best when gambling always to know how much is owed you on each bet, the advice of Kenny Rogers ("There'll be time enough for countin' when the dealin's done") notwithstanding. In any case, if a player had reached out and grabbed the dealer's wrists and turned his hands up, he would have found a chip expertly cupped in each palm.

A dealer constantly rearranges the player's bets. It's a shell game: shuffling, stacking, rearranging. The player is never aware of the palmed chips, because the dealer always returns his hand to the bank and touches his own chips. That is how the stolen chips are deposited back into the bank. The amount is small, but the action is constant, and the take for a year runs into the millions of dollars.

The technique on the roulette wheel is different, but the results are the same. A good wheel man knows how to spin the ball away from a heavy bettor. Certain numbers are grouped together on the wheel, so if the bettor has big money on these numbers the wheel man manipulates the ball so it lands in another section. A good wheel man develops a deft touch spinning the ball, and can amaze initiates with his accuracy. The same is true when a bettor is heavy on certain numbers that are clustered together. The wheel man can direct the ball away from that cluster. He never minds if the small bettors win, as long as he keeps the heavy bettors away from their colors and numbers. It is a good idea to avoid roulette wheels where the croupier does not give the ball a fast spin.

Most players at this time believed the casinos in Nevada ran an honest game. They reasoned that the odds favored the casinos and therefore no need existed to cheat. The players were suckers.

They did not realize how much the casinos hated to lose even one penny, and how they constantly pressured their dealers into doing their dirty work for them. The suckers should have understood that the casinos merely mirrored the morality of much of the country: cheating, fraud, and deception were names of the game, the person who refused to cheat often did not get ahead, and people who did not get ahead were phantoms, shadows in a vacuum, nothing; worse, in Nevada, they got fired.

I closed my eyes to what was happening, but I made sure no one cheated me. Women continued to stuff notes in my pocket, and I gave them a tussle whenever I could. And I met other sorts, too, less savory. One of these was a small-time hoodlum named Emmett Thresher. Emmett's wife was the sister of a major Mafia figure in the East, and he tried to use this connection to secure small favors.

"I'm sending my wife over to your table," Thresher told me. "I want you to arrange for her to win."

Thresher had done his homework. He knew I was a top mechanic and could fix it so players could win or lose.

"I can't do it," I said. "I promised my boss I'd protect his shift."

Emmett Thresher smiled. "If you change your mind, let me know."

He came in the next day with the same proposition. I said no. Then I saw him a week later in a club I was visiting.

"I'm sending my wife out to your place tonight," he said. "This time you had *better* set some money off to her."

I didn't want anything to do with him. I said no and walked away.

When I reported for work that day I knew something was wrong. People avoided me as if I had something they might catch. At the end of my shift I was told I was no longer working for the Riviera. I asked for an explanation but none was given. I had been fired and that was that. My boss had taken the night off, so I went to see him the next day.

"Don't panic," he said. "I'll see that you get put back to work."

Despite other shortcomings, my boss was a man of his word. I reported as usual for work the next day, and he took me aside. "Do you know Emmett Thresher?" he asked.

I said yes. I told him about what he had asked me to do.

"Thresher called the casino manager," my boss said. "He told him you were stealing money from the club."

"That's a lie."

"I believe you."

"What can be done?"

"Stay calm. I'll talk to the big bosses. You'll be back on the job tomorrow."

My boss overestimated his influence at the Riviera, but he argued up a storm for me. He argued so hard he also lost his job.

I tried to find work with other casinos, but they wouldn't hire me. They wouldn't even listen to me. I had been fired from the Riviera for stealing and none of them would take a chance with an ex-convict, particularly one so adept as a mechanic that not even other mechanics could spot what he was doing.

I knew I couldn't call the Governor. Although he probably would have helped, he had already done a great deal for me, and I didn't want him thinking I was a crybaby or a parasite.

Instead I paid a visit to Sheriff Ralph Lamb's office. Lamb had said to come to him if I needed help, and that was precisely what I needed. I wanted to explain to him what had happened, to see if he could use his influence to get me back on the payroll. Lamb was a very important man in Las Vegas.

"The Sheriff," said a deputy, "is attending a convention in the Midwest. He won't be back for two weeks."

There was nothing for me to do except wait for Sheriff Lamb to return.

6

Waiting for Sheriff Lamb to return was not at all unpleasant. During the day I enjoyed the company of my sons, taking them to movies, swimming, on trips to Lake Mead. At night I played "21." It was not necessary for any of my dealer friends to lay money off to me: I could usually beat the tables legitimately. I knew more about the game than almost any dealer in Nevada. My bank account was solid and there was very little to worry about.

Then Peggy called and asked me to come to her house for dinner. "I have something important to tell you," she said.

I accepted, not knowing I was in for an upleasant surprise.

The dinner was nice enough, and Peggy and her husband were cordial. After we ate, Peggy sent the boys outside to play.

"Roy and I are moving to Houston," she said. The words hit me like a punch in the stomach.

"Houston?"

"Roy's been offered a very good deal there. We couldn't turn it down."

"What about the children."

"They're going with us, of course. You can visit them whenever you like."

"In *Houston*?"

"You fly to Los Angeles all the time."

She had not changed. She was still sticking it to me. I bit my lip and checked my temper.

"Send me your address," I said. "As soon as you're relocated."

"That would be only right."

It was going to be rough without my sons. Taking them places, sharing love with them, just being with them had been the high points for me since leaving Carson City. I thought of moving to Houston, but that wouldn't have worked. There was nothing I could do there, and it would be madness to seem to be following Peggy around. I knew I would have to settle for occasional visits.

Sheriff Lamb decided to spend a third week in the Midwest, but it didn't matter. I found a job without him. A casual acquaintance, Barry Churchman, worked at the Silver Slipper, and he got me on the graveyard shift as a "21" dealer.

The job did not last long. Each night when I returned from a coffee break my boss asked me to sign a "fill slip," which meant someone had won money at my table while I was away. When a dealer signs a fill slip for one hundred or five hundred dollars, the boss is supposed to have new chips on hand and place them in the rack. Then he stuffs the fill slip into the money box underneath the table. Instead, my boss was pocketing the chips, which never had been lost, and having a friend cash them in later. I kept signing fill slips, but never saw the boss replenish the rack with any chips. It was clear to me that my boss had found an interesting way to steal.

Just to protect myself (I knew the reason), I asked why I was told to sign so many fill slips, but never got an answer. Two nights later I was fired for being late. I believe I was actually fired because the boss knew I was onto him and wanted me out of the casino.

It was too bad. Even someone being generous could at best call my Las Vegas employment record spotty, though the truth was that most of the jobs I'd lost had been because of someone else. I hadn't stolen that money at the Mint, though the entire day shift had been fired for it, and instead of being rewarded for my conduct with Emmett Thresher, I'd lost my job. Well, I would miss the Silver Slipper. It had been a good place to work. Showgirls, cocktail waitresses, and dealers came in and played at the end of their shifts. A swinging place. Stan Kenton, Redd Foxx, Dinah Washington, and Gracie Allen had played at my table. These and many other entertainers came to the Silver Slipper to hear Charlie Teagarden, a sax player, the brother of Jack. Phil Harris, falling-down drunk, would come into the lounge, actually fall down, and then sing songs from the prone position. I found out that some of the stars who, for laughs, pretended to be lushes on the air, actually *were*.

You could hear all kinds of good stories in the Slipper lounge, from the cocktail waitresses talking about the foibles of gamblers trying to pick them up, from the showgirls who were constantly receiving marriage proposals from rich Texas and Oklahoma oil types, and from the dealers with their endlessly interesting tales of gambling. One of my favorites was about the dishwasher at a local greasy spoon who went into a Strip casino with $9 and built it up to $22,000 with a phenomenal streak of luck at the crap table. Then the dice turned on him, and he lost everything.

"How did the gambling go last night?" a fellow dishwasher asked him the next morning.

"I lost nine dollars," was the reply.

For those who wanted to relax and have a good time, the Silver Slipper lounge with Charlie Teagarden providing the entertainment could be counted on to provide a serene oasis safely isolated from the hurry-up pressure-cooker grind of Las Vegas. There were spots in the lounge where you could have a quiet talk with a friend, and others where you could be boisterous and let everything hang out.

Sheriff Ralph Lamb came back to town, but I did not go to him. He would never have believed I was bum-beefed on *three* jobs.

A few nights after I'd been let go at the Silver Slipper, Barry Churchman called me at my apartment. I had met Barry a couple of times, he was just a guy who was around, and there was nothing to distinguish him from a thousand other people I'd run across. He was an average-looking person, average height, average weight, nothing about him really stuck out. Though he didn't seem to have a job, I understood he owned a nice home in Las Vegas.

"Can you meet me at the Slipper?" Churchman asked.

"What's up?"

"Someone here wants to meet you."

I've mentioned that meeting Ned Coleman at the prison in Carson City was the single event that most dictated the direction of my life. The individual I was now about to meet holds second place in that department, a very close second.

I arrived at the Silver Slipper just at the start of a shift change, and Barry was waiting and guided me into the cocktail lounge. Sitting alone was a huge man who filled half of a booth. From the size of his torso he had to be six feet four inches tall and weigh some 270 pounds.

"I'd like you to meet Glen Grayson," Barry said.

Glen extended an enormous hand that completely engulfed mine. "Sit down," he said.

Barry and I started to slide into the booth. "Not you, Barry," Glen said.

Barry did not argue. He walked over to the bar and sat down out of hearing range.

"Care for a drink?" Glen asked.

"I don't drink."

"That's in your favor."

I did not know what to make of this enormous, friendly man from Fort Worth, Texas. And, of course, I had no idea at the time how important he would become in my life.

"I heard about your bad luck," Glen said.

"It's not so bad."

"That's right. Besides, you've got a job if you want it."

"What kind of job?"

"I need a man I can trust. Someone who is smart and knows the casinos, and knows how to keep his mouth shut. I've checked on you, and I think you're that person."

"If it's illegal," I said, "count me out."

"I know about Carson City. You won't be going back there."

"How do I know you're not a snitch? How do I know you're not an FBI agent looking for a gold star after his name?"

"Have you ever heard of a crossroader?"

"Every dealer in Nevada knows about crossroaders," I said. "They hustle the casinos."

"And I think you would be just fine for what I have in mind. I hear you learned from Ned Coleman."

Glen took a sip from his drink, leaned forward, and once again it was impossible not to marvel at the sheer bulk of the man. And I had to admit he had a winning personality. I soon learned it was impossible even for those who suspected he was cheating them not to like him. Glen could talk you out of your last dollar, or risk his life for you. He could be brutal if crossed, but was quick to forgive.

Glen loved women. He wanted to climb into bed with all of them — individually or collectively, young or old, it made no difference. Glen had been married several times, I never found out exactly how many. He was too much for one woman. There was no way one woman could take his daily diet of sex. He spent a good deal of time and money on the prostitutes of Nevada, which contributed to my old acquaintance Joe Conforte's pocketbook. Most women were dazzled, excited, awed, enchanted, and overwhelmed by Glen, yet they all left him after a short time. He was too crude. Glen spoke two languages: English and Profane.

"Well," said Glen, "you're looking at the King of the Crossroaders, the best ever to set foot on the planet."

Humility was not one of his virtues. I sat impassively, waiting for him to go on.

"Ask around town," Glen Grayson said. "You'll find out I'm telling the truth."

Later I did ask around, and learned Glen was everything he said he was — and much more.

"All right," I said. "Let's assume you're telling the truth. Is there any money in hustling?"

"More money than you ever dreamed of."

I toyed with the ash tray on the table. I knew hustling was not against the law. Nevada, believe it or not, was so wide open in 1965 that no legal protection was afforded the casinos against even the most flagrant type of cheats. Crossroaders were a thorn in the side of the casinos, but the amount stolen was so minute and penny-ante compared to the fortunes the gambling houses were raking in that they never bothered to get laws passed. Other methods, like breaking legs, existed to discourage crossroaders.

I sat in the booth at the Silver Slipper, thinking hard. Glen was right when he said I would not end up in Carson City, but I might wind up dead. Then again, what chance did I have succeeding as a legitimate dealer? It was a long way back to that donut shop in Visalia.

"What do you say?" Glen asked.

"I want to think some more."

"Can you give me an answer tomorrow?"

I said I could and Glen gave me a phone number to call.

"If your answer is yes," Glen said, "there will be a bonus in it for you." He didn't explain about the bonus, and I didn't ask.

"Barry Churchman drove me back to my apartment, and I spent a couple of hours thinking about the strange offer I'd received. I decided I had no qualms where hustling casinos was concerned, and certainly the money was attractive. There was no telling how much that could be, but I figured it was a lot. The chance of getting caught, actually, was the biggest — the only —

worry. I wondered about Glen Grayson, considered and then rejected the idea of checking him out through Ned Coleman. Ned would surely know about him, but there was no telling who might be listening in on that prison phone. Instead I decided to visit the Plush Horse, a piano bar, a quiet place where Las Vegas insiders relaxed after a day of working or gambling. Without giving any information away, I thought, I might be able to learn something about Glen Grayson.

The bar was cozy and dimly lit, and so was the small room which adjoined it, with tables and a piano at the far end. The crowd was good-sized, the usual mixture of dealers, gamblers, cocktail waitresses, showgirls, prostitutes, and even a few pit bosses. Almost every dealer in Las Vegas came from some other town, often Chicago or New York, and ventured west to Nevada because he'd known someone who could get him a job. Dealers were usually gamblers themselves, though more than most people they had reason to understand that bucking the house odds was hopeless. Dealers seldom had much money, and lived eternally from paycheck to paycheck, when they could get back to the tables as players and hit that million-to-one hot streak.

The gamblers who frequented the Plush Horse were more successful bettors than the dealers. They had to be because they survived on their wits, without the cushion of a regular paycheck to forestall disaster. Usually the gamblers were older guys who had hung around pool halls and race tracks as children. They were extremely careful bettors, always looking for an edge, and often their knowledge of gambling was encyclopedic. Greed was a vice they'd learned to control. When they got a little bit ahead, they quit, and waited for another day. Many of them likely would have been big successes in business had they spent the same long, mind-bending hours learning a business that they devoted to keeping afloat as gamblers.

There was a difference between the dealers and the successful ("successful" means eking out a living) gamblers. The gamblers probably would have welcomed the opportunity to align themselves with Glen Grayson, *if* they believed they could get away with it. The dealers were trapped gamblers, trapped in their own compulsion and addiction, who found their greatest thrill in taking a chance. Maybe the ultimate thrill was losing, since they preferred taking a chance to a sure thing. The enjoyment for them was making the bet and sweating out the result, not winning the bet.

The prostitutes (there probably are more prostitutes in Las Vegas, per capita, than anywhere else in the world) were an interesting crowd. Many of the ones I met had a deep but hidden hatred of men, and a certain low self-esteem. I think a lot of them had been abused as children. Anyway, several of them told me they were getting back at men by taking their money and "not really giving them anything" in return. They viewed sex as a form of stealing, a way to rob the men who were the cause of their problems in the first place, and their bodies as not important at all. Most of these women were not supporting a drug habit or a brutal, demanding pimp, as many are today, but were waging private wars against men.

There were a few pinball machines in the Plush Horse. These were the rage in Las Vegas before the introduction of the various video games: video poker, video horse racing, video dog racing, video blackjack. The dealers liked to play the pinball machines. It was action, and a few of them thought they'd get a fairer shake with them than they would against a human being. The gamblers stayed away from the pinball machines, sipping beers and talking in low tones.

I tried to bring the subject around to crossroaders as I circulated between the bar and the piano lounge, and if I discerned interest, to Glen Grayson himself. It was just a subject I was interested in, I said, because I was fascinated by people who would dare to steal from the mighty casinos. "Oh, it goes on all right," a gambling old-timer conceded, "and some of those fellows are mighty slick. You can look right at them and not know they're cheating you blind."

"Ever hear of a fellow named Glen Grayson?"

"Why are you interested in Glen?"

"I heard his name. That he was good. I find people like that interesting."

"You a writer?"

"I'm a dealer. Or I was. Got bum-beefed at the Silver Slipper."

"Well, you heard right about Glen Grayson. He's plenty good. If anyone's better, he's the best-kept secret in Nevada."

"You know him, then?"

"No. My friend," he pointed to a man at the end of the bar, "over there does. He could tell you about Glen Grayson."

I bought the man a beer and headed for the end of the bar. "Excuse me," I said, "but I've heard you know Glen Grayson."

The man was perhaps sixty-five, bony, with a wrinkled, weathered face, and he wore a western hat. He looked like he had prospected for gold, and he had.

"Why do you want to know about Glen?"

"I've heard about him. It's like if someone knew Babe Ruth. I'd want to find out what Babe Ruth was like."

"You aren't a cop." The man was looking at me in a not-unfriendly manner, more amused than anything.

"No."

"Well, sit down. I'll buy you a beer. I'll tell you about Glen Grayson."

"I'll buy *you* a beer," I said.

The prospector had met Glen only twice, both times at whorehouses, but Glen had made an impression and my newfound friend had a thousand stories. Glen hired himself out to casino owners who wanted to put a rival out of business. Mostly this occurred in small towns or foreign countries where the target casino did not have a big bankroll backing its action. In these instances Glen collected two ways: he kept the money he won, and he also received a fee from the client who wanted the competition eliminated. "You have to be pretty good to bust a casino," the prospector said, "even if it's a little one."

There was no bravado or phoniness or exaggeration in the older man's voice. He spoke with a flat western twang, matter-of-factly and with little intonation. He was simply telling the truth.

"Glen does a lot of work in Nevada?" I asked.

"That's a good word. Work. That's how he thinks of it. I'd say he's done more than just about anybody."

"A lot of people seem to know him. How come he never gets caught?"

"Ever try to grab quicksilver?"

"Still, it seems everybody knows him. That can't help in a business like his."

"Son, you just don't understand."

"Tell me."

"He's too good for them. He's like the boxer Willie Pep used to be. Nobody could lay a glove on him. He was smarter and quicker than anybody else. That's the way Glen is. And I'll tell you something else. It will sound odd, but he's about the most honest dude you'll ever run across."

"Honest?" I laughed.

"Thought it would sound strange to you. But he wouldn't touch a penny except for those casinos."

"He a rich man?"

"He's got plenty."

"Why does he keep doing it? If I had enough money, I'd stop."

"He *likes* it boy. That's why he doesn't stop. He likes it."

I mingled with other customers that night, a few of whom also knew Glen Grayson or said they did. Not a single one thought he had retired on his laurels. "He's out somewhere hustling, you can bet on that and take the money to the bank," a pit boss told me.

"Wouldn't think a man in your position would like him much," I said.

"Don't have to like him to respect him."

"Wish you could catch him?"

"Sure. But it's not apt to happen. He's too well known, and too big physically to hide who he is. No, I imagine he uses others now. And since they're his people, they'd be pretty hard to spot."

I stayed a little longer — the quiet, dark atmosphere of Plush Horse was inviting — and then I walked out onto Sahara Boulevard and caught a cab back to the apartment. I lay in bed for a long time thinking about what I'd heard.

"Count me in," I said to Glen Grayson when I called him the next morning.

"You've made the right play," he said.

We met that night at Barry Churchman's home in West Las Vegas: Glen Grayson, Rollie Malone, Jackie Gillitzer and his girlfriend Jan Deerwood, Don Allison from Reno, and of course Barry Churchman. The seven of us would become perhaps the most skilled and audacious crew of hustlers Nevada has ever witnessed.

Barry Churchman had laid out three or four quarts of Chivas Regal, which I soon learned were drunk only by Glen and Rollie, and several bottles of wine and cases of beer. This was to be a get-acquainted party, and while trying to be sociable, I nonetheless found myself trying to measure the others. I guessed, correctly, that if we were going to succeed, each individual would have to be able to trust the others implicitly.

Don Allison and Rollie Malone were leaning on the bar in Barry Churchman's den when I joined them, and it took only an instant to realize how different those two were. Rollie was five feet ten inches and 240 pounds, thick and broad with the arms of a weightlifter and a silly I'm-only-half-there smile on his face.

"We ought to have some girls here," were the first words he said to me.

"I take it you like girls."

"Girls and fighting."

I soon enough learned this was true. Rollie loved a good brawl, and he managed to get into plenty of them. He was also in constant heat, a big healthy kid who could only be called an erectomaniac. In this, and many other ways, he resembled Glen.

In the beginning we would have to practice much longer with Rollie than with other crew members. He was clumsy around the tables, fumble fingered, but, oddly and inexplicably, when he finally caught on he became one of our best crew members.

Rollie Malone would go to bed with any woman in skirts, and bashfulness comprised no portion of his makeup. Rollie would hit on a guy's wife or girlfriend, and he would do it in the man's presence. He embarrassed me in the early stages of our friendship, but in time I learned to accept him and even to enjoy his antics. Certainly he was an original. And Rollie was intensely devoted to the crew and particularly to Glen, whom he admired above all others.

Once Rollie and I went to a gymnasium to work out, and he decided he wanted to spar with me. "You don't know how to spar," I said. "You have no control over yourself. You're a barroom fighter and never hold anything back."

"Come on, John. I won't hurt you."

"You're a madman, Rollie. I know you. You'll just come out swinging and never stop."

"I promise. We'll just spar."

I foolishly agreed to spar with him, and what happened was just what I expected. At the opening bell he came out flailing — whap, whap, whap — sweating, grunting, windmilling punches, a perpetual motion machine bent on destruction. He must have thrown three hundred punches, most of which I blocked, and all the time he had a smile on his face and a crazy look in his eyes. He was like a bowling ball with arms.

Rollie had one way of fighting, and that was straight ahead and keep throwing bombs. He came out the same way in round two, a wildman, and I started to talk to him as I dodged punches and tried to stay out of his way. "Now take it easy, Rollie," I soothed. "We're supposed to be sparring." He unleashed a left hand in response that I actually heard whoosh as it went past my right ear, and an overhand right at my nose that hurt just to block.

"Dammit, Rollie, slow yourself up," I urged, and he answered with an uppercut, a bolo, that started on the floor and seemed destined to end up in the heavens. *Bang, bang, bang* he beat on my shoulders, and in close tried to rupture my kidneys with those cement-block hands. "Rollie, I'm going to have to hurt you if you keep this up," I warned. But he kept wading in, punches coming as fast as the eye could count, a happy smile on his face.

I stepped back and a little to the side, and clipped him on the point of the chin with a clean left hook. Anybody with even minimal amateur experience could have done the same thing. Rollie went down as if pole-axed, and wasn't himself again until I was back in my street clothes leaning over him in the dressing room. "That's what I call fun," he said. "We'll have to do it again."

Don Allison was a different sort entirely. I didn't think you'd ever find him in a boxing ring or a brawl, though I suspected he could take care of himself. This Reno cowboy could have passed for just about anything, and whatever it was, you just knew he was able and competent. He was as soft-spoken as Rollie was loud.

"Why did you join this lash-up?" he asked me, that first night in Barry Churchman's split-level home.

"For the money," I said. "I want to live a certain way, and that takes money."

"Glad to hear it."

I would get to know Don Allison very well. He was a generous man, exceedingly loyal to the crew, mild-mannered, jealous of his privacy, and possessed of a colossal cool that never allowed him to panic in a rough situation. Don Allison had also become a crossroader for the best of reasons, the money, which he intended to use to fulfill a lifelong dream of his: the purchase of a ranch in northern Montana. But I didn't know any of this until much later. At Barry Churchman's home I was sizing up my new partners, and Don Allison looked like one who should wear very well.

I saw a lot of Barry Churchman, our host, on that first night, and I had a vague feeling of unease whenever I talked with him. He seemed nervous in a shy, underhanded way, and either edgy or embarrassed that such an unsavory group could be gathered in his home. I believe my first unfavorable impression of Barry proved correct. He was a whiner, a complainer, and he had no stomach for hustling craps, where the rewards were great but so were the dangers. Barry usually had a reason for not playing: a boxman knew him, a dealer knew him, someone in the casino knew him, or he imagined the joint was full of cops. Barry's mother had come from Poland, and Barry himself was very religious. He attended mass and had communion each Sunday, and went to confession regularly. His personal life was his own business as far as the crew was concerned, but what bothered us was his always pulling back, holding us up. We were thoroughly fed up with Barry by the time he decided to leave the crew. No one was sorry to see him go, least of all Glen Grayson.

This night Barry alternated between clucking like a mother hen around Rollie Malone, changing ashtrays with sudden, lightning-like movements, carrying a rag over his arm ready for Rollie to spill part of his drink, and worrying out loud that the police might have staked out his house. Since this was our first time together as a crew, the stakeout seemed highly unlikely. As far as Rollie was concerned, he should have been told to be careful. What actually happened was that Rollie became tired of Barry's playing the role of nursemaid, and began a wild dance in the center of the carpet, a drink held aloft in each hand.

I didn't talk much with Jackie Gillitzer, the diminutive Peter Lorre look-alike, who spent most of the evening huddled with Glen Grayson. Jackie always looked like he was guilty of something, even if he was just taking a dip in a pool, and I think he made Barry Churchman even more uptight than he normally would have been. I would soon find out that Jackie Gillitzer was an excellent craps hustler, a master slot cheater, and outstanding on the "21" tables. Twenty years before Glen Grayson had enticed him into leaving Chicago for the more profitable pastures of Las Vegas.

At "21" Jackie Gillitzer played the bend, putting a crimp or slight bend on certain cards, the nine to the king. Thus, he could tell approximately what the next card would be, a tremendous advantage. When he was sitting at the table with a stiff or breaking hand, and he saw a face card coming up, he would not take a hit. He would leave it for the dealer, hoping the high card would bust the house's hand. Jackie Gillitzer made hundreds of thousands of dollars cheating the "21" tables.

No one could argue with Jackie's record of never having been caught cheating, and the fact that Glen Grayson trusted him implicitly spoke volumes about his character, at least where crew members were concerned. I've never believed the axiom about honor among thieves, I've known too many thieves, but it held true for our group.

Jackie Gillitzer had a wife in Reno and a girlfriend in Las Vegas. Every penny Jackie hustled was spent taking care of his two women in high style. They kept him going full speed and he was deathly afraid of both of them. But he also loved them both and he never got out of line.

"I'm Jan," was the way I met Jan Deerwood. She was dressed in a dazzling party outfit, which showed off her generous, lust-inspiring body.

"I'm John," I said.

"Think we'll own this state before we're through?" she asked. She was looking at me with frank blue eyes — there was absolutely nothing coquettish about this handsome woman. I would learn soon enough that Jan Deerwood was a chameleon and could play any role. Tonight she was a partygoer, a glamour queen, but on another occasion she might wear a conservative, proper business suit and pass for a lawyer or the vice president of a big accounting firm.

"I hope we make enough so I never have to work again," I said.

"It will get in your blood. You won't be able to stop until somebody makes you."

"That the way it is with you?"

"Oh, hell no. I'm keeping my eyes open waiting for something better. Glen — bless his heart — is a good guy to hook up with, but not forever. I want the quiet life."

Jan, two inches taller than Jackie Gillitzer, her boyfriend, and a million times better-looking, didn't strike me as someone who would settle down. She was what is known in Las Vegas as a scuffler, someone who is always hustling and never pays for anything. She'd find a way to beat a restaurant out of a 99¢ breakfast, and walk out with the salt and pepper shakers in her purse. At this time, certain casinos would offer thirty dollars in free play on the dice tables, so long as you bet the money at one of their tables and could prove you were from out of town. The idea was to lure tourists into the casino, where they would then feel obligated to play.

Jan could prove she was from anywhere, and so could the friend she brought with her. They would each get the thirty dollars in house chips, and one would bet the come line, the other the don't-come line. Unless the shooter crapped out on the first roll, they won sixty dollars and, not feeling the slightest pangs of conscience, exited as winners. The casinos, always slow to catch on despite their image as smart guys, finally changed the rules of the giveaway to require that players had to bet on the come line.

Jan had more and better clothes than the Governor's wife, and she never paid for a single outfit. She was a master thief. She would dress in maternity clothes, wearing a fiberglass shield shaped like half a medicine ball underneath her dress, and it was nothing short of remarkable how many dresses and other outfits she could stuff inside. No one, of course, would ever think to question such an obviously pregnant lady.

Jan had money — the phrase about still having the first dollar you ever made applied to her. She just couldn't bring herself to pay for anything. She ate filet mignon a lot, because it came in a small package easy to conceal. She was so adept at switching jewelry (a fake for the real thing) a magician wouldn't have known, yet at times she employed no ruse at all.

The trick was to act like what you were doing was perfectly normal. Store cops are on the lookout for people who appear furtive (Jackie Gillitzer would have been arrested even though he was doing nothing — he survived in casinos because a lot of people look guilty, and are), sneaky, like they are up to something. Jan always looked like what she was doing was perfectly natural. I once saw her go into a big department store, pick up a television set, and walk out with it.

The highest compliment I suppose could be paid to Jan, if you look at it in a certain way, was that Glen Grayson recruited her. Glen had all the patronizing attitudes toward women that typified men of the nineteenth century — where he would definitely have been more at home, on a riverboat perhaps — yet he unhesitatingly chose her to be part of what he wanted to be the finest crew he'd ever assembled, a sort of capstone to his career.

Anyway, this night at Barry Churchman's home was the first time all members of the crew were together. These crossroaders, carefully selected by Glen using a formula only he fully understood, would hustle more money than any other such crew in the long history of gambling.

7

We soon found out the crew was compatible. Glen Grayson had hand-picked each member, and he was an excellent judge of people. On our first night together after the party we exchanged hellos and handshakes while Barry Churchman served sandwiches and coffee. Then we sat down and listened while Glen explained his scheme, his method for beating the craps. It was ingenious in its simplicity, which it had to be because the more complicated the method, the greater the risks.

"We have an immediate advantage," Glen began. "Casino bosses believe they have all the smart guys on their payroll. They're smug, and this will help us in the long run."

Maybe so. But the success we eventually had was a result of our coordination, courage, skill, and teamwork, not smugness on the part of casinos.

The plan was for two people to steal a die from a crap table. Glen appointed me crew chief of this part of the operation because I had worked the pits before and was adept at sleight-of-hand. I was to stand next to the stickman, and Rollie Malone was to position himself at the opposite end of the table, farthest from me. Rollie was chosen, as I've said, because he looked and acted like a yokel, a big, friendly, gullible country boy who could not possibly be involved in hanky-panky. Rollie was to make one-dollar bets on the field and wait for the dice to work themselves around to me.

When the stickman emptied the bowl of dice in front of me, I would select a pair, and with a flick of the wrist I would send them hurtling to the other end. But the trick was that I had *thrown only one.* Rollie would do a double-take, pretending the other had hit him and fallen to the floor.

"Where's the other die?" the stickman would ask.

"On the floor," Rollie would say.

"One down!" the boxman would holler, and the porter would search for the lost die, which was still in my hand.

It was all done so quickly it really appeared as if both dice had been thrown, and one had bounced off the table. Occasionally we would vary the method. I would actually throw a die off the table, and Rollie would put his big foot on it and retrieve it later.

The stolen dice were then mailed to New Jersey where we had two different sets duplicated: one would be a carbon copy of the casino's dice (we thought they would be handy to have, in case we wanted to rig them later), and the other would be dice which had only fours, fives, and sixes on them. In other words, they were the same dice the casino used, but it was impossible to throw a one, two, or three because on our cubes those numbers no longer existed. The idea was to switch the new dice into the game, have bettors ready to wager on the field, and through a complex set of diversions win two, three, four bets at the most before the casino knew what was hitting it.

It was a ballsy play. It would not take a particularly sharp-eyed dealer to see that three numbers were missing from the dice. Good-looking Jan Deerwood would have to provide an understated but eye-diverting spectacle, and other members of the crew — asking for change, spilling a drink, *something* — needed to draw attention away from the play.

Of course, winning a field bet was nearly a cinch under these circumstances. The only number that could beat us was an eight — two fours. Any other combination and we won.

It seemed suicidal, listening to Glen explain it, but when we saw it demonstrated we began to believe it just might work. The stickman, while the dice were sitting on the table, couldn't see all the numbers. One was face down on the felt, and usually two others were facing away from him. If we — and particularly Jan — could keep him distracted, there was an excellent chance the play would work. Of course, we weren't going to be able to stand around the same table all day doing this. The idea was to get in and out as fast as we could. In addition, this method of beating a crap table, effective as it would turn out to be, was rudimentary and crude compared to other plays we would develop.

The firm in New Jersey charged us thirty dollars for each set of dice we wanted duplicated, and Glen would keep all the rigged cubes in a suitcase with sliding doors. We estimated it would take a year to fill the suitcase with matching dice from casinos all over Nevada.

Glen was finished explaining the plan. "Are there any questions?" he asked.

There were none. I could see Barry Churchman squirming, wanting to ask why we had to use his place to meet. But Barry wasn't then, or ever, going to risk upsetting Glen.

"If any of you ever talk about this to someone outside this crew," Glen said, "I'll take a big Louisville Slugger baseball bat and cave in your skull. Is that understood?"

Everyone nodded.

A year was a long time to wait to put the scheme into operation, but Glen had this figured out also. Most slot machines in Nevada had Ace locks, and the versatile Jackie Gillitzer was expert at decoding them. Crew members would walk into the casino, surround a machine, and pretend to be playing. Actually, we were merely providing cover for Jackie. He was very short and was dwarfed by the rest of us, and as we screened him from prying eyes, he would stand up to the machine and decode the lock with his Ace pick. If a change girl happened down the aisle, one of the crew — usually the chivalrous Don Allison — would stop her and ask for a roll of dimes, anything to get her attention and prevent her from seeing what was happening. A security guard who found his way into the area would be asked directions by the gorgeous Jan Deerwood. Jan could deflect the attention of the most conscientious guard.

When Jackie was finished we would go out to our car and make a key for the machine he had been working on. The key we made for a quarter slot machine would open every quarter machine in the casino, and the same was true for every fifty-cent machine and dollar machine. Even though I'd worked in casinos I hadn't realized such was the case, but a moment's thought explained why it couldn't be any other way. Most casinos had hundreds of slot machines, and it was simply too inconvenient to carry hundreds of keys.

Eventually Jackie Gillitzer decoded almost every Ace lock in Nevada, and each of us had large rings of keys. No matter where we went, we could open a slot machine, set the reels, put on the jackpot, and walk away, leaving it to a confederate to pull the lever and win the money.

We were never caught decoding the locks or with our hands in the machine. We had some close calls, a few footraces out of the casinos, but we invariabley avoided jail and the strong arms of the security people. And we learned something about the casinos, at least one of them. At this sterling establishment we put on a particularly large jackpot and the casino manager was actually counting the money out into the hands of our collector when the casino owner happened by. Upon hearing what had happened, that such and such machine had paid off, he removed the money from the collector's hands and said, "Sue me. Or go to the Gaming Commission. I don't care, but you're not walking out with this money."

It was clear what had happened, and the collector wisely chose not to argue. But I've always wondered about that casino manager. He was taking a huge chance, a giant gamble. He knew he had been cheated because that particular machine had been rigged so it *couldn't* pay off. But what if we had decided to make an issue of it? We'd have exposed ourselves as cheats, it is true, but the casino owner would have been out of business. You are not supposed to have slot machines where the jackpot can't be hit. What happened was the sprocket for the fourth reel had been filed down so the final seven could not line up in the window.

A lot of new slot machines began to appear in Nevada in 1968, and it wasn't readily apparent how they could be opened. Our activities would be considerably curtailed if we couldn't figure how to get inside these slots. All of us discussed the problem and decided we had to get our hands on one of these new machines so we could study it. We tried to buy one, and went directly to the manufacturer. The company wouldn't sell to us. Nor would it sell to any of our contacts who worked in casinos. It was apparent that the joints were tired of being ripped off and had clamped a tight security lid on the whole project. There was only one thing to do.

Three of us went into the targeted casino. While I busied as many security guards as I could with some fabricated tale of woe (I'd been the victim of robbery — someone had grabbed my cup of coins), Rollie and Jackie Gillitzer, dressed as workmen and looking to all the world as if they belonged there, wheeled a dolly into the casino, disconnected the machine, and in front of God and everybody just wheeled it out and put it in the trunk of my Buick convertible. With this job completed, I pretended to be disgusted with the lack of help I was getting from the security personnel, and walked away from them and went outside.

We couldn't close the trunk lid, so we threw a blanket over the purloined slot machine. There was a moment of suspense when, driving down Las Vegas Boulevard, I glanced into the rearview mirror and saw the blanket lying in the street behind me. I slammed on the brakes, jumped out of the car, and retrieved the blanket. No one seemed to notice that I had a big slot machine in my trunk. Of course, once we had the slot safely in Jackie's house and could study it at our leisure, we figured out the technology. The casino, meanwhile, was left with a gap in one of its slot machine banks, like a missing front tooth. But what could it do? Surely it couldn't get rid of all those other expensive machines.

It was interesting. Time and again a manufacturer would come out with a device it would label "burglar proof," and time and again our ingenuity enabled us to find ways to prove it wasn't.

The slots for us were only a sideline, a means to an end, although we did win more than a $1,000,000 from them. The purpose of the slots was to provide an income, and also to reimburse us for the money we spent for tools, hotel rooms, airline tickets, car rentals, and other expenses. We never lost sight of our bigger goal, but it was enjoyable watching a jackpot being collected, especially with a crowd looking on. Everyone would become excited — the tourists, the change girls, even some of the dealers. They were happy to see someone win, and of course they all believed it had been accomplished on the square.

Most dealers I knew secretly rooted for the players. They knew the many advantages the house had and didn't mind seeing it lose money. Of course, there were exceptions. Some dealers identified with the house, fantasized that they themselves might own a joint some day, and worked to take every nickel the player had. Other dealers were simply competitive, and to alleviate boredom imagined the game was them versus the players. These dealers really wanted to win, not for the casinos but for their own egos. Still others felt that if they didn't win they might be fired.

After Glen had gotten our attention with the talk about what he would do to our skulls with a baseball bat should any of us succumb to the temptation of bragging, he announced that he had arranged for a crap table to be delivered to Barry's home in the morning. This was the first any of us, including Barry, had heard about the crap table, and he opened his mouth to complain, then thought better of it and clamped his jaw tight. He had the only place we could use in Las Vegas that was large enough to accommodate a crap table.

"We've got a lot of practicing to do," Glen said, almost as an afterthought.

I returned to my apartment feeling good. It was a racy thing we were going to do, switching those "tops," the dice with three numbers missing, and we could all end up in the desert with bullets in our heads. The opposite side of the coin was the very large amount of money we could win. The more I dwelled on the possible consequences, the more I alternated between fear and exhilaration. Whatever, I knew I'd go ahead. It was a chance to do something far out of the ordinary — about as far from a donut-shop operation as I could get — and I was eager to see how it would turn out.

I wonder if I hadn't known ever since I'd taken those long lessons from Ned Coleman that it would come to something like this. What did I think I'd been doing, learning all those moves? I hadn't thought about it, during or after; I'd just gone ahead and learned them, and never dwelled on the why.

After showering and climbing into bed, I turned on the radio, set it to self-destruct in sixty minutes, and shut off the lamp. The eleven o'clock news was on. The announcer said someone with a shotgun had blown out the upstairs and downstairs windows of Emmett Thresher's home. Neither Thresher nor his wife had been in the house, but it must have scared them a great deal, because a week later they left Las Vegas for good. The last I heard he was a front man for a mob hotel in Chicago.

The next morning I arrived on schedule at Barry Churchman's split-level house to begin practicing with the crew. Glen took me aside. "Satisfied?" he asked.

He winked and smiled, and only then did I realize what he had meant when he promised a bonus if I joined up with him. Frightening Emmett Thresher was Glen's way of sealing our partnership.

For the next month we met twice daily at Barry's house. We spent two hours in the morning and two in the afternoon perfecting the play. Glen Grayson was a man who demanded perfection, and the sessions were gruelling, exhausting, and as well organized — each minute accounted for — as a Vince Lombardi training camp. Glen used both sarcasm and abuse whenever a mistake was made, and never tired of reminding us what the cost of that mistake could be. After thirty days he was satisfied we had it down right.

Our first target was the Fremont Hotel in downtown Las Vegas. We could hear the "Howdy Pardner!" greeting emanating from the Pioneer across the street, and the midday heat slapped me in the face when I stepped out of Glen's air-conditioned Cadillac. It was 112 degrees in Las Vegas, and my brain seemed to be spinning in dizzy circles. I told myself to get control, and forced it to happen. Across the street I could see Jackie and Jan, and a block or so away Don, Rollie, and Barry. They would converge on the casino when Glen and I went inside.

Glen seldom stepped into a casino anymore. He was too well-known; his presence, innocent or otherwise, was bound to cause suspicion in the minds of those who guarded the house's lucre. But today was an exception. Glen wanted to watch, albeit at a distance, this first time we'd be putting the plan into effect.

We split up when we were inside the Fremont. He took up a watching post near a bank of slot machines, and I headed on rubbery legs toward the designated crap table, imagining that every eye in the casino was on me. I fantasized that the crew had a Judas in its midst (wouldn't a casino pay for news we were coming?), that we'd be grabbed the moment we made our play. It all seemed a bad idea, and I wanted to bolt and run before the worst happened.

Instead I stood at the crap table, next to the stickman, just where I was supposed to be, and waited for the others to arrive. *Glen has been doing this for years and hasn't gotten caught*, my mind told me. I'd been around gambling long enough to know that you should bet on streaks, and Glen's had lasted a lifetime. I could actually *feel* myself calming down. My hands weren't shaking, and I no longer feared that my legs were about to crumble underneath me. What would be would be, I thought, not a very original notion, but I knew all I could do was make certain I performed at my best.

Still, I wasn't completely comfortable. Athletes will tell you there's a big difference between performing on the practice field and performing under pressure, and you'll never know how you'll do until you're under game pressure. I'm sure this holds true for many professions. Ned Coleman had said I had all the moves, but he'd warned I might not have the heart or guts for it. I thought I was about to find out.

The crew members, as planned, spaced their arrivals at realistic intervals; no sense in barging in as a gang and drawing unwelcome attention. I occupied myself by placing dollar bets on the come line and watching the Fremont's extraordinarily long bar. A football game was playing on the television set, and I would have wagered I could pick out every single customer who had a bet on it.

We had already duplicated the Fremont's dice, plus some from a few other casinos, but we were still eleven months and many pairs of dice away from a full-steam-ahead assault on Nevada's crap tables. Glen had simply thought it would be a good break from the monotony of the practice sessions to give the plan a try at the Fremont. Being a cautious man, extra careful, he would not have given the go-ahead if he hadn't been confident.

Glen's confidence turned out to be misplaced.

It was just unbelievable what happened. We had practiced and practiced, and when the moment arrived we responded like clowns.

Barry Churchman and Don Allison were the bettors. Theirs was the *easiest* part of the whole scam. Each was to place a maximum bet, $500, on the field when I got the dice and put an unlit cigarette to my lips, the signal that I had switched the duplicated dice for those of the casino.

Barry and Don put their bets in the wrong place and we lost!

I had imagined many things going wrong, but not this, not something so basic as making the wrong bet. I'd thought we could sleepwalk through that part of the play. It was Roy Riegels running in the wrong direction in the Rose Bowl, or Wrong Way Corrigan, or even that announcer getting President Herbert Hoover's name hopelessly mixed up.

I was just stunned when I saw what happened, and sick when I saw the dealer picking up our $1,000. All I could think to do was brush the crew out, get away from the Fremont, go back to the drawing board or forget the idea. It didn't matter. I was in a state of shock.

Glen Grayson had watched the play from his post by the slot machines, and when we met outside he was almost hot enough to boil. Curse words foamed from his mouth, and I thought he might hit one of us. Glen was an impressive man when he was angry.

"We're going back to Barry's place," he growled. "I can't believe what I saw in there. You're all going to practice until you drop dead or convince me that it's safe to turn you loose again."

We had blown $1,000 to the play. It was not a lot of money to Glen, but the loss was frightening because of its implications. If we couldn't even make the right bets, the simplest part of the operation, how could we ever expect successfully to pull off the much more sophisticated maneuvers?

Glen had cooled off by the time we arrived at Barry's house. "It's okay," he said. "We'll make it up."

The length of the practice sessions increased. When we made mistakes Glen scolded us like he might little children, but he was just as ready when praise was merited. He might have been a good and determined teacher, alternately cajoling and threatening. He's had numerous other crews before, but he talked as if this would be his last one, and he wanted it to be his best.

Two weeks later we tried again, starting at the Stardust on the Strip, and everything went without a hitch. As always we converged on the casino from different points, and I was surprised to find I wasn't nearly as nervous as I'd been that first time at the Fremont. It was like a second parachute jump, Glen later explained, not nearly as bad as the first. And once we succeeded at the Stardust, we just kept going.

That first weekend we worked Friday night, Saturday afternoon and evening, and Sunday afternoon. Sunday nights were usually dead in Las Vegas: the weekend crowd was headed home. We wanted to work only when a casino was busy, bursting with customers, because then we were less likely to be noticed. Our profit for the four sessions was slightly over $23,000.

Before going to work, everyone had counted his own bankroll. We each knew the amount of money we had when we started. I had $230. When we arrived back at Barry's house late Sunday afternoon, we emptied our pockets onto a coffee table.

"Now get yourselves even," Glen said.

I reached down and picked up $230. The others straightened out their accounts.

"Take your expenses for the weekend," Glen said.

This amount varied, but averaged out to $270 per person.

"We split the rest seven ways."

My share was more than $2,600. I had never earned so much money for so little work, and it felt like finding the end of the rainbow. I slipped the money into my billfold and pondered the pleasant problem that it was now bulky and difficult to fit into my back pocket.

Everyone had a different way of storing their winnings. Barry Churchman had a wall safe, which he thought no one knew about. Rollie Malone simply stuffed his money into a pocket, where it was readily accessible for whatever adventure he had planned for the week. Jan Deerwood attached hers to a diamond-studded gold money clip she'd boosted from a Reno jewelry store. Don Allison tucked his neatly in a breast wallet, where it would remain until his bank opened Monday morning. He was very serious about buying that ranch.

"It's only the beginning," Glen said, when we were ready to go our separate ways. He also said the $270 we had deducted for expenses was too high. He cautioned us to keep the "nut" down.

Occasionally on weekdays we'd hit three or four slot machines, and we continued to accumulate more pairs of dice. We went after the bigger money on weekends at the crap tables. Over the next four weekends we worked our scam in Reno, Carson City, Las Vegas, and again Reno. Each of us *averaged* more than $2,500 a weekend, after expenses. Glen called it "peanuts." I called it heaven.

We never stayed at the casino hotels we were going to hustle. If someone was onto us — and no one was — we were less likely to be harassed at some other place. Also, a motel could be checked out of much faster than a casino hotel.

Glen Grayson rarely went into action with the crew. He knew everybody in the gambling business, and they knew him. Usually such an arrangement would have spelled the end of a crossroader's career, but Glen's organizational talents allowed him to continue through us. The worst thing that can happen to a crossroader is to be recognized by pit bosses and dealers. He's out of action, often quite literally, if his face becomes too familiar. Crossroaders are made to feel very unwelcome in casinos. When a hustler is spotted, security is called and the cheater is thrown out, or into jail. Since Nevada had no laws against cheating, the charge was usually vagrancy — a fifty dollar fine and the cheater was back on the street. Still, it was not a good idea to get busted. The police got a good look at you, and before you knew it you were dodging security guards, dealers, and the cops. If a crossroader was alert he could see the steam coming and leave the casino without being told.

We worked three more weeks, with the same gratifying results. Then Glen, ever cautious, decided it was unwise for all of us to

continue living in the Las Vegas area. Jackie Gillitzer, Jan Deer-
wood, and Don Allison moved to Reno on a permanent basis.
Glen, Rollie Malone, and Barry Churchman remained in Las
Vegas. I went to Los Angeles.

When I arrived in Los Angeles, I called Delores, the doctor's
wife from Beverly Hills. She put me in touch with a real estate
agent, and I was able to rent a beautiful home on the ocean at
Newport Beach. The agent must have been doing Delores a
favor, because this was January, 1966, and I was able to get the
place for $200 a month. It was a steal, with plenty of room, and
the Pacific Ocean for a backyard.

Life was idyllic. Morning and evening meals were eaten on the
beach, and nights were spent sampling Los Angeles' abundant
entertainment possibilities. Warm afternoons were whiled away
under the sun. Nights were always cool, perfect for sleeping.
Existence was drowsy, serene, happy. I imagined that no rich
industrialist or Arab potentate lived any better.

Even Peggy seemed to have mellowed. She overcame her
suspicions and agreed to let our sons visit me once a month at
Newport Beach. Life really was sweet. I had accumulated a
$20,000 nest egg and was living like a rich, idle playboy. Glen
said there was no limit to how far we could go, and I believed
him.

Delores was a regular visitor at the beach house. She had
become serious about me, and talked about divorcing her husband and marrying me. I liked Delores — she had style and
warmth, and I admired her truthfulness, her absolute honesty
and lack of guile — but I knew I wasn't ready for another
marriage so close on the heels of the last one. Also, I admitted, I
enjoyed the beach outside the back door, which was crowded
with beautiful young California girls, and I didn't think I wanted
to surrender the field for just one woman.

I hadn't been as honest with Delores as she was with me. I'd
told her I made my money gambling, never mentioning that the
way we did it wasn't gambling. The gambling aspect intrigued
her, and she aften asked if she could go along with me. She also
wondered if I was hanging out with mobsters, a subject that held
an endless fascination for her. She thought the life was glamorous, different from what her conservative doctor/husband provided, and it was no use telling her most women would gladly
trade places with her. Nor was there any point in saying the

actual "work" I did was far more dangerous than glamorous.

I'd told Delores I was married, and that my wife refused to give me a divorce. This ploy didn't work. Delores said she would retain a top-notch lawyer and pay the legal fee. Next I tried to play the wronged and long-suffering husband.

"I don't like my wife," I said. "But I can't divorce her."

"Why is that?"

"Because of my children. The court would give them to her, and I'd never see them again. It's for sure that a judge wouldn't approve of my gambling."

Delores tried a different tack. "I have my own personal fortune," she said. "You could live well the rest of your life. You'd never have to worry about money."

This made me angry. It sounded as if she were talking to a gigolo, someone who would panic at the thought of losing his weekly allowance. I insisted we leave things as they were.

"I don't want to continue this way," she said. "I don't want to share you. If it's impossible for you to get a divorce, then I think it's best we stop seeing each other."

To her consternation, I agreed with the analysis. I suspect it was a bluff, and she hadn't expected me to call it. She was not unlike a few other women I've known who have money and use it to buy a younger man. But Delores was also different from these women. She left without a scene and we parted good friends. We still are.

Every three weeks or so Glen Grayson would telephone and arrange for the crew to meet somewhere in Nevada. We would work a weekend, divide an average of $25,000, and return to our respective homes. We had not yet gotten into full stride. We were a team of good horses, and Glen was our crafty driver/trainer, warming us up before we went for the really large stakes.

Our moves around the crap tables and slot machines were so well-coordinated and smooth that it would have taken a stop-action camera to tell we were hustling. The naked eye just couldn't pick it up. Besides biding time while we picked up additional sets of dice, Glen wanted us to get experience under true hustling conditions. The moves we employed were already second nature to us, but the repetition was insurance against ever making a first mistake, which likely would be our last. Also, we were warned constantly about the danger of overconfidence. It was something which at first I believed I would never be guilty of, but as success piled upon success with astonishing ease, I found it was indeed something to be guarded against. Jan Deerwood and I were the two who always looked the calmest, and though I can't speak for her, I know appearances in my case were often deceptive.

8

When I wasn't hustling in Nevada, I was attending parties at various houses along the beach. Often actors, writers, and directors were present, and a few professional athletes could be counted on to drop by. The music was good, the Beatles and Elvis and Bob Dylan, and the conversation stimulating. At one of these parties I met June, a professional sun worshipper. June was young, fun-loving, golden brown, and very beautiful. We swam together during warm afternoons, talked and made love in the cool evenings. I had never been so content.

June introduced me to Stan and Betty. Stan was a fireman, a hard worker, an honest, stand-up guy. Betty was a cute blonde from Torrance who enjoyed swimming and surfing and reading F. Scott Fitzgerald. Stan and Betty had been married about a year and were trying to scrape together enough money to buy a house. Like most young couples with only a high-school education, they were finding it difficult — no, impossible — to put up a down payment.

Stan, Betty, June and I hit it off right from the start. It was a friendship that happens now and then — the right chemistry, the right vibrations. Stan was everything I had once attempted to be — foursquare middle class — and I seemed to represent to him the glamorous life that was passing him by. He was stolid middle-class, all right, but in his heart were Walter Mitty dreams.

Betty was seven months pregnant and larger than most women at this stage. She was younger than I by twelve years — I was thirty-six — and impressed by the money I carried, especially the hundred-dollar bills. June had told them about me, so they knew

I made my living as a "gambler," although of course not even June knew about the crew or its methods at the crap tables.

I invited Stan and Betty to my house one night for dinner, and they were good enough to pretend to enjoy the meal and compliment me on it, even though I am a terrible cook.

"Why," asked Betty, only half joking, "don't you take Stan and me to Las Vegas? Maybe we could win enough money to make that down payment on a house."

Half of Betty was serious, however, and I did not know what to say to her. I knew how much a down payment meant to them, but more was involved. This was a couple that drove a station wagon and had all the baby furniture picked out and bought in advance. They liked things like bridge and canasta. I was not sure Betty and Stan could do what was expected of them, I had no idea what Glen Grayson's reaction to the suggestion would be, and, most important, I had grave doubts whether this nice couple should in any way get caught up in the world of crossroaders. Winning enough money for that down payment might be no favor at all.

"I'll think it over," I said, stalling, but I knew Betty would bring the subject up again.

Friday came, and with it a call from Glen, and I had to go back to work. I drove to Las Vegas, a lonely ride through the desert that keeps you alert only because so many drivers are traveling so fast, and met the crew at Barry Churchman's house. We practiced for an hour in his basement, not unlike a professional team warming up, and then drove out to the Strip. Friday night was good. We netted more than $10,000 almost as easily as if we'd just had to stoop down and pick it up off the floor. By this time we had dice that matched those of almost every casino in Nevada.

On Saturday afternoon we were in the Fremont Hotel in downtown Las Vegas, scene of our original debacle. The midday action had not yet begun, so we bided our time (we certainly weren't going to play at a table with just the casino people present), waiting for the place to become crowded.

Rollie Malone noticed the jackpot on one of the progressive slot machines was up to $1,800. "Let's take that one off," he said. "It will cover our nut for the weekend."

An old woman with blue hair, one of the legendary little old ladies of Las Vegas, was pulling the handle of the machine we wanted. When she finally gave up and moved on to another, five of us moved in. Jan Deerwood disappeared and joined Glen

Grayson outside. Her appearance was scheduled for later, at the payoff.

Four of us — Don Allison, Rollie Malone, Barry Churchman, and I — huddled around Jackie Gillitzer and the target machine. Jackie opened the door with his key, kicked the reels loose, and set the sevens in line. The entire operation look less than thirty seconds, but the old woman had seen us! From the look of shock and disgust on her face (how could this be? how many times had this one-armed bandit robbed her?) an observer might have thought we were sticking up an orphanage.

The woman with blue hair screamed and ran in search of a change girl. The change girl called a slot mechanic. While this scenario was being acted out, the five of us left as casually as we could through a variety of exits. Jan Deerwood entered to collect the jackpot and put on a good act as another change girl counted out the money. Jan explained how she would tell all her friends back home about winning at the Fremont. Of course, the change girl had an act of her own. She was as excited as Jan; she seemed to be overjoyed that someone had won so much money. Actually she could care less. In any case, when the slot mechanic arrived, he found not five sinister thugs but a jubilant, dancing, delighted blonde being congratulated by other patrons on her good fortune of winning an $1,800 jackpot.

What could the slot mechanic do? He would have been shouted down, shamed as a poor loser, brought disgrace to the Fremont, had he made a fuss about the jackpot. Instead he accused the old lady of seeing things. This was some gratitude, she sniffed, she was simply a good citizen who had seen bad guys cheating the casino, and she had done her duty. This was the thanks she received?

Actually, the slot mechanic was not naive at all. He knew the Fremont had been taken. But if he admitted it, he would also be admitting he had let someone come in, open one of his machines, and win the money. There was nothing he could do but vent his frustrations on the old woman.

It was a close call, and Glen was anything but pleased. He was sure we somehow had bungled the operation, and he berated us as individuals and as a crew. Glen did not appreciate suspense and hair-breadth escapes. "In this business you only have to be caught once," he never tired of pointing out.

Jan Deerwood's collecting that Fremont jackpot was typical of her nerve. She knew we'd been seen opening the slot. A lot of it was adventure with Jan. What if we *had* been seen? She'd just bluff it out. Crossroading, like everything else Jan did, was *fun* for her, and without risk there wasn't any fun.

The weekend concluded on a happy note. We netted $32,000 and change, and before we went our separate ways had a sumptuous dinner at the Stardust Hotel. Glen mentioned he had to visit Los Angeles on business, and I offered to drive him.

It was late as we crossed the desert, and the moon and stars were bright as jewels. Glen was in a mellow mood. I could tell that despite his constant criticism he considered us the best crew he had ever assembled, and I believed this might be the time to talk to him about Stan and Betty.

"It doesn't take a whole lot of skill to collect a jackpot," I said.

"Ummmph," he said.

"I mean, it's necessary and all, but the individual only needs to act excited and hold a hand out."

"The most important part," Glen said. "What good are we doing if we don't get the money?"

"I'm talking about skill. It's not a skill job, like Jackie opening a slot, or switching new dice into a game."

"What are you leading up to, John?" Glen didn't like the sideways approach to anything.

"I know this young married couple, and . . ."

"You think they'd be just fine as collectors."

"Not for long. But they need a little money for a down payment on a house. You know how tough that can be." I doubted if this last was true. Glen had been hustling one game or another almost since he'd left the cradle. But he had a sentimental streak that could occasionally be touched, so I laid it on with a trowel. "Their names are Stan and Betty. He's a fireman. A hardworking guy, Glen. She's pregnant. They really deserve a break."

"You think this is an easy job?"

"No. I'm just saying they could be our collectors for a short time. Till they get the money for the down payment.

"I misjudged you if you're saying this is easy. The people we take money from are the best in the world at hanging on to what they have."

"Stan and Betty would be in your debt forever if you helped them."

"If I'd wanted beginners, I'd have raided a grade school."

"If Stan and Betty have a boy, they'd probably name him after you." I knew this was going way too far.

Glen snorted, lit a cigar, and looked out the window. Everything was flat and desolate, and the road was built for speed. You could go as fast as you wanted on this road, and the cops usually wouldn't bother you. Glen didn't speak again until we were on the outskirts of Los Angeles.

"If they're your friends," he said, "you can bring them next weekend. We'll see if we can help."

The following Friday I drove Stan and Betty to Las Vegas. They were eager, thrilled, expectant, almost like little children in anticipation of a first visit to a carnival. We went directly to Barry Churchman's house and I introduced them to the crew. Everyone seemed to take a liking to them including Glen. Stan and Betty really were a pleasant couple, typical Southern California kids. Betty, even with her swollen stomach, was extremely attractive. She had a figure that could launch a thousand kids.

We ate at Barry's house, and Glen made his singular impression on Stan and Betty. He told them exactly what to do, and while leaving out the baseball-bat threat, which was inappropriate, made it clear that absolute secrecy was expected. Glen decided we should get money for Stan and Betty by beating the slots.

"They've never collected a jackpot before," he reasoned, perhaps trying to convince himself the idea was a good one. "No one in the casinos will recognize them."

We drove out in several cars to the Sahara Hotel and surveyed the slots. The big payoff was a $3,700 jackpot.

"Let's take it," Glen said.

"Don't be nervous," I said to Betty.

"I can't help it," she said.

"Everything will be easy."

I bought a roll of quarters from a change girl and ambled over to the machine we intended to take off. I started to play the machine, because it was important to get at least two or three 7s or bars in the window. This facilitated getting them all in line when we opened the door, and speed was crucial to our operation. We figured we had to open the door, put the jackpot on, and close it in thirty seconds.

Betty was standing to my left, right up against me. I could feel her trembling, partly from fear and partly from excitement. Stan stood next to her. He had been in dangerous situations fighting California brush fires, but nothing like this. Glen was on my right. Usually Glen avoided direct action, but he felt his presence would provide a steadying atmosphere for our tyros. Regardless, the machine was surrounded.

Glen unlocked the door. I pulled the handle and broke the reels lose. I held the door open, just enough for Glen to slip his hand in and set the reels in place. When he finished, I pulled the handle down, and Glen held the reels in place until they all were locked. Then he jerked his hand out and I closed the door. Glen locked the machine, and he, Stan, and I split, leaving Betty alone with her jackpot.

Betty stood bravely in front of the machine like an old pro until we were safely out of sight. Then she launched into what was not entirely an act. She squealed, hollered, and became very excited. She and her unborn baby jumped up and down for joy. A change girl came over to see what was going on, and she found a young, pretty, pregnant girl standing in front of a $3,700 jackpot. The change girl was overcome with genuine happiness for someone else. She hugged Betty and kissed her, and hugged and kissed her again. The two of them danced around in circles locked in a warm embrace. Other patrons and casino employees gathered to offer congratulations.

Betty collected the money, and left as soon as it was safe to do so without arousing suspicion. I stayed in the background to make certain no one followed her into the street to mug her. When she was safely in the car with Glen, I got into another car and followed them back to Barry's.

"How did it go?" I asked Betty.

"Terrific!" she said. "It was more fun than I've ever had. They were actually happy I won."

"Maybe the change girl and the dealers were," I said. "Don't be so sure about the management."

We decided on the Mint, drove downtown in several cars, and selected a jackpot worth $1,800. Jackie, Don and I put it on, and Betty collected the money. In an hour we had earned $5,500. I told Glen we should get started on the craps tables.

"I'm not sure they can handle it," he said. "The slots are safer."

"They'll be all right," I said. "I explained to them on the way from Los Angeles. They know each is supposed to put $500 on the field when I touch the cigarette to my lips."

"I don't want to rush it," Glen said. "Let's let everybody calm down."

Glen was the boss. We drove this time to a motel room he had rented earlier, had coffee, Cokes, and sandwiches, and laughed and laughed about what we had done.

Stan and Betty were amazed it was so easy to make money, and we kidded them about their enthusiasm. They wanted to work all night.

"At the rate we're making money," Betty said, "we can't afford to take this coffee break."

"The casinos will be there for a long time," Glen said.

Glen was still not satisfied that Stan and Betty could handle the action at the crap tables. He wanted to test them once more, this time under real fire.

"Before we see about the craps," he said, "I want to try one more slot machine.

The Fremont Hotel had a machine paying $3,700 on the jackpot. It was extremely tough to crack because it was located next to the main doors that opened onto Fremont Street. Also, it was a double-door machine that would require greater coverage. Single machines were easy, all that was required was the lining up of three or four reels at most. With a double-door machine we had to open the door wider and reach across *six* reels. To add to the problem, the change booth was right next to the machine, and the girl in the booth was elevated high enough to look over everyone's head. Glen was being a real ball breaker. If Stan and Betty were going to make money, he reasoned, they would have to work for it.

"How," I wanted to know, "are we going to open the door and roll the reels with that damn change girl staring right over our shoulders?"

"It can be done," Glen said.

Glen told Stan to purchase a cup of quarters from a change girl on the floor, and to take them to the change girl in the booth. "Tip them over inside the booth," Glen instructed.

Stan did as he was told, while six of us surrounded the target machine. When Stan was two steps from the change girl, Jackie Gillitzer inserted the key into the lock. Stan "accidentally" tipped over his cup of quarters and the change girl dutifully bent down to retrieve the coins. This was all the time we needed to set the reels and clear out.

Betty stood there alone and collected her second $3,700 jackpot of the night.

We reassembled back at the motel. There was no doubt it was going to be a good weekend.

The main shows would break on the Strip in thirty minutes, and the resultant crowded casinos meant that was the time we should be ready at the crap tables. We had to get with it if we were going to hustle the craps.

Glen Grayson was now satisfied Stan and Betty could hold up their end, so we drove out to the Tropicana Hotel. I went inside alone to see what kind of action it had. Although Glen was in charge, he let me run the crew, and I controlled the play once we entered the casino. I selected the table and decided how long we would stay and how much money we would take. Glen trusted my judgment, and I never let him down.

The action inside the Tropicana was ideal for our purposes. The place was humming with gamblers. I returned to the parking lot and signaled the rest of them to come in, and they wandered inside singly and in pairs. We took every precaution to avoid being identified as a group.

I met Glen in the parking lot and told him what I'd observed in the Tropicana. Glen reached inside his special suitcase and removed a pair of dice we'd had prepared in New Jersey to match those used in the Tropicana.

We were going to switch our "tops" into the game. The switch was simple enough, but doing it took a lot of guts. The hard part was keeping the boxman and dealers from examining the dice while they were still lying on the table.

Now that practice had made us more sophisticated with the tops, our betting was more finely tuned, and now not even throwing an eight could defeat us. To win the money, we placed the eight, nine, and ten, made a field bet, and bet the eleven and twelve. We knew for certain that at each table we targeted we would win between $8,000 and $10,000 using the tops. We always aimed to get three rolls of the dice, and might go for a fourth if the boxman was asleep.

Each member of the crew had to be on his toes, and the more people we had betting, the better. But the important part was perfect execution. It's just not possible to overemphasize this fact: if we messed up, we very well could end up dead in that desert.

When the Tropicana stickman emptied the bowl in front of me, I switched the tops into the game. The crew received my signal that tops were being thrown, bet accordingly, and when the dice settled at the end of the table, the stickman called the number. He then raked the dice to the middle of the table, directly in front of the boxman.

Most boxmen, out of habit, routinely pick up the dice and examine them. To prevent this disaster from occurring, Jan Deerwood, in a low-cut dress, would lean over with a twenty-dollar bill and ask for change. The boxie's eyes would focus on Jan's breasts, distracting him long enough for me to get the dice safely into my hand. To deter the stickman from rolling the dice over with his stick, I would hand him two dollars and say, "Put the boys on the eleven."

A bet for the dealers made them feel good, and took their minds off what was happening and onto their own wager. Should one of the dealers, who stood on either side of the boxman, have nothing to do, he was handed money by a member of our crew. It was essential to keep the dealers and the boxman busy until the dice were back in my hand. It was a super-risky play. A daredevil play. When we did it, we did it right.

After the third or fourth roll, I would cut the dice out of the game, brush the crew out of the casino, seven myself out with the legitimate dice, and leave.

I was expert at sizing up a craps crew. That is why Glen Grayson delegated so much authority to me. I could tell if the craps crew was alert and sharp, or bored and half asleep, if they were hawk-eyed veterans or inexperienced. There were a lot of inexperienced people working the casinos of Nevada.

Glen Grayson always remained in the parking lot when we shot craps. He was, as I've mentioned, too well-known to go in with us. I would enter the casino with the tops in my jacket pocket and select the table with the greatest amount of action, and the crew would assume their positions. My position was next to the stickman, on his right side. If it was impossible for me to get next to the "sticky," I would allow one player between us, but never more than one. It was vital that I stand as close as possible to the stickman: the distance to the end of the table was shorter.

That night at the Tropicana a spot was open next to the sticky and I moved in. The dice worked their way to me, and I gave the signal to the crew to get ready. The stickman emptied the bowl of dice in front of me. I picked out two of them, set them down on the table, made a few small bets, and checked to be certain the crew was prepared. I touched the cigarette to my lips, the signal to place the bets as soon as I picked up the dice. I saw the wagers come down on the table, in the field where they belonged. Stan and Betty had done what they were told. Don Allison and Jackie Gillitzer handled their end, as usual. Rollie Malone and Jan Deerwood were ready if needed to distract the stickman or boxman. I flicked my wrist and the dice flew across the table.

"Nine in the field! Pay the field!"

The stickman raked the dice back to me. Rollie kept the dealer occupied while Jan Deerwood entranced the boxman.

I checked the crew. We had just won $2,000, and they were busy collecting the money. I waited for them to get ready, then fired the dice again.

"Twelve in the field!"

The payoff was two to one, and we were $6,000 ahead. One of the bosses seemed a little spooky about the last toss. I stalled by placing a few insignificant bets, and decided we could get away with one more roll. I put the dealers up with a $5 bet on eleven, waited for the bets to come down, and threw.

"Eleven in the field! Pay the field!"

The dealers were happy. They had $75 to put in their toke (tip) box. "Thank you for the bet, sir," one of them said.

We were ahead $8,000. We had not encountered any steam from the casino, but I thought it was best to leave. I brushed the crew out, switched the dice, and a few moments later sevened out and left the table. Everything had been routine, just the way we'd planned.

Success on the crap tables always depended upon how much steam we received, or how the bosses reacted to the play. The vast majority of bosses believed our play was legal and never knew we were hustling them. An alert few would sense something was wrong but could not figure out what it was. I had a knack for knowing when it was "tom" (no good) in a casino. I would quickly brush the crew out and we'd hit another place.

The important thing was not to get caught. The consequences could be dire, and Glen always insisted we err on the side of caution. Certain casinos took pleasure in breaking arms and ribs if they got a crossroader in the security office. All of the casinos employed gorillas, but not all of them used force. The ones that didn't simply detained the crossroader until he could be arrested on that vagrancy charge. The ones who did use force did not care if they were working over a man or a woman, an old person or a youngster. Occasionally a gorilla would grab a person he suspected of cheating, but who wasn't, and break some of his bones. The casino then got a lawsuit for its efforts.

A favorite method of cheating among certain crossroaders was to switch decks on a "21" dealer. A clever cheat could palm a new stacked deck into action, or the dealer might cooperate with the play. Jackie Gillitzer recounted what happened to a fellow suspected (actually, he was innocent) of switching decks in a Strip casino. He was taken out to the desert where his fingers, jaw, and several ribs were broken, plus he suffered a punctured lung and fractured skull. The man's wife went to get him after receiving a phone call saying where he could be picked up. It took a year of treatment in Las Vegas and Detroit hospitals before the man was even halfway back to normal.

The crew was hardly given to moralizing. We just didn't spend time worrying about right or wrong. Each of us had a variety of reasons for what we did. What chiefly motivated me was the money. I'd never had much, and now a whole new world was opened up. Don Allison had a more specific goal, that ranch he'd always dreamed of. Jan Deerwood and Rollie Malone, I'm sure, loved the adventure. Glen and Jackie, I suppose, had done it for so long they couldn't imagine another life. So although we didn't spend time on the niceties of ethics, I think each of us did do some rationalizing, and we couldn't help, as professional cheats, noticing a very blatant double standard: it was all right for the casinos to cheat their customers; it was not okay for someone to cheat the casinos.

As I've said, much of this has changed since our heyday, when it was very difficult to get a fair shake in Nevada. Today, if a person wants to be cheated, he needs to go to small outlying towns. Here, the gambling establishments cater largely to individuals just passing through, on a hunting trip perhaps, and stopping for lunch or breakfast. Of course, they will place a few bets before getting back on their way. These out-of-the-way casinos know they have to grab the money fast, as they will probably never see the individuals again, and it is tremendously difficult to win even a single bet. On the other hand, the larger casinos in Las Vegas, Reno, and Tahoe, who don't have to grab every penny waved in front of them, and with much more at stake if they're caught, now seem to run a pretty straight show. It's helped also, I think, that much of the mob mentality that previously prevailed has been replaced by corporate thinking with its longer-range goals.

Anyway, when we were making a shambles of the law of averages, the owners and managers kept their dealers so afraid of losing their jobs that they took advantage of every little move they could. Some dealers who cheated the players at craps thought they were impressing their boxmen. There were "21" dealers who considered it a triumph to hustle a player out of a two-dollar bet.

There are many ways to cheat at "21," the most common being for the dealer to change his hole card. If a dealer holds seventeen points, with a ten or a face card showing, he simply substitutes a face card for the seven, giving himself twenty points, usually a winning hand. This is done by sliding the top card down (he knows it's a face card because he's seen it by crimping the deck) while palming the seven to the bottom of the deck. Another method is to second-card the player. When shoes (boxes containing four to eight decks of cards) were introduced in Las Vegas, it became more difficult to cheat on either side of the table. Still, as we knew, a smart dealer could second-card from a shoe. But just as casinos became more expert with their methods, so did crossroaders, and ways were found to *switch an entire stacked shoe* into the game.

When that weekend with Stan and Betty concluded, all of us gathered at the motel to split the take. The difference between my two friends and members of the crew was glaringly obvious. The crew was relaxed and subdued. Stan and Betty were bubbling with enthusiasm. They thought the world was free. Our take just for Sunday had been $17,000 and change.

"I want to do this another time," Betty said.

The look on Glen's face told me that was unlikely. He had the crew he wanted and saw no need for additions.

We never did tell Stan and Betty what it was I did at the crap table. Stan couldn't figure it out, and it bothered him. Had he known what I was doing, it was conceivable he could form his own crew and go into business for himself. The more competition we had, the more difficult it would be for us to win, though if Stan had made a move on his own the result would almost certainly have been disastrous for him. Glen Grayson was constantly afraid of being caught, and Glen was the best in the world at what he did.

Stan and Betty were in ecstacy all the way back to Los Angeles. *Each* had won $4,900, a one-ninth share. "We couldn't have saved this much money in ten years," Betty said.

"I'm glad you're happy," I said.

"We really hope we can do it again."

Between them they had $9,800, more than they needed for a down payment on a house. They would even have enough left over to furnish the new home.

Before we left Las Vegas, Betty laid out all their winnings on a bed and Stan photographed the loot. Then Betty made a fan out of their hundred-dollar bills, and Stan snapped another picture. They were two happy kids. They had eaten in choice restaurants, slept in luxurious quarters, made a pile of money, and it had all been free. Everyone was delighted. Even the casino owners, because they did not know they had been taken.

It was late Sunday evening when we arrived in Los Angeles. There was just enough time to stop at a favorite Chinese restaurant. After dinner I dropped Stan and Betty off at their apartment, then drove to my home in Newport Beach.

June was waiting for me. She looked as beautiful as ever, but I kissed her once and went straight to bed. Working a weekend in Las Vegas was exciting and rewarding, but it exacted a terrific mental and physical strain. I was totally exhausted.

The telephone jarred me awake at 9:00 a.m. "Why don't you and June come over and have breakfast with us?" Betty asked.

I didn't want to leave the beach, but I knew this was Betty's way of thanking me for the weekend. I said we would be there in forty minutes. I rolled out of bed, showered and dressed, jumped into my car, and June and I drove to their apartment. Betty had baked a Quiche Lorraine, which was delicious.

The sun was climbing higher in the sky, and I wanted to be on the beach with June. We finished breakfast and got up to leave.

"When are we going to Las Vegas again?"

Betty had been bitten by the bug. Just one weekend, and she wanted to become a crossroader. I felt maybe I had made a mistake taking Stan and her to Las Vegas. Now it was my duty to edge her back into the world of middle-class America.

"Not for a while," I said. "Maybe not ever. Glen doesn't like to use the same people too often."

"We were good, weren't we?"

"You were fine."

"Then why wouldn't he want to use us again? We're ready any time."

"You were fine, Betty, because you were with people who knew what they were doing. You weren't given the dangerous jobs, or the ones that require special skill. I wish you'd follow my advice. I think the world of you and Stan. I knew you wanted that house and I thought I'd help. But you shouldn't think about going on with the Vegas business."

"We could learn the things you know. We'd be willing to do our share. I'm sure you weren't born with a pair of dice in your hands. You learned. So could we."

"The security cops in Vegas could get a make on you and Stan. You could both end up in jail, or worse. I wouldn't want anything to happen to either of you."

"We're not afraid."

That was one of the problems. A healthy amount of fear is *good* for a crossroader.

I was beginning to think I had created a monster. My motive had been good, the desire to help a young couple, but I could see the result turning sour. Betty had tasted the "good life," and she wanted more. What was a down payment on a little house when she could buy a large, luxurious one? And Stan was talking about quitting his job as a fireman. They envisioned tall stacks of hundred-dollar bills, an endless series of exhilarating betting *coups*, when what was more likely, almost certain, was an arrest record and lives shattered by a get-rich-quick dream turned into a nightmare.

But how do you get this across to people you like? How does an artist tell a friend to stop painting, that the friend simply does not have what it takes? "Life is good for you," the friend might reply, "and you just want to keep everything for yourself."

Life was good, but not for a moment did I believe I could keep going on as I was. It would end. I just hoped not in disaster. I was saving almost everything I won and was looking into possible business opportunities for when the inevitable day arrived. I really had been giving it a lot of thought, and although the odds were bad (not many crossroaders got out in time), they weren't hopeless. For Stan and Betty, the middle-class couple Peggy and I once aspired to be, they were.

I tried again to talk to my two friends. Scaring them didn't work, and talking about right and wrong would have sounded absurd coming from me. I tried logic: if this were a viable way of making a living, the profession would be incredibly over-crowded.

Nothing worked. I just hoped later they would come to their senses, though I had grave doubts.

Finally, June and I drove back to Newport Beach and our special, private place on the sand.

I really was enjoying life to the hilt. A few mornings after the breakfast with Stan and Betty, I asked June if she would like to fly up to San Francisco for dinner, and she said she would love it. I made reservations and the next morning we hopped a flight north. I leased a car at the airport and we drove to Golden Gate Park, where we rented two horses and rode along the beach. We had lunch in the park, then visited the Palace of Fine Arts. We ate dinner at the Wharf and arrived at the airport in time to board a late flight back to Los Angeles.

It was past midnight when I got June home. She said it had been the greatest day of her life, and I believed her. It had been a pretty good one for me, too.

My main worry these days was what to do with the large amounts of cash I was accumulating. I did not want to entrust the money to a bank. Banks are hand in glove with the IRS and report large deposits to the agency. Nor did I want to keep all the money at home. So I dug holes all around the Los Angeles area and buried the loot. I used redwood boxes to avoid the danger of someone happening by with a metal detector, and tried to select spots that were unlikely to be dug up by a housing developer or a power company. I buried the money at night. During the day, a casual observer, watching from a distance with binoculars, might have spotted me. Or so I thought, anyway. I figured that being careful was the only protection I had.

Glen called a week after my trip to San Francisco. He said he was flying to Los Angeles, that he had something very important to discuss with me. Glen did not use the phrase "very important" loosely.

I was waiting at the airport when Glen arrived. We drove to my home, and he insisted we walk along the beach.

"This is something big," he said.

"I figured it was."

"We're going to Europe. Istanbul. There's a casino that just opened there, and it's giving strong competition to an established club. The club wants it put out of business. One of the owners contacted me last week. He wants us to go over there and shoot the new club out of its bankroll and close it down. He figures we'll have to win $400,000 to bankrupt the operation. You should get a passport right away, and whatever shots you'll need."

"Why doesn't the club handle it themselves?"

"They don't have the personnel. Also, they figure it's better if outsiders do it. They don't want to steam up the Government of Turkey."

I had never been to Europe, and the trip appealed to me. So did the excitement, and the thought of all the money we were going to make. I believed nothing could compare to the satisfaction and thrill of teaming with a crew of professionals in a contest of wits against a mighty casino. Our crew of crossroaders thought of ourselves as Davids against a powerful and dangerous Goliath.

I asked Glen if he wanted to stay overnight with me, but he said he had arrangements to make in Las Vegas. I drove him to the airport, and started making my own preparations.

In ten days we were ready. George, Rollie, Don, Jackie and Jan assembled at my house. Barry said he couldn't get away, but we suspected he had a case of nerves. We left the cars at my home and rode in two cabs to the airport to board a flight for London.

We stayed in Great Britain two days and did some sightseeing. We saw Big Ben and Windsor Palace. One night I went to Ladbroke's, a gambling house, and won the equivalent of $2,000 playing "21." In a private room at Ladbroke's were some Arab sheiks spending money as if there were no tomorrow. I would have loved to get them into a card game.

In Istanbul we checked into the hotel whose casino we intended to break. This was a change in our usual routine, but necessary because we were unfamiliar with the Turkish capital.

Glen and I shared a room. Other crew members were lodged strategically throughout the hotel in order to appear not in mass. We changed clothes after checking in, went down to the casino, and sized up the craps. The casino itself was much smaller than even the tiniest American version, and far more elegant. The ambience was subdued, the decor tasteful. It was an elaborate playpen where you'd expect to find bored jet-setters, people with titles like Earl and Duke and Baron, and wealthy, sophisticated international financiers. Aristotle Onassis had played here, I was told. No one said anything about a dress code, but I sensed right away that our casual attire was not what management intended. This very chic casino had a low, tasteful hum, unlike the raucous, constant buzz of a Nevada joint, and everyone was extremely polite. It was assumed that all of the players had fat bankrolls. There was no one here who'd ridden in on a Greyhound bus with twenty dollars and hopes of parlaying it into a fortune.

We intended to steal a die off a table and have it duplicated in the United States. Fortunately, the dice used on all the tables were identical, so one duplicated pair could be used everywhere.

That first night I played a little and made an evaluation of the dealers. They were amateurs, friends of management who knew little or nothing about the gaming business. They were patsies for any scuffler who wanted to whack them out of their money.

It occurred to me while I was playing that we wouldn't have to steal a die. We could take a picture of them and send the picture to New Jersey in an air mail letter. To maintain a low profile, Glen was playing the role of a tourist, and he took a picture with the camera he wore slung around his neck. He instructed our man in New Jersey on the size and color of the dice and told him to rush the order. Eight days later — eight days spent learning the incredible history of the Turkish capital — we had our dice and were ready to go to work.

The first night we won a tidy little bundle of $120,000. It was just fantastic the teamwork we'd achieved, and the red carpet was rolled out for us. Management did not want us to check out with its money. They need not have worried, at least not yet. But everything was on the house: food, drink, we were told even our rooms were paid for.

Glen Grayson was reliving his youth. He could join the game without fear of being recognized, rather than have to lurk in a parking lot wondering how we were doing. Even the sophisticated Jackie Gillitzer was having a good time, although this old-time hustler complained that there was no challenge, that we were shooting fish in a barrel.

However, Glen was hot to bust them and get back to the United States. He had heard chilling tales about Turkish prisons, and all of us knew there *were* laws against cheating in Turkey. But Glen Grayson was indeed King of the Crossroaders, and despite his impatience to hit them and run he told us we should lose the next night. This would give the casino hopes of recovering its losses, and allay any doubts management might have about us. On the second night, betting witlessly, we gave the casino back $15,000.

The third night was different. I went to the table and waited for the dice. This was old hat for me by now, and I felt supremely confident.

The stickman, a kid out of high school, probably a nephew of one of the owners, emptied his bowl in front of me. I picked up two dice. My own dice were tucked in the palm of my other hand.

The crew was all in place. They looked like high rollers — they were — and they came out betting big. I whipped the dice to the end of the table, caroming them off the wall, and it was pay-up time for the casino. I did it again, and again, and again. Then I switched back the casino's dice and breathed easier when I sevened-out.

That's the way it went for an hour. I would roll four winners, then lose. The casino took a $110,000 shot in the cash register.

It was time to worry. Glen and I slept in shifts, and so did the other members of the crew. Glen had his baseball bat with him, and we alternated sitting at the door inside the room cradling it in our laps. Glen believed it was better to defend himself with a baseball bat, rather than a knife or a gun. Either of these could inflict fatal injuries, and Glen did not want a murder rap hung on him, even if it was self-defense. There was always the likelihood of a frame.

We were not really afraid of management. It did not figure they would try to knock us off, especially since their losses had been split evenly among our crew, which they did not know was a crew, and several bettors lucky or smart enough to cash in our "hot" streak. The danger, we felt, might come from an adventurer who saw in these improbably "lucky tourists" an easy target.

The night passed without a problem. The bosses were still forcing smiles the next day, like actors in a toothpaste commercial. We had taken them for $215,000, to the brink of bankruptcy, and like punch-drunk pugs they wanted another chance at us.

The game was rigged — possibly the more alert among them even suspected it was rigged — but they were eager to play some more. What a reversal! Usually it is the poor bettor who wants to get socked in the wallet one more time by the house, but here it was the house begging to be frisked.

We spent the day touring Istanbul. No one had a make on us, and it was fun wandering the city not worrying about security guards or cops. Glen loved his role as the tourist, and he snapped pictures of everything. Jackie and Jan stayed by themselves. Rollie went off in search of a whorehouse. Don visited a horse auction. It was crucial we not be identified as a crew.

Early in the evening Glen and I had a marvelous Turkish dinner, compliments of the casino, and made ready for our final assault on the money.

There was a late-night flight to London, and we planned to be on it. Glen rounded up our luggage while the rest of us were positioning ourselves in the casino. He tipped the bellman ten dollars to get our bags out of the hotel unseen. He also made a deal with a stewardess to smuggle the money out of Turkey.

This last was not hard to arrange. He had dinner with the young woman, made her a generous offer, and settled everything before the dessert. Stewardesses didn't have to go through customs; all she had to do was carry the money through in her overnight bag.

When Glen had completed the arrangements, he came down to the casino and lost a small bet. This was the signal for us to move. We were so precise, six people perfectly synchronized, that we had the casino down $140,000 in less than an hour.

The casino owners were a sorry sight. All of them gathered at the craps table where we played, hoping for a change of luck, a miraculous reprieve (for it seemed the dice had forever turned against them), but in reality what would happen was the final destruction of their business.

Right near the end they called in an expert to check the dice. I saw him coming and switched their dice back into the game. The expert found nothing wrong with the dice, of course, because he was examining his own, and when he shrugged his shoulders and left, I palmed our pair back in.

The owners finally had to announce the house was closed down, out of business, bankrupt. We cashed out amid sub-zero stares, and so did a number of gamblers who'd thought I was riding a lucky streak and jumped on. But no more was there any pretense of friendliness. I was short-changed $1,000 on the count, but it would have been madness to complain.

The crew left singly. It was like a controlled dash toward a fire exit. We wanted to get out with a speed approaching that of light, but we didn't want to arouse suspicion. Don, the cowboy with the drawl, left first. Then Rollie, the hick from Texas — he spotted an attractive socialite on his way out and for a heart-stopping moment I thought he was going to slow down and proposition her. Next Glen, that camera still slung around his neck. The jockey, Jackie, and his flashy girlfriend, Jan — she looked annoyed that the casino had no more money for us to win. I was the last to go. With every step I waited for a hand to clutch my shoulder and beckon me back.

We stayed away from one another at the terminal. I couldn't relax and unwind until the plane cleared the runway and adjusted to its heading. I knew the others were drawn tight as piano wire, also. Then, as we climbed into a night cloud, I leaned back, thought of the money we had won — nearly $400,000 — the dangers we had endured and conquered, and I opened my mouth and out came an ear-shattering whoop. A number of people on the plane were taken by surprise.

"That's not very professional," Glen said. He was smiling.

"I guess not," I said.

"Well," said Glen Grayson, King of the Crossroaders, "this time was something special."

My share of the take was about $60,000. That was one thing about our crew. Glen might be our heart and soul, but everything was shared equally.

We checked into the London Hilton. A few hours later we got a call for our steerman, one of the owners of the rival casino. The news was out that we had broken the house, and he said he wanted to come to London to show his gratitude.

He took the six of us to dinner. He and Glen regaled each other with stories of the great crossroaders, and the rest of us sat entranced the entire evening.

Toward the end of our stay in London, Glen became restless. It happened all of a sudden, eight hours before our flight left for the United States. It was the only time I ever saw him get reckless.

"Let's go to Ladbroke's," he said. "We can take it off for five or ten thousand dollars."

We were exhausted, drained from the experience in Istanbul, but no one refused Glen when he was ready for action. I think what Glen wanted most was to perform as a participating partner with the crew for a last time before the recognition factor made that impossible back in the United States.

Glen searched in his briefcase and found a pair of dice that resembled those used at Ladbroke's. Jackie, Glen's comrade through twenty-two years, raised his eyebrows, shook his head and shrugged. But he didn't say anything.

We drove to the club in two cabs. This gambling club was plush. Sound was absorbed by an acre of carpet. A winding old staircase led to a room where roulette and baccarat were played, and there were many private rooms with thick walls. Waiters in Ladbroke's intimate dining room dressed in tuxedos and were stiffly formal (incidentally, there are many Ladbroke's in London — they are betting parlors — but this was private and for the well-heeled).

We set ourselves up at a craps table, and I switched the dice when the bowl came around to me. It was more profitable than even Glen had bargained on. No one knew us, and we were so proficient at what we did, there was no suspicion we were together. We walked out of Ladbroke's $39,000 richer.

"You're going mad," Jackie said to Glen.

"I think you're right."

The trip to Los Angeles was long and tiring, and the sun was setting when we put down at Los Angeles International Airport. We cleared customs, Glen contacted the stewardess he had arranged with to smuggle our money in, and we caught a pair of cabs out to my house on Newport Beach. I was so tired I wanted to collapse.

June had stayed at my house while I was away. Someone had to watch it and the cars. When we arrived I could see June out on the beach, soaking up the last of the sun, and I didn't disturb her. The crew went into the house and split up the money.

June came in off the beach and all of us sat around talking, joking, relieving our tensions. The crew departed for their various destinations about 10:00 p.m.

June and I were alone. We went to bed together, but I could not respond to her coaxing. Part of me was still in that casino in Istanbul, and I kept thinking about all the money I had, and that there was more to be buried.

I considered going into a legitimate business. The donut shop had been a disaster, but if I had something bigger, I thought, I might become more professional about its operation. Going back to jail held no appeal at all. The thought that I could have been thrown into a Turkish jail made me shudder. But now wasn't the time to quit, I thought. I'd come this far, I might as well go on a little longer. I was still a young man, I told myself, and there was plenty of time to settle down.

Nonetheless, I'd keep my eyes open.

10

June and I had three good days together. We made love in the sand dunes and in between the sheets. We went for long walks on the beach, and when we felt too warm we took a dip in the ocean. At night we dressed up and went to fancy restaurants and for drives along the shore.

June was good company. She was easygoing and she laughed a lot. She also had talent. She was a fine painter and recently had had her own exhibition. I was enjoying every moment with her, not even thinking of the time when it would end.

Then Glen called. "I want you to work this weekend," he said. "I'll contact the crew and meet you in Reno."

I really wanted more time off after the Istanbul caper, but Glen must have figured we were on a hot streak, that there was no sense in backing off for a while.

Glen had made a reservation for me at the Hacienda Motel, and I flew to Reno on Friday. Glen was at the airport to meet me, and he was on edge.

"There are people in a car out in the parking lot," he said. "I think they followed me here."

Glen drove while I kept an eye on the mysterious car. It pulled out behind us and followed us along the highway.

"You're right," I said. "We've got a tail."

"I wonder who's got it in for us."

"I wonder who doesn't."

"You know what I mean."

Glen made a few turns around the city, and when he figured he had shaken the other car he drove me to the motel. I carried my luggage to my room, hung up my clothes, freshened up, and then went out to meet the rest of the crew.

We ate dinner (for the price, Nevada has the best food in the country), and then it was on to Harrah's. We were going to shoot some craps. I got the dice in my hand and looked up to see if the crew was ready. They were, but so also were what seemed to be the entire Reno police department. They had just suddenly appeared, as if from the woodwork. I hurriedly brushed the crew out, rolled a loser, and joined them outside.

"What's the matter?" Glen asked.

"The joint is crawling with detectives."

We got in different cabs and went back to the motel. I arrived before Glen, and when his cab pulled up he didn't release it. He stopped just long enough to tell me to take another cab and meet him in a bar across town. He was waiting when I got there.

"I want you to go back to the motel," Glen said, "and clean up my room. The craps are there in my suitcase. There's also a box of craps under the front seat of my car. Get them out of there in case a bust is coming. I don't have to tell you the heat we'll face if the cops get those craps."

I had the cabdriver drop me a block away from the Hacienda Motel, and then walked directly to the coffee shop. I ordered orange juice and looked around. Cops are usually recognizable, no matter how much they attempt to conceal their identity, and I didn't notice any. I drank the orange juice, went up to Glen's room, and cleaned out his suitcase. Just looking at his counterfeit collection of dice made me tremble. Name a casino in Nevada, and we had duplicates of its dice. If the police got their hands on this treasure trove of evidence, there was no telling what they could pin on us. It wasn't as if we were innocent.

Next I went out to the parking lot, to Glen's car. The dice were exactly where he said they would be, and I walked across the parking lot to another car Glen had rented for me. I slid the dice under the front seat of the car and put the key in the ignition. Before I could start the engine I felt something cold against the back of my head: a .357 Magnum pistol.

The hand holding the gun was shaking so violently I thought I was going to be killed right there. I was too frightened, too paralyzed, even to tremble. I tried to think of my enemies. Emmett Thresher came quickly to mind, but that did not seem logical. Thresher wouldn't contract a hit on a crossroader. I thought of Carson City, but I'd made no enemies there. Visalia? I gave away more donuts than I sold. Then it occurred to me: Istanbul. The owners of the bankrupt casino had contracted with an assassin to repay the hustlers who had busted them.

I considered ducking, or whirling around and disarming the man. I put the thoughts out of my mind as fast as they entered. My brains would be all over the windshield. Still, I wondered about the guy in the back seat with the gun. Who was he? If he was a professional, why was he waiting, and why was he shaking so much? It's incredible all the things that go on in your mind — quite logical things — when you're in mortal danger.

"Put your hands over your head," the man ordered.

I did exactly as I was told. I did it in slow motion. I certainly didn't want to upset him any more than he already was.

"Now get out of the car, very slowly."

I had not slammed the car door, and I eased it open with my foot.

"One sudden move and you're dead."

My mouth had gone dry, turned to cotton. I got out of the car as carefully as I could.

Suddenly I was surrounded by cops. There must have been fifteen of them, and I couldn't imagine what was going on. They did not need an army of police to arrest one crossroader.

"Start walking," said a cop who seemed to be in charge.

He directed me to a motel room on the ground floor. When I entered the room my knees buckled. In the window, pointing out into the parking lot, was a .30 caliber machine gun mounted on a tripod. Also in the room was what appeared to be a complete radio command post.

"Where are your guns?" the cop in charge asked.

"I don't have any guns."

"We're not going to take any shit from you. Tell us where they are, and do it right now."

Once I realized I was dealing with the police instead of a hit man, my courage began to return. "Are you feeling okay?" I asked. "Why would a gambler have guns?"

"Do you know Charlie DuCharme and Ray Lechner?"

"Sure. I know them." DuCharme was a former pit boss at the Riviera who'd been caught stealing chips. Lechner was a burglar. The two were in Glen's circle of acquaintances.

"Well, we have solid information that you came to town to break them out of jail."

"I didn't even know they were in jail."

I said it so matter-of-factly that he could tell I was giving him the truth, and he knew he had made a mistake. He tried to bail himself out of an awkward position.

"Where's your buddy Glen?" he asked.

"He went to the airport," I said.

The leader went on radio and ordered two squad cars to the airport to pick up Glen. But Glen was not at the airport; he was waiting for me at that bar.

The officer in charge was now certain I had come to Reno to gamble, not to lead a jailbreak. It wasn't just my attitude that persuaded him. I had almost seen something click in his head. The information he'd received was wrong, and he knew it.

I learned Glen's motel room had been wired for sound, and I'd been picked up because I was overheard talking to him. The officer called in his army, including two who had been on the roof, and sent them on their way. I sensed it was a letdown for some of these police officers — they had counted on a shootout, had psyched themselves up to kill someone. Instead they loaded their equipment and hauled me off to jail.

I was booked for vagrancy. As I was signing the papers, Glen was escorted in by *six* officers. They had found him waiting in the bar for me to show up with his dice. Glen posted bond and we left the police station together.

We went back to the motel and checked my rented car. Miraculously, the police had not searched it, and the dice were safe. This was a lucky, lucky break. We had invested a fortune in money and time in those dice, and their loss would have been incalculable.

Glen bought dinner for the crew, who were anxious to learn what had happened. They were afraid one of the casinos had gotten wise to us and dealt with us in their own way.

"I don't think we should work this weekend," I said. "There's too much steam in this town right now."

Glen didn't argue. He realized that the crew thought we had gone back to work too soon after the difficult job in Istanbul, and was willing to concede a rest might be good for all of us. Glen drove me to the airport, and I flew home to Los Angeles.

On Thursday I was back in Reno, where I had to appear in front of a magistrate on the vagrancy charge. The judge listened patiently to my story, fined me fifty dollars for vagrancy, and told me to "hit the road." The bad part was I got my picture in the Black Book, a publication distributed to casinos to help them identify crossroaders. I was described as an accomplice of Glen Grayson, as a craps cheater, a slot cheater, "21" cheater, armed robber, and murder suspect. All of it was true except the murder business, which was thrown in to make me appear particularly heinous. The armed robbery part stemmed from my driving that getaway car for Happy Heagen.

The two trips to Reno cost me four hundred dollars, and I had not made a penny for my efforts. Worst of all was getting my picture in the Black Book. Now the casinos had a make on me.

The slots began to appear more attractive as a source of income. I urged Glen to ease off the crap tables.

"We should beat the slots only to get our nut back," he said. He always considered our winnings from slot machines to be small-time stuff.

Glen was either fearless or crazy — or maybe those two are one and the same thing. I pressed my point and he got testy.

"What's the matter with you?" he asked. "Are you losing your nerve?"

"I'm not losing anything. I'm trying to keep my head, and also to use it."

It could be dangerous standing up to Glen, but I had to occasionally or he would run roughshod over me. Glen could be violent, and physically he was extremely powerful. This time he controlled his temper.

"I'm listening," he said.

"There's a lot of money to be made off the slots. We can do good for ourselves over the next five or six months, until the heat is off. Nevada isn't going to dry up."

"So?"

"So it's clear as crystal. We stay away from craps for five or six months. We pocket easy money from the slots. The jackpots, I'm sure you've noticed, are getting bigger and bigger. The joints are using the bigger payoffs to lure the suckers. I say we go after those jackpots. When things return to normal we go back to the craps."

"I don't like it," Glen said. "We're at our peak now. We might lose our edge on the crap tables."

"We can practice at Barry's house."

"It's not the same. Also, I'm beginning to wonder about Barry."

"That's your business."

"Well, I'm worried about Barry."

"He's all right," I said. I don't know why I said it.

"I'm not so sure."

"We could set up a crap table at my place on the beach. We won't lose our edge."

Glen said he would think it over, and for me that was a victory. The next Wednesday he called me and agreed to my plan. We would concentrate on the slots.

Glen's hunch about Barry Churchman turned out to be right. The day after Christmas, Barry said he was quitting the crew. He went off on his own to beat the "21" tables, using every method known to crossroaders; he was good, and when he cheated he made plenty of money. But Barry Churchman had a flaw, a sickness, which was that he liked to gamble on the square. He knew he could easily defeat the casinos by cheating, but he loved nothing better than attempting to beat them legitimately. And at this he could only fail.

Compulsive gamblers have discovered what one writer has called the most painful and complicated way ever devised to commit suicide. Many of them do take their own lives, when they see what they have done to their families or when the law or the mob is about the swoop down on them for the money they obtained illegally to gamble. Many compulsive gamblers claim they merely want to win money, but I wonder. Barry Churchman knew how to win money but could not avoid the lure of games he more than anyone else knew were rigged in the house's favor.

Barry took to hustling six months at a time. He would accumulate fifty or sixty thousand dollars, then he would blow it all back in a month shooting craps, never more than five hundred dollars at a time. He would sit in a bar, drink, brood about his misfortune, go to the bank and withdraw five hundred dollars more from his safety deposit box. When that was lost, he would repeat the routine, over and over, until the bank was closed. This way, unconsciously, he'd found a way to "die" not just once a day, but many times. He was dragging it out.

None of the casinos would issue Barry a marker, which enraged him (though he could have solved the problem by drawing more money out of the bank), so the process of losing would continue until he was completely tapped out. Then his wife would fight with him. She would threaten to leave and he would promise never to gamble again. Their tortured, merry-go-round existence went on for four years.

One day Barry was arrested by the Las Vegas police for dealing in stolen jewelry. The police said they would drop the charges if he became an informant, and Barry, like so many compulsive gamblers, was basically a weak individual and agreed to go along. He put the finger on a number of people around town, although he seemed to stay away from us. I believe it was because he feared Glen's baseball bat.

The Las Vegas police set Barry up in his own bail bond business so he could keep in touch with thieves and hustlers. He was permitted to continue his traffic in hot jewelry, and to go on some small-time scores with local punks. It was all part of his cover.

Then Barry was caught transporting stolen goods into California, and the FBI became involved. The arrest precipitated a big fight between the FBI and Sheriff's Department, and the FBI refused to back off. They did so only after the Sheriff used his considerable political influence. The FBI agreed to reduce the charges against Barry, but insisted he serve a short sentence in the federal camp at Lompoc.

The FBI was holding a prize prisoner at Lompoc, a high Mafia mobster, and Barry was persuaded to obtain information from him. He did his job so well he was released in four months.

Barry was the first member to leave our crew. With each fresh revelation about his activities I reminded myself how I had vouched for him to Glen. But Glen never said a word. He was simply grateful our weakest member was gone.

Barry is a free man today, but he walks a thin line between life and death. He purports to be a solid, standstill hustler, but he continues to finger people. Usually they are petty thieves whose misfortune was that they always outsmarted the police. Their cunning enraged the cops, and always made their punishment more severe.

The gray, shadowy world of the informant is not to be recommended to anyone. The informant is hated by those he snitches on and despised by the police as well. A good detective will readily admit that one good informant is worth more than a dozen expensive crime-fighting computers, but the detective does not and cannot like the snitch, nor his own reliance on him.

I remember a phrase perhaps Barry should think on: What Goes Around, Comes Around. Karma.

11

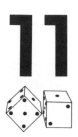

Before the crew assembled again in mid-January, 1967, we lost Don Allison. That likable cowboy, so steady, so adept at blending into a crowd, did what he said all along he would do and used his carefully conserved winnings to buy a ranch in northern Montana. All of us were happy for Don. A crossroader winning spectacular sums of money is one thing, but the rarest of the breed is the one who can walk away on top.

We threw a party for Don when he announced he was retiring, and Glen opened his wallet wide in sparing no expense. I predicted that Don would miss the excitement and be back with us within a year, but again I was proved wrong. Don made a big success of his ranch, and if he was ever tempted to rejoin us, he never succumbed. That night I felt both envy and happiness for him. I hoped I also could leave on top, and told him so.

"You just quit cold turkey," Don advised. "Do it all of a sudden and never look back."

In mid-January, 1967, at my house in Newport Beach, Glen made plans for a series of raids on Nevada slot machines that was probably unprecedented in the history of crossroading. It had been agreed that for six months we would hustle only slots. The work would be almost relaxing compared to the pressure cooker at a crap table. We would never be in a casino more than five minutes, which greatly reduced the risks.

I kept a record of the crew's successes over the next six months:

LAS VEGAS	AMOUNT WON
The Stardust	$ 35,000
The Mint	$ 33,600
The Tropicana	$ 32,500
The Sahara	$ 32,400
The Desert Inn	$ 31,100
The Riviera	$ 28,600
The Golden Nugget	$ 28,500
The Fremont	$ 27,500
RENO AND LAKE TAHOE	
The Mapes	$ 36,000
The Wagon Wheel	$ 31,000
Harrah's	$ 28,500
Harold's	$ 28,400
CARSON CITY	
Nugget	$ 18,600
ELKO	
Commerce	$ 12,200
WINNEMUCCA	
Star Boiler	$ 11,000
ELY	
Ely	$ 10,500
TOTAL	$425,400

My share, after expenses, was just short of $60,000, and it had been accomplished with some new people. The core of the crew, of course, was still Glen, Rollie, Jackie, Jan, and myself, but we brought in other people when Glen deemed it desirable. Stan and Betty, to their delight, were permitted to work with us, and occasionally Glen brought in hookers he particularly liked and trusted. We spread our action over all three shifts so the same person was not too often seen collecting a jackpot.

Many of the casinos at this time gave S&H green stamps to anyone winning a jackpot, and soon we had dresser drawers filled with stamps. It was fun watching the women debate over which one should be allowed to keep our mountain of stamps.

The casinos took such a working over from us that eventually they changed their payoffs. Some reduced their jackpots to $250, while others simply eliminated the big-payoff machines entirely. The casino bosses knew their machines were paying off too regularly, but they couldn't figure out what was wrong. Even top-level management became concerned. Private investigators were hired, but they found us as hard to catch as the security people did.

The toughest slot machine to beat was the piggy-back. It was a six-reel slot with three reels waist high and three reels shoulder high. The hinges were on the back of the machine. Lifting the door high enough for Jackie to get his head inside was difficult and hair-raising. It would have frightened the devil himself. Jackie had literally to be on his toes to beat it, but the payoff was $5,000 so we went ahead. I think also Glen had a bit of the mountain climber in him and was attracted to the piggy-backs simply because they were there.

Harrah's, in downtown Reno, had several piggy-backs. They also had a man who walked the rafters on a catwalk, looking for cheaters and other undesirables. A two-way mirror enabled him to observe the players without their knowledge, another example of the advantage the house has. It was against the rules for bettors to photograph the interior of a casino, but it was perfectly okay for security people on catwalks to take unauthorized pictures of the players.

In order to hustle certain casinos, it was necessary to bribe the man in the sky. The security guard in the rafters during one of the shifts at Harrah's was doing business with us.

Glen ordered a transmitter and receiving unit, made up especially for the crew, and the transmitter was in the hands of the skyman. I wore the receiving unit like a garter around my leg. On the garter were two pieces of metal, each the size of a five-cent piece, and a wire ran from the garter to a set of small batteries strapped to my waist. The transmitter was also powered by batteries.

The skyman watched the pit bosses and change girls while we did our work on the floor. If he spotted anything unusual, he would hit a button twice, which told us heat was coming down. We then would back away from the machine. Later we used this same system on craps and "21" tables, a further refinement on an already effective method of cheating.

When a boss suspected a player of cheating, he would telephone the skyman and say something like: "Watch the guy in the maroon jacket on table number four. He may be pulling something on us."

If the skyman was on the take, he would watch us for ten or fifteen minutes, then call the boss and tell him we were straight. The skyman would also keep an eye on his boss. If he thought the boss was becoming too spooked, he would give me three shots of juice. A single shot from the skyman was the signal to go back to work.

The transmitter sent a slight electrical charge through my body, which could be increased or decreased by adjusting a rheostat. When the receiver was properly adjusted, the amount of electricity flowing through the body created no more than a pleasant tickle.

The first time I wore the garter was in Harrah's. I wanted to be sure to receive the signals, so I turned the juice up as high as I could. We arrived at Harrah's fifteen minutes ahead of schedule, and I sized up the place and allowed time for the skyman to spot me. There were six of us in all, four regulars and a pair of hookers who were friends of Glen. Glen himself remained outside.

The machine we had targeted was at the end of a row of ten slots. At the opposite end was a change booth. The girl in the booth had a good view of the floor and of us.

I played the piggy-back for a few minutes to get some bars in the window, then Jackie moved in and opened the back door. Jackie had his hand in the machine and was turning the reels when Rollie said, "It's no good."

With what seemed a single movement Jackie had his hand out of the machine and the door closed. But it was a false alarm. Just a customer interested in playing the same machine.

"You're wasting your time," I said to the customer. "We've been playing this machine all day, and we're not leaving until we beat it. You know how it goes." *Get out of here, you idiot,* is what I wanted to tell him, you might be mistaken for one of us, and you wouldn't want to hear how dangerous that can be.

The customer smiled and moved on. The skyman hit the juice once to let me know everything was all right, and I almost jumped out of my shoes. I felt like I'd been hit with a bolt of lightning. I tried to get my hand inside my shirt to adjust the voltage, but before I could, that snappy skyman hit the juice again to show me the coast was clear. My knee convulsed into the air and almost hit me on the jaw. I thought I was going to die.

"What's the matter with you?" Jan said.

"That asshole upstairs is trying to electrocute me," I said.

"Well, turn the power down."

"What do you think I'm trying to do?"

"And stop making a spectacle of yourself."

Jan could be a real sweetheart.

The change girls started down the aisle to see what the fuss was about, and the madman in the rafters hit the juice twice more to warn that danger was coming. This time I was sure I would die. The two jolts, one right after the other, nearly knocked me down.

"I've got to get out of here," I said. My ears were smoking.

Jan intercepted the change girl and asked for a cup of dimes. Clumsy Rollie blindly ran into the two of them and the dimes scattered all across the floor. I staggered off to the men's room, found an empty stall, and turned the juice to very low.

Now I was determined to get that piggy-back. We reassembled at the machine. Jackie opened it, rolled the reels around, closed it, and we cleared out of the casino. One of the hookers collected the jackpot.

We went to the Wagon Wheel at Lake Tahoe, where there were several $5,000 slot machines all in a row. We selected one of them, huddled up to it, put the jackpot on, and left, all in under three minutes. The second hooker collected this jackpot, and the Wagon Wheel's management tried to make her believe they were happy to see her win.

Before the night was over we drove to Harold's and took off another $5,000 jackpot. We had $15,000 for the night, and more was waiting whenever we wanted it.

In August, 1967, Glen dropped a bombshell. He had been

offered a job as a pit boss at the Silver Nugget in North Las Vegas, and he said he was going to take it. The crew thought it was a joke and enjoyed a good, hard laugh.

The King of the Crossroaders going to work as a pit boss? It was like having the fox guard the henhouse.

But Glen was serious. He said we could keep the crew together, that he would help us however he could, but he made us promise we would never hit the Silver Nugget during his shift.

The Silver Nugget must have figured it was cheaper having Glen on the payroll working for them than outside ripping them off, but there was more to it than that. No crossroader would dare come into the Silver Nugget while he was on the job. He could recognize all the moves, and some that hadn't been invented yet.

Glen was paid as much as any pit boss in Las Vegas — $200 a day. He could live quite well on that, and with his extraordinary skills he could easily steal an additional $300 a day from the casino. Five hundred dollars a day, minus heat and high taxes, was a tempting inducement.

Glen also would be free to strut around town with his chest out. Sheriff's detectives couldn't touch him because he was legitimate, backed by a major casino. None of the other casino managers would dare hassle him either, and that too was flattering to his ego.

The crew figured that sooner or later Glen would be back with us, that he could not remain out of the action forever. Glen knew, all too well, how boring life could be and how monotonous it was to work a life away for a pension that wouldn't keep a dog or a cat alive. Glen had beaten every joint in Nevada and quite a few outside of Nevada, and it seemed preposterous that all of this was behind him.

As long as Glen stayed out of other casinos, he was assured of his job and his privileged status. But of course he got restless. After just four months on the job, he went out to the Sahara and beat one of their craps tables for $5,000. A bigshot at the Sahara called Glen's boss at the Silver Nugget.

The next day Glen was called into his boss's office and told he was bringing down too much heat on the Silver Nugget, that he could not keep his job and hustle at the same time.

Glen smiled and really did not pay much attention. He was confident of his importance to the Silver Nugget and knew he was worth every penny he earned and stole from them. He was not only a shield against crossroaders but also the best man in the business at switching craps into and out of a game. He could switch dice on a hot shooter without anyone ever knowing what hit him.

Nothing happened to Glen because of the Sahara incident. He continued to prosper in his respectable life, while what remained of the crew scuffled around the state.

We would go to Reno for a few weekends, then Lake Tahoe, Las Vegas, Carson City. We even made one-night stands in little towns like Ely, Elko, and Winnemucca, beating the slots and, just to keep in practice, when everything seemed extra safe, bringing out the dice and taking off an occasional craps table.

We did just fine, and all of us were more than compatible — we were friends — but we did miss Glen and wished he was with us. I had saved a considerable amount of money from the years of hustling, but I figured retirement was still quite a distance in the future.

Rollie and I became especially good friends during the time that Glen was on the shelf. No matter how close we became, however, I never rode in a car he was driving. He was the world's worst driver, and demolished every automobile he ever owned plus a few owned by friends.

Rollie wrecked his first car on his way out of Beatty, Nevada, when he and a high-school pal were on their way to a whorehouse. A guy ran a stop sign in the desert, and Rollie hit him broadside doing 80 m.p.h. A person can see for miles in the desert, but Rollie claimed he was a victim of bad luck. No one was killed, but Rollie's car was totaled.

His next car was a Mustang, and on a trip to Reno, again on a flat stretch of desert, Rollie hit a steer that was crossing the highway. Rollie was traveling 100 m.p.h. an hour, and he totaled the Mustang *and* the animal. "Stupid steer should have seen me coming," he reasoned.

Rollie was versatile. He next drove an Impala off a cliff after a night of gambling. It happened near Lake Tahoe. He was airing the vehicle out down a mountainside, there was ice on the road, and he slid into a canyon. Another car went onto the scrapheap.

Then he bought a Porsche, a vehicle the salesman assured him was impossible to roll over. Rollie believed him and tried to negotiate a curve at 120 m.p.h. The Porsche careened off the road, landed upside down in an irrigation ditch, somersaulted an additional two hundred feet, and came to rest against a dirt embankment. The Porsche was demolished and Rollie sustained a concussion.

After Rollie was discharged from the hospital, he purchased another Mustang. On a skiing trip to Oregon, his car left the road and smashed into a redwood tree. This time Rollie's neck was broken and it was four months before he was released from the hospital.

"Cars are too dangerous for you," I advised. "Why not try something safer?"

It was bad advice. Rollie bought an expensive speedboat and took it out on Lake Mead for the maiden voyage. He traveled less than one hundred yards in a wild, zigzag fashion before tearing its bottom on a rock.

The crew had been without Glen for just six months when Rollie surprised us by announcing he was getting married. Though still in his early twenties, he was someone you thought would always be a bachelor, and for a while we thought he was putting us on.

The crew voted to give Rollie a wedding present. We made excuses to him and then went out without him and worked an abbreviated weekend, winning $15,000. We bought round-trip tickets for a honeymoon in Hawaii, and gave the rest to him in a sealed envelope.

"Shucks" — he really said *shucks* — "you guys" — one of the *guys* was the abundantly endowed Jan Deerwood — "shouldn't have done this."

The newlyweds stayed in Honolulu for three weeks, and the hotel accommodations didn't cost a cent. Rollie beat the bill. It was his habit to check out without paying, and at this, just as at hustling, he was a master.

Marriage was supposed to calm Rollie down, to satisfy his voracious appetite for women, but it didn't. One month after he returned from Hawaii, and we had finished hustling the slots for a night in Carson City, he asked me to ride with him to the Moonlight Ranch, a whorehouse. That was all right with me, but when he insisted I go in with him, I said no.

"You never know," he said. "You might find a girl you really like."

"That's right, I'll never know."

Rollie kept teasing and joking, and before I knew what was

happening I was walking inside with him. His genuine good nature could disarm anyone.

The Madam recognized Rollie the minute he walked in and called out all of her girls. Any customer would be given a choice, but since Rollie was a regular, no one was held back. About all I knew about houses of prostitution, which flourished in certain areas of Nevada, was that there were ordinances detailing how far they had to be away from churches. In any event, Rollie chose what he deemed to be the most attractive of the girls and took her off to one of the private rooms. I simply shook my head when the Madam looked at me inquiringly.

Whorehouses never held any appeal for me, although I had no problem accepting them morally. If people wanted them, and no one got hurt, what business were they of anybody else?

I started to thumb through a magazine. It was one of the girlie publications, packed with pictures of women with silicone breasts. One of the prostitutes walked over and slapped the magazine out of my hand. Then she wheeled her spiked heels and returned to her seat.

"This isn't a library," she said.

I stared hard at her for a minute or two. But I could understand a little bit what she was feeling.

Rollie the Rabbit returned a few minutes later. He had balled his prostitute, paid the twenty-dollar fee, tipped her another twenty dollars, and we were back in the car on the road to Las Vegas, all in about ten minutes. He was that fast.

Rollie and I traveled a lot together, and I always drove. Together we made a pile of money, and usually had a good time. Rollie was an amazing individual, a real dingbat, but capable, and like Glen he inevitably got the money. It was Jan's opinion that Rollie didn't really want to be a crossroader, that he did it because of Glen, whom he idolized. Rollie's "craziness," she thought, was a sign of something deeper. Jan could have been right, but she was another, I believed, who could have fascinated a whole battery of psychiatrists for a long time.

Rollie had a friend, a boxman at the Sahara Hotel in Las Vegas, who wanted to make some money. Having a boxman on our side would increase the odds in our favor, and Rollie told him we would be coming in to work the craps.

We arrived on schedule, positioned ourselves at the table, and when the dice came around to me I gave the signal. We won nearly $33,000 before we backed away from the table. The boxie took a coffee break and I met with him.

"I've never seen anything like that," he said, "and in case you wonder, yes, I've been around. Why don't you people come back in and win some more money?"

That would be veering from our usual routine, which was to get in and out of a casino as rapidly as possible and to make sure a safe amount of time elapsed before we visited it again. But that table, with the boxie in our corner, did seem ripe for the picking. I agreed to hit it again. We quickly made another $12,000, but then noticed a boss had spotted one of us, probably me, and almost surely because of that mug shot in the Black Book. I saw the steam coming down, really heavy this time, and I brushed the crew out.

Rollie, bless his heart, did not leave with the others. He must have sensed that this time we could be in deep trouble, and he stayed behind to make sure I would be all right. The casinos had recently become very much aware of the activities of crossroaders and were determined to put a stop to the activity. There was no telling what might be done to me. I had to stay cool, not just bolt and run, to give myself every chance. Suddenly the casino seemed like a giant tomb.

By the time I sevened out, I could see the security guards coming. Rollie and I started to walk, then to jog, shouldering people aside, and in moments we were in full flight. We raced out a side door and across Sahara Boulevard to a parking lot where I had left my car. A security guard was right behind us, furious: "Stop!" he ordered. "Stop, or I'll shoot!" He had drawn his gun, and not for a moment did I think the threat was an idle one. The Sahara management probably would give him a medal for shooting a pair of crossroaders.

I was running for my life, and coming up fast on my parked car. When I got to it I jumped onto the roof. The guard was running so fast he couldn't stop, and he kept on going after Rollie. I got into the car and started the engine.

And couldn't go anywhere! The traffic in that parking lot was ferocious, and every exit was blocked by harried, horn-honking drivers, none of them as anxious as I was. I had seen Rollie race around a corner, chugging his big body up the Strip toward the El Rancho Hotel. Now I saw that the security guard had given up on Rollie and was coming back for me.

I put the car in gear and roared down the sidewalk. Then the guard spotted Rollie again and took off across the intersection after him. He couldn't make up his mind which one of us he wanted.

Rollie barreled into an empty lot and I knew he had to be tired. He was carrying 250 pounds on his frame. But that beefy guard wasn't ready for the Olympics either.

Fortunately for Rollie, the lot was not entirely empty. In its center was a swimming pool that had been drained of its water. Rollie saw the pool and ran around it. The security guard didn't see it and fell six feet to a cement bottom. He broke his leg, and his screams could be heard up and down the Strip.

I drove around looking for Rollie and finally found him, bent over and gasping for breath, just as an ambulance pulled into the empty lot to collect the security guard.

Our boxman at the Sahara was fired. The big bosses decided he was in on the play, although they couldn't prove it. They felt something had not been on the up-and-up, so they terminated him.

I thought about the incident a lot in the months to come. I really believe that security guard would have shot us. It would have been an example to others. I figure there were at least a hundred crews of crossroaders working Nevada at this time (we knew a number of them by sight), and the take was a lot more than the casinos had previously believed. These crews had varying degrees of skill, though probably none attained our level, which is one reason we stayed away from them. We felt we had nothing to learn from them, and we didn't want anyone else copying our methods. Regardless, even an incompetent crew might score now and then, and the casinos wanted it stopped. Had we been shot that day, it would have been hard to justify to a jury, since there was no proof we were cheating. Still, I have no doubt that the casinos, the real power in Las Vegas, could have invented a scenario that would have justified our demise.

A week after the incident at the Sahara Hotel I was back in Las Vegas clearing up some personal business when Rollie gave me a call. "Let's do something," he said.

This meant he wanted a woman. I told him I wasn't interested.

"Okay," he said. "Let's take a shot at the '21'."

That was all we could play. The rest of the crew was out of town, and Glen was still a legitimate pit boss. I agreed to play for a few hours at the Fremont. We found a table that looked good, and I stole a card from the deck. I handed it to Rollie and he started mucking (holding a third card in his hand). The move was simple, and anyone could learn it in fifteen minutes. If Rollie held a face card and a three, he would switch the other face card he was holding for the trey. Instead of sitting on thirteen points — a dead man's hand — he would have twenty, a winner more often than not.

The move had to be made before a "hit" was given. After a hit, the dealer expects the player to put his cards under his bet.

Bosses often are suspicious of winners, because they are not accustomed to players winning. If a boss thinks a player is doing something, he will come to the table and change decks. If a bettor is holding an extra card in his hand and the boss grabs the deck before the player can get it back into the deck, the boss will count the cards and know someone is cheating.

It was my job to watch the bosses. When I saw one coming, I would take the card from Rollie (or whoever in our crew was playing) and put it back into the deck. We took pride that no boss ever got a dirty deck off the table while we were playing.

A crossroader will have no trouble if his point man does the job properly. The reason is simple: a boss always gives himself away. He might station himself next to a player or walk out of the pit to a better vantage point. He might stand directly behind the player or hide among the slot machines. But nothing the boss does will escape the scrutiny of a good point man.

When a boss suspects cheating, he will go to the podium, remove a new deck of cards from a drawer, put them in his pocket, and then walk aimlessly around for a few minutes. Then, suddenly, like an eagle diving on its prey, he will swoop down on the table, remove the cards that are in play, and replace them with a new deck. He might also call the man in the sky and tell him to keep an eye on the suspected cheat. If the skyman sees something out of the ordinary, and if he is not on the hustler's payroll, he will inform the pit boss what is going on.

But the boss still has to take the deck off the table and count the cards. That's difficult to do, and I liked to think it was impossible when I was the point man. A boss emanates vibrations, and a good point man who has been hustling for a few years can detect them.

Bosses hate cheaters, but not because stealing is involved.

Nearly every boss steals from his casino. But in order to steal, he has to maintain a winning percentage some other way. Should a hustler win $5,000 from a "21" table, the pit boss will not be able to fill his own pockets. If he did, he would show a loss for the shift, and the owners would want to know where the money had gone. It is important for a pit boss to weed out the "illegitimate" thieves so the "legitimate" ones can flower their own garden.

We had a good night at the Fremont. We had taken a chance, what with the recently encountered static at the Sahara and my picture gracing the Black Book, but we received no steam and walked away with $2,500 of the Fremont's money.

Rollie wanted more action. "Get some sleep," I said. "Go home."

But I knew he wouldn't.

One of the rules our crew lived by was that we never went into a hotel unless it was to make money. We did not go to any of the shows. The greatest entertainer on earth might be playing, but we stayed away. Our faces were seen too often as it was by hotel employees, and we did not need added exposure.

I left Rollie standing outside the Fremont Hotel, caught a cab, and went to my motel room. I was tired, bored, and lonely. Without Glen the entire scam seemed wrong. We were making good money, but the fun had gone out of it.

I also missed my sons, whom I hadn't seen in several months. I loved my little boys — not so little any more, eleven and fourteen years old — and wanted to have them with me. But that was impossible for a crossroader.

Peggy's husband was doing well in Houston. I was grateful that he was good to my children, but it bothered me that another man was playing Daddy to them. Time was passing, and I worried that they might forget me. I had made only one trip to Houston. On that occasion Peggy actually flirted with me, which made me believe she regretted the divorce.

I fell asleep with those thoughts on my mind.

The telephone rang at 3:00 a.m. It was Glen.

"Are you awake?" he asked.

"I am now. What is it?"

"Do you know where Rollie and his wife are staying?"

"Yes."

"Meet me there as fast as you can."

I reached Rollie's motel at 3:45 a.m., and Glen was already

there. So were Rollie, his wife Ann, and Joyce, one of Glen's girl friends. Rollie's face looked like it had been run over by a Caterpillar tractor. One eye was swollen shut, and his lips resembled the inner tubes of tires. The two women, Ann and Joyce, did not look so good either.

"What happened?" I asked. I figured Rollie had smashed up another car.

Rollie tried to speak, but couldn't. Tiny spit bubbles and an incoherent gurgle were the best he could manage. His entire face was red, blue, and dark purple.

Ann did the talking. She said she, Joyce, and Rollie had gone to the Sahara to catch the late show. They knew it was against the rules of the crew, but they did it anyway. She said they had not gone to gamble, merely to see the show and enjoy a late dinner. The security guards recognized Rollie and were waiting when the show ended. They hustled Rollie and the two women off to the security office. Rollie was handcuffed and strapped to a chair, and one of the guards told him he was going to "whip his ass."

The two security guards worked Rollie over. They were methodical about it, professional, enjoying their work and taking their time. One would drive his fist into Rollie's midsection, and when Rollie's face lurched involuntarily forward, it would be smashed backward by the fist of the other guard. Ann pleaded with them to leave her husband alone, so one of the guards heaved her across the room and over a desk, scraping her shins and bruising several ribs. Joyce tried to defend Ann and was punched around for her efforts. Then the guards returned to Rollie: one in the stomach, one to the head, over and over and over. The women thought he would be beaten to death, but he never screamed. No one would have heard him, and he would not give them the satisfaction.

Glen was silent through the entire narrative.

"Let's go out and do a number on those bastards," I said to him.

Glen had something else in mind. "Can you put Rollie and the women up at your house for a while?" he asked.

"Of course. But . . ."

"Start driving as soon as it's light."

"Won't you need me here?"

"Do as I say! I want you and the entire crew out of Las Vegas until you hear from me again."

That morning I drove Joyce, Ann, and Rollie to my house at Newport Beach. The sun, the ocean water, and the care and attention the women gave Rollie speeded his recovery. After two weeks the swelling had almost disappeared, the purple around his eyes had turned to yellow, and just a few drying scabs remained on his face. He would soon be in fine shape, and he said he was eager to return to work. I told him to stay put, to wait for the call from Glen.

It came on the seventeenth day of our enforced vacation. "Everything has been taken care of here," Glen said. "But I want all of you to stay out of Las Vegas for another week or two."

I decided to spend some time in Houston with my sons. Rollie, Ann, and Joyce stayed at my house, and I caught a flight from International Airport. I checked into a motel not far from Peggy's home, called Glen to give him my temporary telephone number, and made ready to have a great time. Glen had not mentioned what had happened in Las Vegas, but I had a pretty accurate idea.

The next eight days in Houston were among the happiest of my life. My boys had grown into little gentlemen, and I took them everywhere, reveling in their company. The life I had chosen as a crossroader provided numerous rewards in terms of excitement and money, but each night after being with Billy and Johnny I knew I would have traded it all for the opportunity to have watched them grow.

The best times we had were the picnics in the park. We would take cold chicken, potato salad, and soft drinks, pitch pennies into a stream that ran past, join a game of volleyball others had organized, or just talk and get to know one another better.

The call on the ninth day from Glen was the most unwelcome I had ever received from him. "I'm having a pilot and Rollie fly my Cessna to Houston to pick you up," he said.

"I hope the pilot is doing the flying. I won't ride with Rollie behind the controls."

"Do you think I've lost my mind? That airplane cost a lot of money."

I met Rollie at the airport and drove him to Peggy's house. He met my kids and Peggy's husband, we had dinner, and then we talked late into the evening. Just before we left, Peggy took me aside. "I think your friend Rollie is insane," she said.

"Why is that?"

"He keeps sticking his tongue out at me."

"Oh, that. He just wants to go to bed with you. Ignore him. If he bothers you too much, tell me, and I'll have a talk with him."

Peggy did not understand Rollie, and she didn't like him either.

The next morning Rollie and I stopped by Peggy's house on the way to the airport. It was Saturday, my sons were home from school, and I wanted to say one more good-bye.

I kissed them and squeezed them and thought I was going to cry. They begged me to come back soon, which made me feel like a giant, and I promised I would. Then Peggy, Rollie, and I walked out to the driveway to my rented car.

"How would you like to jump in the bushes with me?" Rollie suddenly said to Peggy.

Peggy was dumbfounded. Her face turned bright red.

Rollie rephrased his question: "Wouldn't you like to go to bed with me?"

Peggy started to laugh. Rollie stood there like a wounded bull, genuinely unable to understand why he was being rejected. He was such a big, green, raw country boy — at everything except hustling. He really didn't know what was going on, and he was too hypersexed even to be embarrassed.

"Why didn't you line me up with your ex-wife?" Rollie asked when we were airborne.

"If she'd wanted that, she would have said so."

"Maybe she was scared off because you were there."

"I don't think so."

Rollie was not someone to dwell on an individual woman. Soon he was talking about all the women he knew all over Nevada.

Glen was at the airport when we landed in Las Vegas. On the way into town he explained how he had taken care of what he called "the matter." He had hired two tough brawlers from San Francisco, and they had waited for the security guards outside the apartment building where the guards lived. Each of the brawlers carried a baseball bat — Glen's trademark — and they attacked with a measured ferocity.

Both security guards suffered broken legs, and their faces resembled Rollie's less than a month before. They got the message. Both of them quit their jobs and left Las Vegas. I don't know if they caught on somewhere else, but if they did they would think long and hard before working someone over again.

Had Rollie gone into the Sahara to steal some money and then had his melon thumped, he would have expected it and the guards would have been in the right. As it was, the guards were out of line, and they deserved what happened.

12

Glen Grayson, as we suspected he would, eventually grew tired of being legitimate. One evening after work he stopped at a club to have a few drinks and relax. He became so relaxed that he decided to go to the Tropicana and rip off one of the craps tables. He got it on good, but one of the Tropicana owners recognized him and called Glen's boss at the Silver Nugget. "Fire the bastard," he said.

No longer was there room for discussion. The order was final and had to be carried out, just as would be expected if the Silver Nugget called the Tropicana about one of that casino's pit bosses. The big houses stick together. It's called solidarity.

Glen was called in and cashiered. He had never thought the Silver Nugget would let him go — he was too valuable — and it was a hard blow for him to accept. Once he realized it had really happened, he thought, characteristically, about revenge.

Glen called me in Newport Beach. "Come to Las Vegas," he said. "I've got something for you."

When I got there the next day, what he had for me was a key. "It's for the cashier's cage at the Silver Nugget," he announced proudly. "Close to $80,000 is kept there at all times. Half is yours if you take it off. The other half I'll split with the cashier. He's in with the play.

"All I have to do," I said wonderingly, "is walk into the cage, put the money in a bag, and walk out?"

"That's it."

"What about the security guards? They're not blind. They'll see me."

"They won't. Nothing like this has ever happened before, and the casino figures it never will."

"They'll see me," I insisted, "and it'll be back to Carson City."

"Listen to me, John. One of the guards is always stationed at the rear door, and he can't see the cage from there. The other guard is at the front door. He never looks in the direction of the cage. He knows no one would try anything this wild."

"Well, I'll look it over. But I don't think I'll do it."

I cased the casino and did not like what I saw. I decided I wanted no part of it: too easy to be caught. Despite Glen's optimism, he would not be the one inside that cage, nor would he be the one trying to nonchalantly pass the apes who were called guards. If I were caught, there would be no bondsman, no lawyer, no trial — just a bullet in my head, that's how the casino would handle it. I would be buried in the desert, and decades would elapse before some curious archeologist uncovered my bones. I called Glen and gave him my decision.

"You're passing up a good deal," he said.

"It's not my line of work."

It was hard to turn Glen down on anything, but I hoped he'd come to his senses and look for a more sensible way to get even. I didn't say it, but I didn't think I'd mind, nor would the crew, playing some craps in the Silver Nugget.

When I returned to Los Angeles, feeling depressed, I visited Stan and Betty, and this plummeted my spirits even lower. They were not getting along at all. Babies have a way of cramping the style of young couples in southern California, at least couples who have been turned off to the work ethic. Also, Stan was spending a lot of time away from the apartment. He had quit his job as a fireman, and Betty said he had a girl friend. The money they had won in Nevada was being spent on pleasure. They had forgotten about their dream house.

My chief emotion was disappointment. Regret that things didn't work out as they should. I figured I was to blame for interfering in their lives. It would have been better if I'd stayed out. The quest for easy money had changed my life, too, but mine had probably already been off the accepted track when I first went to Nevada.

I knew I loved what I did, and perhaps I was rationalizing when I thought I was somebody special, that the whole crew was special. We did have a gift, though. Very few people, I knew, could do what we did. It had been wrong to allow Stan and Betty to get mixed up with us.

Feeling worse with each passing moment (Stan and Betty were quarreling), I left soon after dinner and drove to the house at Newport Beach. The phone was ringing when I walked in. The down part of the roller-coaster ride was about to end.

"I'm through being legitimate," Glen said.

When had he ever started? I guess he was talking about the job at Silver Nugget, but I knew he'd been stealing there.

"Meet me in Reno in a week," Glen said. "I'll assemble the crew and we'll go back to work."

"We've been working."

"You dummy. You're a disorganized mob without me."

It wasn't *that* bad. But Rollie and I had done some crazy things.

"It's not that bad," I said. I'd been sort of the *de facto* leader of that mob.

"Just be there in a week." Glen was getting angry.

I smiled. Life had returned to normal.

The crew now consisted of Glen, Rollie, Jan, Jackie, Jackie's wife Penny, Glen's girl friend Joyce, and me. There were also a few part-time extras we called in to collect jackpots for us, including Stan and Betty.

No friction existed between Jan and Penny, Jackie's wife. Glen would not have permitted it, nor would the two women, who rightly perceived that hustling was their living and friction had no place among crew members.

Betty's mood gradually became less downbeat. She seemed to adjust to Stan's having a girl friend, and she once again looked lovely lounging around the beach in a bikini. The time she could spend gambling and sunning, of course, was necessarily shortened by the needs of her child.

June and I had gone our separate ways. Kitty was my new regular girl friend, but she was only twenty-one years old, looked even younger, and it would have been unwise to involve her in the crew's activities. My middle-class heart was still partly in Visalia, and I could never accept that what was happening to Stan and Betty — their growing apart — was for the best.

I had a regular bank account but never deposited more than six or seven thousand dollars into it during the course of a year. My growing financial reserves were scattered around southern California, buried at a dozen carefully selected sites. It was the only way to keep the IRS off my back. I didn't want to do business with that bureaucracy. Besides, it should have been checking on the casinos, which each year did not report tens of millions of dollars in taxable income.

The crew met in Reno as planned, and with Glen calling the shots it seemed all the excitement had returned. He constantly was suggesting how we could do things better, more effectively, more imaginatively. He tested us, pushed us, called on us to do things we did not think we could, and this helped us as a crew. We always split the money evenly, but each of us acknowledged that Glen was *primus inter pares*.

There were cars and boats to be won on the slot machines, along with money and those S&H green stamps, so we won cars and boats. We won a fur coat Jan Deerwood fancied, and she griped that she couldn't wear it in Nevada. We won vacations to places like the Bahamas and Hawaii. Glen always griped when we insisted on winning what he called "tourist trinket traps," but I think he was having more fun than he'd ever had.

More important, those first two weekends in Reno we won more than $70,000. I thought I might just be a crossroader forever.

"Next weekend we meet in Las Vegas," Glen said, as we prepared to head our separate ways. "There should be plenty of action."

There was indeed, but all of it was the kind we so conscientiously tried to avoid.

13

I arrived in Las Vegas a day early, on a Thursday, and ran into Joe Conforte on the Strip. I had not seen the Whorehouse King since the days at Carson City.

"What are you doing in Las Vegas?" I asked. "Come to blow all your wife's money?"

"I'm here on business," Joe said solemnly. "I'm going to put a lot of girls to work."

"How will you do that?"

"I'm opening up a house."

"Joe, use your head. This town is full of prosititutes. Besides, the Sheriff won't allow it."

"Screw the Sheriff. He doesn't tell me what to do. I put houses where I want them."

"You're wrong, Joe. You can operate in Reno, and a lot of other countries, but you'll never get it on here in Las Vegas. The Sheriff is too strong. Plenty of people have tried to open up here before. None of them made it."

"Those guys weren't Joe Conforte. They didn't have the money I've got. And they didn't have every pimp in the country bringing them girls, begging me to put them to work."

"The Sheriff doesn't need your money," I said, but Joe wasn't interested in negative conversation.

"Whatever. You look like you're doing good. How about dinner tonight? I'll bring a couple of chippies along."

I met him at the Riviera, having decided that for this night I would break the rule about staying out of casinos when I wasn't working. He had two beautiful young women with him. They must have been new in the business, because they looked fresh and were not heavily made up.

After we ate Joe said he had something to show me. He gave each of the prostitutes a hundred dollars and told them to wait for us in the cocktail lounge. Then he drove me to a motel near the Showboat Lounge. He parked in the lot and stared at the empty building.

"This is it," he finally said, proudly. "This is going to be my new house." He looked at me and waited for approval.

I knew he couldn't do it, and I laughed like a maniac. Joe turned a little salty because I doubted him.

"There's no point in trying to convince you," he said when he cooled off. "Let's hit a few casinos."

"What about the girls?"

"They're big enough to find their way home."

We stopped at three different houses, and Joe lost $1,000 in each one. He had not changed. Losing did not bother him, and he still enjoyed impressing people with his bankroll. He never worked for it, and the money kept arriving by the truckload.

I simply watched Joe throw his money away. In a contest between a casino and him, I supposed I should root for the casino. I knew I should not even have been with him, what with that Black Book containing my picture and the crew intending to work the next evening.

It was late, and I said I had to leave. But I couldn't resist zinging him. "I'll see you up north," I said.

"The hell you will!" Joe bristled. "You'll see me right here in Las Vegas!"

To my great surprise, Joe did open that whorehouse right where he said he would. He got away with it at first because the Sheriff didn't take him seriously.

Joe had thirty girls working in the motel. Everyone in town was talking about the place, which stayed open exactly three days. That was how long it took for the Sheriff to take Joe seriously, and that was how long he stayed in business.

Joe Conforte was arrested, and he and the Sheriff had a talk. I never found out what was said. "I don't even want to think about it," Joe said when I asked.

Joe did call the Sheriff a few choice names, but insisted he left town because business was bad. It cost him a small fortune, and he had had to buy several officials, but it came to nothing. The Sheriff must have shaken Joe down pretty hard before running him out of town, because Joe went to Reno and stayed there. I knew the Sheriff had made a strong impression on the Whore-house King.

Kitty flew to Las Vegas Friday afternoon, the day after my

chance meeting with Joe Conforte, not to gamble or be part of the crew but because we thought we could enjoy ourselves between sessions. That night the crew took off three slot machines and beat a craps table at the Mint. I was back in the motel at 11:30 enjoying a shower when there was a knock at the door.

"See who it is," I said to Kitty.

She looked out the window.

"There are six or seven men. All of them in suits."

The men in suits could only be detectives. I didn't know what they wanted, but I wasn't taking chances. I came out of the shower dripping wet, called Glen, and told him I expected to be in the slammer in a few minutes. I asked him to have a bondsman ready. The knocking at the door became louder and more insistent.

I threw on some clothes, and Kitty opened the door. The detectives came in without saying a word. They opened our suitcases and scattered clothing all over the floor. Then they emptied out the dresser drawers.

"Where are your guns?" the one in charge asked.

I had been down this road before.

"I don't have any guns," I said.

"Where are the diamonds?"

"I don't have any of those, either."

"We have a warrant for your arrest. What does the name Wittenburg mean to you?"

"Something to do with the Protestant Reformation?"

"Don't be a smart-ass."

The detective handed me his warrant. I was charged with the armed robbery of a home belonging to someone named Wittenburg.

I had $6,000 rolled up in my pocket. I figured if the detectives got their hands on it they would put the money in their own pockets. I managed to slip it to Kitty.

I was read my rights, and led outside to a waiting prowl car. The detectives did not bother Kitty.

On the way to the station house I learned the Wittenburgs had been robbed of a considerable fortune in diamonds, fur coats, pistols, and money. The bandits had done quite a job, but I wondered why I had been fingered for it. I thought maybe the casinos suspected what they were never able to prove, that we were cheating them, and had tipped off the police to apply heat. Of course, the cops would be only too happy to oblige.

I didn't make connections with the bondsman, but it wouldn't have mattered. Bail could not be set until the court opened in the morning, so I spent the night in jail. Early the next morning I was hauled out of the cell and questioned. I denied knowledge of the robbery.

"Don't lie to me," the detective said.

I said nothing. This was harassment, pure and simple, and I figured I could take it.

The bondsman got me out at 3:00 p.m. Bail was $10,000, ten percent of which I had to put up. The rest of the weekend was wrecked, but I was not too worried about the case. It turned out I should have been.

I appeared at a preliminary hearing, and the District Attorney told the judge the Wittenburgs had picked me out of a lineup. This was impossible. There had been no lineup. But now I was afraid I might be in serious trouble. The D.A. also said the Wittenburgs had given police an accurate description of me before the lineup, and it was ruled I would have to stand trial. My lawyer thought we would win any fair trial, but it would be costly — and not just in terms of money. Crew members would have to testify I was with them during the time of the robbery, which was true, but such testimony would establish links among us.

But there never was a trial. At the last minute, perhaps afraid to perjure themselves, the Wittenburgs refused to testify, and the judge was forced to dismiss the charges. I was exonerated, but it had cost $7,000.

My freedom ranked among the most short-lived in history. I was rearrested in the corridor outside the courtroom, charged with *murder*, and thrown back into the slammer.

My lawyer called the station house and threatened the Chief of Detectives with every sort of lawsuit he could imagine. The Chief said he was unaware of what was happening and would check on it. He called in the arresting officers, demanded an explanation, and when they didn't have one I was released.

The only reason I could imagine for this abuse was that the casinos wanted me out of Nevada for good. If they were trying to scare me, they were succeeding. Had the Wittenburgs testified, I might have gone to prison for a long time. The murder charge was just harassment, and nothing would stop the police from using such a ploy over and over again. They had done it before to rid Nevada of undesirables, and none had been a bigger thorn in the Establishment's side than our crew. Of course, the casino bosses knew that if I was constantly checking in and out of jails, I could not be hustling them.

I wasted no time getting out of Las Vegas. My recent notion to remain a crossroader through the foreseeable future underwent a sea change: I now considered using the money I had saved to open a business. Don Allison, I thought, had been the smart one, pulling out when he was ahead and buying that ranch in Montana.

Even Glen agreed we should take time off. He set an example by flying to Idaho in his Cessna to fish and hunt.

I called Peggy in Houston and asked if she would let my children visit me. She said yes, and the three of us spent two happy weeks on the beach. It occurred to me that I might be able to have them on a permanent basis if I hooked up with something legitimate and settled down.

My sons returned to Houston only two days before Glen called from Idaho. "I want to work this weekend in Las Vegas," he said.

I couldn't believe it. "Have you forgotten what happened to me?" I asked.

"No one told you this business would be easy."

"Well, I won't do it."

"John, we *need* you."

"It's too dangerous."

"Have you ever gone to jail because of me?"

"Yes."

"You know what I mean."

"I guess not. But there's way too much steam right now."

"We're going to be in Las Vegas this weekend, John. If you don't come, I'm sure everyone will understand."

I knew Glen relied a great deal on me, and so did the crew. The crew could not work the crap tables nearly as well without me. I saw right through what Glen was doing — counting on my loyalty to him and the others — but he had touched on a vulnerable point in my resolve to find a new line of work. I agreed to meet him in Las Vegas, but I also promised myself that very soon I would call the crew together and explain to them why I intended to do what Don Allison had done.

I flew to Las Vegas that Friday, and the crew won almost $45,000 without even a hint of trouble. On Sunday evening, as we were separating, Rollie offered to go with me to the airport. "Only if you let me drive," I said.

Two detectives spotted us driving along the boulevard, pulled us over, arrested us for vagrancy, and once again I was back in jail, this time with company.

An hour after the arrest, Rollie was released on a $100 bond. Before they let him go he was brought into the room where I was being questioned. I could tell by the hard looks on the faces of the detectives that they were finished playing games with us. One of them pointed to me: "Soares," he said, "the next time we catch you in Las Vegas, we're going to kill you." Then he pointed to Rollie: "And anyone seen with Soares is in more trouble than he can handle."

The message was clear, and there was more.

"Do you enjoy flying?" one of the detectives asked me.

I didn't answer.

"We have a helicopter," he said. "If you're seen again in Las Vegas, we'll take you for a ride in the helicopter, and you won't come back."

Rollie was released and told not to forget what he had just heard. The detectives didn't know him very well: he would forget the warning before he hit the street.

In my pocket was an airline ticket to Los Angeles on a flight that left at 10:30 p.m. "If you promise never to come back here," one of the detectives said, "we'll let you go. If not, you'll have to stand trial."

I didn't say anything. My lawyer's advice was to keep quiet in situations such as this. My lawyer had never been in a situation like this, or he wouldn't be giving that sort of counsel. The detectives didn't like the silence. They got sore and bounced me around.

"Okay, okay," I said. "I won't come back."

At 9:00 p.m. they handcuffed me and drove me to McCarran Field. I was detained in a holding room until flight time, and on the wall of the holding room was a *poster* picture of me. No doubt at all remained that the police were very serious.

Ten minutes before take-off the detectives started me down the ramp toward the plane. What occurred next was bizarre. Rollie, of all people, came racing in with my suitcase. He tried to give it to me but I was handcuffed. The detectives could not believe their eyes.

"What did we tell you about associating with this bum?" one of them asked.

Rollie looked puzzled. He had a big, goofy grin on his face. I knew he had really forgotten what the detectives had told him. I hoped the detectives would understand that.

Evidently they did. No one, they must have thought, could be that stupid. Rollie was handcuffed and taken back to jail. This time it cost him $500 to get out, but at least they didn't hurt him.

After everyone was on board the plane, the detectives removed my handcuffs and repeated their threat. I was not sure if they were bluffing. I loved to gamble, but not on my life.

The plane took off and circled McCarran Field, and below me were the glittering lights of Las Vegas. I estimated our altitude at three or four thousand feet. I wondered how long it would take to fall that far, and the thought made me sick.

It took two days on the beach with Kitty to recover from the shakes. Glen must have known just how long it would take, because on the third day he called. He wanted to work the coming weekend in Las Vegas!

I figured Glen might be testing me. He had done it before, making me prove myself under fire, and I had always been up to the challenge. But if that was what he was doing, this time he had gone too far. Besides, I believed I had nothing more to prove to him and resented the fact he might think otherwise.

"You're crazy," I said. "You're absolutely loony. Those cops are serious. I saw them, and so did Rollie. And I never want to see them again."

"It's nothing," Glen soothed. "Everyone gets a little steam now and then."

"It's a lot more than that. Those monkeys want to kill me. And they will if I listen to you."

Glen finally accepted the fact that I was determined to stay out of Las Vegas. Instead he persuaded me to work Reno and Lake Tahoe for three weekends, which might have been what he had in mind all along. We did as well as we ever had, more than $100,000 for the three weekends, and then we took two weeks off. At the end of this short vacation Glen was back on the telephone to Newport Beach. He was beginning to sound like a broken record.

"We're working Las Vegas this weekend," he said.

It was as if he had never heard a word I had said.

A heated argument ensued which ended with my hanging up on him.

The crew worked Las Vegas that weekend without me. They

made good money on the slots, but did poorly on the craps tables.

Glen called again. "You shouldn't have hung up on me," he said.

"I'm sorry," I said. "But I couldn't seem to make you understand."

"Well, I have another plan."

"If it involves Las Vegas, I'm not interested. I'll take my chances in Reno and Tahoe, but Las Vegas is out."

"Listen to me."

"I can't promise I won't hang up again."

"Just listen. I want you to go to Max Factor's in Hollywood. Get yourself made up. Get a disguise. If you recognize yourself, don't come to Las Vegas this weekend. If you don't, the crew will expect you to be here this weekend."

I knew a makeup artist at Universal Studios. He gave me a mustache, lamb-chop sideburns, a scar down the side of my face, and some gray in my hair. I wore glasses and stuffed cotton in my jaws to make my face fuller. The disguise was a beauty. I looked twenty years older, and even Peggy or my mother would not have recognized me.

The adrenalin began to flow again. I drove to Las Vegas early Friday morning, assuring myself everything would be okay, but when finally I stood at the crap table I was shaking so bad I was afraid I would muff it. I suppose it was like riding a bicycle, though: once you learn, you don't forget. We enjoyed a *great* weekend.

14

My line of work virtually assured I would come into contact with a fascinating array of characters and rogues. One of these was Eric Mitchell, a disbarred lawyer who had been caught phonying up medical reports for automobile "whiplash victims." No client of Eric's, as artful an ambulance chaser as ever copied his way through law school, was involved in a car crash without injuring his neck and back, always permanently. But Eric went too far when he added imaginary passengers to a fender bender and claimed they also were grievously hurt. The insurance company got wise to Eric and hollered to the Bar Association. Despite a spirited and sometimes brilliant defense in his own behalf, he was no longer permitted to practice law.

Eric Mitchell telephoned me early on a beautiful May, 1971, morning, just after I had returned from a healthy and invigorating jog on the beach.

"Hey, old friend," he bubbled. "How are you doing?"

"I'm fine," I said. "How are you, Eric?"

"I'm wondering if there's a market in Los Angeles for a pleasure boat."

"There are ten million people here," I said. "I would think someone is looking for a boat."

"Good-bye, old friend," he said.

The next morning at six o'clock I was awakened by a horn blaring away out in the street. Cursing, I got out of bed and looked out the window. Attached to a car driven by Eric Mitchell was something that looked like the Queen Mary. I put on a robe and went outside.

"Eric, why are you making so much noise?" I asked.

"I wasn't sure which house was yours," he said, "and I have to get this boat off the street. It's hot."

"Where did you get that thing?" I asked.

"I drove to Lake Mead yesterday and stole it," he said.

"Well, I don't want it around here."

Eric seemed hurt. "You said you could get rid of it for me," he said.

"I didn't say that. I said there might be someone in Los Angeles interested in a pleasure boat. You didn't tell me it was a forty-foot cabin cruiser. And you didn't tell me it was hot."

"What difference does that make?" He really didn't know the difference. In a later time Eric might have fought off disbarment with a defense of diminished capacity.

"Where do you want me to park it?" he asked.

"Back it into the driveway," I said. Anything was better than letting it draw attention by blocking the street. Then I looked once again at the size of the boat. "Are you sure you can get it in there?" I asked.

"No problem at all."

Eric spent half an hour driving forward, backing up, driving forward again. He left tire tracks all over my carefully manicured lawn, and knocked over several shrubs, before finally getting the Queen Mary into what I promised myself was a strictly temporary berth.

"How much will you give me for it?" were the first words out of Eric Mitchell's mouth when we were inside the house.

"I'm not interested in buying it," I said.

"Make me an offer," he said.

Eric was not easily discouraged.

"I'm going to tell you only once more, Eric," I said. "I don't want that ship."

"What about the buyer you've got lined up?"

"I don't have a buyer lined up. You asked if there was a market for a boat in Los Angeles, and I said yes."

Eric was annoyed.

"That's not what I understood on the telephone," he said.

Eric complained that I did not have coffee perking. I brewed a pot, and he said it was too strong.

"You've put me in a fine fix," Eric said.

"It's your own fault," I said.

Kitty came out of the bedroom. She offered to prepare breakfast, and Eric said not to overcook the eggs. She looked at me and raised her eyebrows, but all I could do was shrug.

"Eric," I said, "you can't leave that ship here."

Tears welled in his eyes. He was a little man, five foot six and perhaps 125 pounds, and he removed his glasses and began wiping them with a napkin. Eric was only thirty years old, but he was shaking like someone three times his age. He confided that life had been very rough for him since he'd been unable to practice law. Kitty, who didn't know Eric, was filled with compassion.

"All right," I said. "You can leave the boat here for a little while. I'll even try to find a buyer for you."

Eric ate his breakfast without further comment, then started back for Las Vegas. I went out in the backyard and took a dip in the ocean.

Eric called at 4:00 p.m. "Have you sold it yet?" he asked.

"You just left this morning," I said.

"I'd appreciate it if you'd hurry up."

I would have told him to shove that ship, but Kitty was standing near me, and all day I had listened to her say how the only thing "the poor man" needed was a break.

"I'll try to do better," I said to Eric.

The next day I called a friend who was active around the marinas and told him I had a boat for sale. He drove over to the house and gave it a look.

"How much do you want for it?" he asked.

"Make an offer."

"Understand, I'm not interested in it myself. But I can help you sell it."

"The boat is hot," I said.

My friend looked at me, then gave the boat a much closer inspection. "It will be easy to get a license," he said, "but I'll have to take the trailer with me."

We unloaded the boat onto blocks and hitched the trailer to my friend's car. He drove to the Los Angeles Motor Vehicle Division and obtained a license for the trailer. A few days later he applied for a permit that said he had built the boat, a permit assuring him of ownership. He drove to my house, picked up the boat, and the next thing I knew it was on a lot in Redondo Beach sporting a FOR SALE sign. The asking price was $10,000.

Eric Mitchell called every day, and I supplied him with progress reports. Instead of being grateful, he grew hot because the boat had not yet been sold.

"It takes time," I said.

Eric continued to call every day. Finally he said he was coming to Los Angeles to pick up his property. He believed he was being ripped off for his luxury liner, and he arrived at my house steaming. I drove him to the marina so he could take a look at his prized possession. When he discovered he would receive only a quarter of the sales price — half was going to the lot dealer, and a quarter to my friend who licensed the boat — he got in a beef with the guy on the lot. He vented the rest of his anger on me. He said I was trying to rob him.

"Eric," I said, "if you think you can do better somewhere else, please try. I'm not getting a penny out of this, I was just trying to do you a favor. Now you come and insult me and my friends."

Then came a reply I couldn't believe, even from Eric: "All right," he said, "I accept your apology; you can keep trying to sell the boat — but I warn you, you don't have forever."

Two weeks later the boat was sold. When Eric made his daily telephone call, I told him he could come and get his money. He said he would drive to Los Angeles to pick it up, but he flew instead. I met him at Intenational Airport rather than have him visit my house.

"Make me a promise," Eric Mitchell said when I handed him the $2,500. "Promise you won't come around trying to do business with me again."

Bernie Borderman was another one-of-a-kind only Las Vegas could have produced. Bernie was a craps dealer at the Riviera, and people in his profession were one of the reasons there was no more pressure than there was on crossroaders. The dealers, being much more numerous, stole a great deal more money from the casinos than the hustlers did. Bernie and other Riviera employees were so adept at stealing that management finally had to close its doors for a while and reorganize.

Bernie Borderman contributed more than his share to the Riviera's financial woes. I once suggested to him that he join our crew, but he refused, calling us "small-timers." I'm not sure Bernie knew how much we were making, but then again, maybe he did. Bernie drove big cars and wore flashy rings, which seemed to me to be rubbing salt in management's wounds.

Bernie Borderman was a riot at a party, if you liked the type. He specialized in eating ground glass and lifting refrigerators. He had legs like the trunks of oak trees.

Eventually some eastern bigshots traveled to Las Vegas to straighten out the Riviera. They grabbed a few dealers and put the fear of God in them, but somehow they overlooked Bernie. I mentioned to Bernie over breakfast one morning that he should take it easy for a time. But his theory was that now was the most propitious time: the bigshots had made their point so strongly they would never suspect someone would continue to steal.

Bernie Borderman had been an All-American wrestler at Oklahoma State and could take care of himself. Sometimes this can be a liability. The casino goons might decide to go easy on someone with less than the strength of King Kong, but they take no chances with a Bernie Borderman. When Bernie was ultimately discovered to be stealing, three goons pounced on him and nearly killed him, though not before he busted up two of them. He broke a few bones, and had a few broken, but the outcome was never in doubt. College wrestling, no matter what the level, is a child's game compared to the alley tactics the casino goons employ. For a week it did not seem Bernie would make it. When finally he was released from the hospital, he moved to California and opened a sporting-goods store.

Sully Kelly, the guy who persuaded me to leave the donut business, was another craps dealer who would gladly have worked without salary just to keep his job. His pay was tiny compared to what he was able to steal. But Sully had no style, no class.

Sully Kelly specialized in stealing from drunks, a helpless group at a gambling table. However, stealing from drunks often requires the highest level of skill on the part of the dealer — not because the drunk is alert, but because the pit boss is. The contest then, as beautiful in its own way as a fencing match between two champions, is between the dealer and the pit boss. The dealer wants to steal for himself; the boss wants the casino to reap the windfall (with some for himself, of course).

Rich drunks are welcomed by everyone in a casino except the other customers, whom they annoy. Poor drunks are shown the door. The idea that what a casino fears most is a drunk on a hot streak is so much malarkey, an invention of the casinos themselves. A drunk's hot streak can be terminated any time the house wants it terminated. What the casinos most fear are their own employees, and perhaps a crusading politician who might put a stop to the lucrative practice of skimming. The employees are a reality; such a politician has not yet existed. Nor is he likely to, as long as the casino owners are the main contributors to election campaigns in Nevada.

Sully Kelly was working at the Sahara Tahoe when I decided to visit him. He was dealing craps. As I neared his table, he said in a voice loud enough to be heard ten feet away, "Jesus Christ, don't steal anything from here!"

As I said before, Sully had no class. I had not come to hustle the casino, but to talk to him, and if he was worried about the former all he had to do was give me a signal and I would have passed. He did not do the right thing (not to mention the trouble I could have had), and I've never spoken to him since.

Sully eventually lost his job at the Sahara Tahoe, but went on to land a better one in Las Vegas. I understand he is still stealing his end each day. I don't wish him any bad luck. I hope he steals a million dollars.

15

In the middle of 1969 I developed a further refinement of our method of cheating craps. Instead of having to steal a die off a table and having to mail it to New Jersey to get a duplicate made, we could simply walk into a casino and start playing right away. All that was involved was a basic adjustment, and it was surprising no one had thought of it before. What we did was use the casino's own dice.

When the stickman emptied the bowl of dice in front of me, I selected two but threw only one. Rollie went into his act of being hit, and of course the porter was unable to find the one that had fallen to the floor. I passed it back to Jan, who walked it around to Rollie. Now — on the very next roll — we were ready to go into action. The entire crew, and especially Glen, thought it was amazing we hadn't thought of this before. "Maybe we're not as smart as we thought," he said.

The new play simplified our operation. We did not have to switch dice and send to New Jersey to have sets made up.

Even with the new method and my Max Factor makeup kit, I never entirely dislodged from my mind the vision of that helicopter ride with the police over the Nevada desert. I reminded Glen that I preferred to work the northern part of the state. He said he understood.

Many times when the crew worked Las Vegas, I stayed in Newport Beach. On one of these occasions, a hot May, 1970, afternoon, Kitty and I lay on the soft sand and soaked up the delicious California sunshine. We had an early dinner and went to bed. We made love several times before dozing off to sleep, and the last thing I remember thinking was how lucky I was.

At 3:00 a.m. I was jolted awake. I wondered who was calling at that hour.

It was, of course, Glen.

"You have to come to Las Vegas and bail us out," he said.

"What the hell are you doing in jail?"

"We're not in jail. We're working this weekend, and we're stuck $26,000."

"I don't want to go to Las Vegas. It's not safe for me there."

"Wear your old-man outfit."

"Be a good loser, Glen. You can afford it."

"It's not that simple. I brought out some big bettors from New York, and I can't send them back home stuck to the play."

Glen was right. The big bettors paid us to tell them when and how to wager, and we had promised one another we would never hang them up. It was one of the rules we lived by.

"I'll drive to Las Vegas," I said.

"Take an airplane."

I was testy. "Are you sure you're sober?" I asked. "It's three o'clock in the morning here. There aren't any planes at three o'clock in the morning."

"Then drive. But get here as quick as you can."

Kitty was awake, and she prepared breakfast while I dressed. At 4:00 a.m. I was ready to go. I kissed Kitty good-bye and told her I would be back late that night. Then, as I had so often, I drove across the desert to Las Vegas.

I arrived in town and went directly to the motel were the crew was staying. My disguise helped assure that I would not be recognized by some eager-beaver detective.

The crew was waiting in the motel room and seemed happy to see me. They had tried making money with my method and had lost to the play. None of them could make the dice work the way I could, but mostly they had been unlucky, running up against an extraordinary string of ones and twos.

Glen said there was no time to rest. The bettors from New York had to catch a 9:00 p.m. flight home.

We worked three different casinos on the Strip, and by 6:00 p.m. we had won $46,000. The bettors from New York did all right also.

I felt I could relax. I had my end of the take in my pocket and the work was finished. I removed my makeup and sat around the motel room having a few laughs. Glen, Rollie, Jackie, Jan, Joyce, and Penny, along with the Eastern bettors, smoked a few numbers and blew their minds. When it was time for the New Yorkers to leave, I said I was headed back to Los Angeles. Glen shook my hand and thanked me for helping him out of a tight spot. I said I was sorry for getting hot with him over the telephone.

Before leaving the motel I called my bondsman to say hello. It was prudent to stay on good terms with him. Members of his profession were the Patron Saints of Crossroaders.

My bondsman invited me over for a cup of coffee, and I couldn't refuse. I was just outside his office when an off-duty detective recognized me. He raced across the street with his gun drawn.

"Don't move!" the detective ordered.

This time it's really bad, I thought.

My bondsman, thank God, saw it coming down and hurried over to the jail to get me out. He knew he had to get the bail up immediately, or something serious could happen to me. He also called my lawyer, just to be safe.

I was booked and deposited in the receiving tank. Already inside were three hippies from Santa Monica, tapped out, and unable to make bail. The charge against them was the old reliable, vagrancy. The police had to maintain the city's image of affluence, which meant they were supposed to keep the streets clear of those who could not afford to lose money. Hippies are not known as high rollers, but they could provide a convenient free labor force to keep the parks pretty.

Bond for the three hippies was $50 each. It could have been 50 cents each and they wouldn't have been able to meet it.

"If I bail out," I told them, "I'll go your bail."

I could see they didn't believe me. Perhaps someone had made a similar promise one time and never followed up. Anyway, I talked with the hippies, who were good people, honest and naive. They had not yet been chopped up by the real world, and I liked them. I would get them out if I was able.

A pair of detectives came to the holding tank, opened the cage, and pointed at me.

We walked down a long corridor. We had traveled quite a way before one of them spoke: "Well, hotshot, are you ready for that helicopter ride?"

I got sick to my stomach. I wanted to yell to the hippies, tell them I was going to be killed, but before I could get out a word I was hurried through a back door and into the parking area. A prowl car was waiting, but so was my lawyer!

"Where are you taking this man?" he demanded. The detectives stammered, stuttered, searched for something intelligent to say, but it was beyond their capabilities.

"We want to question him in private," one of them finally managed.

"He's no longer your prisoner," my lawyer said.

We went back into the station house, back to the main waiting area. My lawyer sent for the bondsman, who had been covering another exit, and he had the necessary release papers ready.

At the bondsman's office, enjoying that delayed cup of coffee, I gave him the names of the three hippies in the holding tank and asked him to get them out. He drew up more papers, went to the police station, and was back in thirty minutes with the hippies.

"I'm driving to Los Angeles in a few minutes," I told them. "You're welcome to ride along if you like."

They were three happy kids. They were out of the tank, and they had a free ride home. I hoped also they had learned a valuable lesson about Las Vegas. We left town at 11:00 p.m. and stopped in Barstow, where I treated them to a meal. They kept promising to repay me, but this time I was the cynical one. I dropped them off in Santa Monica and drove on home. I never heard from them again.

Six months passed. It was December, 1970. In the six months I came no closer to Las Vegas than the five hundred miles of desert separating it from Reno, and I only went to Reno a few times. I loved my life in Newport Beach, and I had all the money I needed. Even the crew seemed to be cutting back some.

Glen called just before Christmas. I hadn't heard from him in more than a month.

"I think it's safe to do Las Vegas again," he said. "The police seem to be cracking down on dope parties and pushers. They're not so concerned about crossroaders any more."

"I don't believe you," I said.

"Use your head. There's so few of us we're no longer a threat. It's not like twenty years ago when everyone was hustling."

"Those detectives seemed pretty interested when they had me six months ago."

"Times change. If you don't trust me — and why you wouldn't I don't know —then check with your other contacts. You know plenty of people in Las Vegas."

I did check. I called my bondsman, my lawyer and a variety of acquaintances I had made over the years. They supported what

Glen had said. The anti-hippie, anti-demonstrator, anti-counterculture backlash of the comfortable middle class had spread to Las Vegas, and the police were only too happy to be the whip hand of that backlash. Las Vegas was hardly a hotbed of radicalism, but the vogue was to pursue pot users. Also, as Glen said, few crossroaders remained active in Nevada, and the best of them — our crew — had remained virtually inactive.

I decided to give it another whirl. There was the risk of jail, or worse, but the money was so easy to take.

When I once again met with Glen in early January, 1971, I learned the crew was using increasing numbers of new people. I worried about the new recruits, but knew the core — Glen, Rollie, Jackie, Jan — was solid and reliable.

The new people were mainly middle-class men and women who were willing to chance jail to hold on to a tenuous affluence. Their lives were tied up in suburban homes, mortgages, swimming pools, payments on a second car, a boat, a recreational vehicle. The risks they assumed were not as great as ours, but they were nonetheless risks.

In any case, I was happy to be back with my friends again, in action on the Strip, the gambling center of the planet.

We began our play at the New Frontier, then went on to the Tropicana and the Desert Inn. We won $36,000 in what seemed no time at all.

We ran the winnings to $50,000 while still at the Desert Inn. A boss was watching so closely his head was almost lying on the table. I signaled the bettors to place another wager and rolled the dice again. The manager moved into the pit along with the boss.

I should have brushed everyone out, but I didn't. I was in a state of high exhilaration. I wasn't nervous, I wasn't afraid, there was no quick heartbeat. I was high on the knowledge that I was the best and was beating them right in front of their eyes.

Our winnings rose to $60,000. The people in the pit were like madmen. I wanted to go on, show them what I could do to them, show them I could own their whole damn casino if I wanted, but I knew they wouldn't stand much more. I was on a terrific, suicidal high, but I knew it wasn't fair to take the crew down with me. I brushed them out, sevened-out, and started to back away from the table.

"Don't move too fast," a voice said. "Do it nice and slow and come with us."

It was one of my detective friends. I knew I was going to jail again. The casino manager had looked in the Black Book, recognized my picture, and called the police.

For some reason I was not frightened this time. I had given them a premier performance, they had no idea how, and at the moment nothing else mattered.

My arrest ended the play for the weekend, but Glen, as usual, had been right. The police had cooled off. No threats were made to me, I was in jail only two hours, and the bail was just $500. I knew Glen would be furious with my hotdog behavior, especially my not wearing a disguise. In the future I would be more careful.

16

It was April, 1972. We had completed three weekends of work in Reno and Lake Tahoe, and Glen decided the crew could use some rest.

Glen flew his Cessna to Idaho to fish and hunt. Rollie said he was going to visit every whorehouse in Nevada, a monumental task, but one I was confident Rollie could manage. Jackie took his wife Penny to New York City for the horse races and some Broadway shows. Jan Deerwood split for Fort Worth, Texas, headquarters of a rich oil man who had proposed to her. I drove home to Newport Beach.

One hot, sparkling afternoon I was out on the beach, loving the ocean breeze and the sound of the surf, the beautiful girls in bikinis, even the impromptu volleyball game I thought of joining, when Kitty called to me from the house. I had a long distance call.

There was no way I could ever have forgotten the voice on the other end. It belonged to Ned Coleman, my old friend from Carson City, the man who had taught me to deal cards. He had just been released from prison after nearly eleven years.

"Where are you?" I asked.

"Reno."

"You're coming to Los Angeles. I insist on it."

"I *have* to come to Los Angeles. I'm arriving at three o'clock tomorrow afternoon. Will you pick me up?"

"Wild horses couldn't keep me away."

Kitty asked who it was. "A dear friend," I said. "A very valuable friend. Someone I owe a lot to."

Kitty and I drove to International Airport the next day. We arrived thirty minutes ahead of Ned's flight and were in a coffee shop when its impending arrival was announced. At the gate where he would deplane I noticed several detectives milling about, probably there to find out who was meeting Ned. I wasn't going to let their presence spoil our reunion.

I saw Ned coming down the ramp, and he looked much older than I remembered. I threw my arms around him and hugged him for a long time. He was very thin and his body shivered in my embrace. I introduced Kitty, and I could see he approved.

"How about coming to my place?" I said. "Plenty of room and sunshine, and you can treat it like it's yours."

"I'd like to go to my former wife's apartment," Ned said. "I want to change, and relax for a few minutes."

I'd forgotten he had been married. "Of course," I said. "We'll pick up your luggage and be on our way."

"What luggage do you think I'd have after eleven years in the bucket?"

We both laughed. "You're right," I said. "Let's get the hell out of here."

We got in my car and drove along the freeway. "Where did you get the clothes you're wearing?" I asked.

"My ex-wife brought them to me at Carson City."

I would never have told him the clothes had gone out of style eleven years ago.

Ned's ex-wife was waiting for him, a plump, pleasant woman with a wistful smile. Her manner was kind, gentle, and I sensed she still cared about Ned. But his pace of living had just been too fast for her, a girl from a small town in Minnesota. When he went to jail for life, the pressure mounted and finally she divorced him. But between the two of them in the apartment that afternoon was an affection and deep respect for each other that was present in few married couples I'd ever known.

Ned showered and changed into a suit that also was eleven years old. His ex-wife had kept his clothes for him. I told myself to forget about being Cupid, they were older than my own parents, but in retrospect a little push right then might have allowed me to report a happier ending.

Marcia, Ned's ex-wife, chilled martinis for him, and we sat and talked for hours. Then I took Kitty and Ned to the Mediterranean for rare prime rib, the best in southern California. Marcia wouldn't go with us — she said she would be "in the way" — but she told Ned he could spend the night in the apartment. After dinner and more talk, I dropped him there and promised to pick him up at eight the next morning.

I was early at Marcia's apartment building that morning, but Ned was already waiting outside.

"I didn't expect this," I said. "I thought you and Marcia would want to be together longer."

"She doesn't need to be hurt any more."

"Maybe you can help each other ease the hurt."

"I don't know."

"Do you need money?" I asked. "I have plenty of money. I'd be honored if you'd let me help you."

"I don't need money," Ned said. "You already sent me enough."

Our first stop was the parole office in Los Angeles. I read a newspaper in the car while Ned talked to his parole officer. When Ned came outside he looked even more depressed.

"What's wrong?" I asked.

"Please drive me to Balboa Island," he said.

On the way Ned told me he was going to live on Balboa Island with Bob Sorensen, once a gambler but now a prosperous retired real estate agent. Balboa Island was populated with upper-middle-income and rich people. I thought that would be good for him, but there were two stipulations in the parole agreement that upset Ned: he could not leave Balboa Island without permission from his parole officer, and he could not engage in gambling activities for the *rest of his life.* If either stipulation was violated, he would be sent back to Carson City.

I met Bob Sorensen, who was the same age as Ned, about seventy. Sorensen had a guest house in his backyard that Ned would use. Sorensen himself was an old crossroader gone straight, and the three of us exchanged stories the rest of the morning and into the early afternoon.

"Let's go, Ned," I finally said. "Let's take a ride."

"Where are we going?"

"Trust me."

"Trust him," Bob Sorensen said.

When we were in the car, I told Ned I knew a place on Balboa Island where he could get some great clothes.

"I don't want charity," he said. "I won't accept it."

"This isn't charity. I wouldn't have a dime if it hadn't been for you."

"I want you to know I'm paying Bob Sorensen rent."

"I never thought otherwise."

We went to the best store on Balboa Island and picked out six pairs of slacks, a dozen shirts, two pairs of shoes, and three sports jackets. Ned thought the bill was outrageous. He had been in prison a long time.

We had dinner at the Jolly Roger.

"It's going to be hard for me," Ned said. "I don't like being restricted. I thought things would be different when I got out."

"You're not restricted," I said. "You can leave any time you want. Just call the parole officer and tell him you're taking a trip."

"I have to tell him where I'm going. Who I'll be seeing, and why. I won't really be free."

"I know you're nervous," I said. "And I know it's not my hide I'm talking about. But you really will be able to leave the island whenever you want to. No one's going to be following you. Just be careful and there won't be anyone the wiser."

It had gotten late. I drove Ned home, telling him I would call him in the morning. I stopped at the Lighthouse in Redondo Beach and listened to the smooth, mellow jazz of the Ramsey Lewis Trio. I thought about Ned Coleman, about my own life and how he'd enabled me to change it, and about how much I wanted him to be happy.

"I'll pick you up at six o'clock," I told him when I called the next morning.

"Where are we going?"

"The Reuben E. Lee. It's a ship. Great seafood."

"Where is it?"

"Newport Beach."

"I can't go there."

"Yes, you can. I want you to trust me, Ned."

Kitty and I picked Ned up at six. He was on edge, afraid someone would spot him and finger him to his parole officer. He didn't enjoy the dinner — baked sea bass — or the show, and said he never wanted to violate his parole again. I told him to loosen up, but prison had taken some of the spunk out of Ned, and he was deathly afraid of going back.

The crew had a weekend planned in Las Vegas. I told Ned to call me in three days and he did.

"Come over when you get a chance," he said.

"I'll be there in thirty minutes," I said.

Ned was waiting outside the guest house when I arrived. He did not look well at all. His color was unhealthy, his hands shook, and in his eyes was the look of a man trapped.

"What's wrong with you?" I asked.

"Living here is worse than being in prison."

Ned had no friends on Balboa Island and nothing to do that interested him. Being confined there was almost like Carson City. I could tell something else was bothering him, too, something serious, but he wouldn't tell me what it was.

"Could you get me some pills so I could relax?" Ned asked. "I can't sleep at night."

"What kind of pills?"

"Valium."

"I don't know where to get them."

"Do you know someone who works in a doctor's office?"

"I know a girl in Manhattan Beach who works for a doctor."

"She can get some for you. Doctors always have Valium in stock."

"I'll get in touch with her."

"Can you do it today? I need them."

"I'll go right now. I just wish you weren't so uptight, Ned."

I drove to the clinic in Manhattan Beach where Sharon worked, and told her about Ned's condition. She said she could help, went to a back room and returned with a quart jar filled with green triangular-shaped tablets. I offered to pay her, but she said it was on the house.

"How did you get so many?" Ned asked when I handed him the jar.

"I told my friend I needed some pills. This is what she gave me."

More than two months passed, during which I visited Ned whenever I could. He enjoyed my accounts of the crew's activities, but argued that eventually I would be burned out of all the casinos. He said it was just a matter of time before — even using elaborate disguises — I would be recognized by all the major houses.

Kitty and I took Ned to dinner at least once a week, and he asked about all his old cronies in Nevada. He never tired of telling and listening to stories about the great crossroaders. He would enjoy reading today about the super-jackpots ($250,000 and more) being won in Nevada. He would never for a minute believe that crossroaders weren't involved.

Then one night when I was in Reno with the crew, I put in a call to Ned to find out how he was getting along, but there was no answer. I tried a little later — still no answer — and became worried. Ned was almost always at the guest house.

Finally I called Marcia, his former wife. "John," she said, "Ned died."

I couldn't think of what to say. Ned Coleman dead? He'd been a second father to me, always patient and solicitous, the most understanding of men and a superb teacher. I knew Ned had trained others besides just me: such legendary casino managers as Carl Cohen, Johnny Hughes, Johnny Maizon, Phil Zholut, men responsible for the early growth of the gambling industry in Nevada.

"What killed him?" I finally managed to ask.

"No one knows." I could tell she was close to crying.

"Wasn't there an autopsy?"

"No. They said it wasn't necessary, that he died of natural causes."

I could feel Marcia's pain coming through the telephone. Even though they were divorced, she had never stopped loving Ned. But there was really nothing I could do for her.

I did not believe the medical authorities. I did not believe Ned had died of natural causes. Except for his nerves, he was a very healthy man.

Several months later I learned what had really been bothering Ned since his release from prison. He knew some things about certain casino bigshots that put his life in danger. My friend was put to sleep because he knew too much. Now he rests in a cemetery in Los Angeles — dead of "natural causes."

17

The money was not coming in as fast as before. Rollie and I hit the slots now and then, but Glen was spending most of his time on his ranch in Idaho. Jackie had opened up a business on the Boulder Highway. Jan, though still joining us in various hustles, was thinking of marrying the Fort Worth oil millionaire. I wondered, twenty years from now, what his good-old-boy friends would say when they let her in a card game and she cleaned them out.

This was fall, 1972, and Rollie and I had added a number of new wrinkles to our repertoire. At roulette we became skilled at "past-posting," which was placing a bet *after* the ball had fallen on a number. There is a brief moment when the dealer looks at the wheel to find out what number has come up. At that exact instant we placed our bets. We also would drill a hole into a roulette wheel that was not being used at the time and insert a fine wire into the hole that would knock the ball off the rail it was riding on and assure that the ball would drop onto a certain area of the wheel. This guaranteed us an enormous advantage.

Our job was always made easier when a celebrity was playing at the table. Casino employees would invariably pay more attention to the celebrity than to us. One night in the Flamingo, Rollie and I were at the crap table where Jonathan Winters was playing. He was on a terrible losing streak but was taking it with good humor. The dice came around to me. I was going to throw one, and Rollie was going to set the other one down. If I threw anything but a one or a two we would have a winner. Of course, we could do this over and over again, because the die I kept in my hand would then be walked around to Rollie by an accomplice.

"Bet on the field," I suggested to Jonathan Winters.

He looked at me strangely, hesitated, and decided to ignore me. I rolled a four and he would have won.

"Bet on the field," I said.

Again he ignored me, and again he would have won.

The third time he did bet on the field, but this time I rolled a one.

I guess Jonathan Winters was just an unlucky gambler. The one time he did take my advice, he lost, despite having the odds two to one in his favor. I would have liked to have rolled again, but three times was all we could rationally risk.

Another time I was playing "21" at the Silver Slipper when Frank Sinatra and Dean Martin came to the table. I was mucking (holding a third card) and with these two famous people playing, there was virtually no chance I would be discovered. Sinatra lost five or six bets in a row. "This guy," Sinatra said, referring to the dealer, "doesn't want to make any money," and with that he and Dean Martin walked away from the table.

But despite our successes, increasingly confined to Rollie and me, the years were rolling by, I was getting older, and it was more difficult than ever to be a crossroader. The steam was once again rising around the craps and "21" tables, and the casinos were taking their $5,000 slots out of action. Maybe this was someting positive the crew had accomplished. The odds were 64,000-to-1 against a player hitting the jackpot on a dollar slot. Oddly, many people did not seem to care. The harder it was to win, the more they would try. Tell a player he can't beat a machine and he may stand there for twenty years pulling the handle.

Many changes had taken place in Nevada since the crew first started to hustle the casinos. The houses had learned to overcome a number of their previous errors, and hustling the slots was mainly being accomplished by casino employees. I think also the more professional approach adopted by the corporations that were taking over the joints, as opposed to the mob with its scattershot and cocky attitude, made life tougher for hustlers. But I'm also convinced that as long as gambling exists, there will always be people who'll find ingenious ways to cheat.

Another minus for crossroaders occurred when the Nevada State Legislature finally passed a law that enabled the district attorneys of the various counties to prosecute cheaters. A cheater found guilty could be sentenced to ten years in prison, a formidable threat that forced many crossroaders into legitimacy. I was one of them.

I decided to open a restaurant on LaCienega Boulevard in West Los Angeles. The area was considered "restaurant row." I hired the best chef available, pretty cocktail waitresses, handsome and efficient waiters, top-notch bartenders, professional kitchen help, reliable janitors, and a reputable bookkeeper. An interior decorator transformed the restaurant into what many customers considered the most pleasing dining atmosphere on the boulevard. I had a well-known advertising agency handle publicity, and the restaurant received excellent exposure on radio and television and in local newspapers and trade publications. It cost a lot of money — I had to dig up a good deal of what I had buried — but the place was first-rate.

Then I began to miss the action in Nevada. The crew had split up, and only Rollie remained active. I guess I was like a retired war horse, champing at the bit for one more battle, and Glen, now a prosperous rancher, must have heard the same bugle call. He telephoned me at the restaurant.

"How's the Restaurant King?" he asked.

"Business is good."

"Are you interested in some action?"

"Yes, if you're involved."

"Is your passport still valid?"

"Yes."

"Have you ever been to Macao?"

"I don't even know where it is."

"It's in Asia."

"That's a big help."

"Well, that's where we're going."

Glen flew to Los Angeles several days later and stayed at my house in Newport Beach while we waited for the rest of the crew to assemble. He enjoyed lobster — a house specialty — at my restaurant, and late at night at the bar he would entertain customers with his stories.

Eventually the crew straggled in. Rollie and Jackie arrived from Nevada (Jan was in Fort Worth visiting her oilman, and sent her regrets). Doug Hinson, a high roller, flew in from New York. The scam was going to be simple. We intended to use tops, the dice with only four, five, and six on them. Glen had obtained a set from an employee who worked the casino in Macao, and already had them duplicated. The employee was part of the competition that wanted the joint shot down, but what we didn't know was that the casino was owned by the state.

The crew flew to Hawaii and stayed for three days. Then it was on to Manila in the Philippines, and finally to Macao. At our destination we learned from a solid source that the authorities had recently caught someone cheating and cut off his hands.

We waited four days in Macao, a tiny Portuguese colony, before going into action. We wanted to familiarize ourselves with the layout and accustom ourselves to the surroundings. We ate Pan-Asian food, saw some shows, played with the girls. Then Glen judged it was time to start work.

The casino, if anything, was smaller than the one we'd bankrupted in Istanbul, but it catered to the same rich clientele, only this time most of the gamblers were Oriental. Glen, Rollie, Jackie, and Doug placed field bets, and I handled the dice. Zip, zip, zip, working with perfect synchronization, knowing bone-deep we were the best who had ever done this, we won a quick $65,000 before I brushed the crew out. It was great to be back in action, or so I believed.

Glen and I shared the same hotel room, and at 4:00 a.m. there was a loud knocking at our door. I opened it, and standing impatiently outside was a platoon of Chinese armed with *machine guns*. They pushed past me into the room and began turning it upside down. I didn't have to understand what they were saying to know what they wanted.

The local officials had been more alert than we anticipated. They had checked out Glen and me and found out that we were notorious crossroaders. Fortunately, they failed to run checks on Rollie, Jackie, and Doug.

Glen and I were taken in a van to a prison that must have been built in the fourteenth century. The stone slabs were two feet thick. We were locked up in a room with ten other prisoners, all Chinese except a twelve-year-old-boy who *said* he was Portuguese (he spoke some English, a bit of Portuguese, and fluent Chinese). The boy was in jail for stealing rice.

The authorities confiscated all the money we had, which was $25,000. They wanted to know what had happened to the rest, but we said that was all there was. We certainly weren't going to point them in the direction of the other crew members. It was during our first morning in prison that we learned the casino was state-owned and the authorities were boiling over losing so much money. They didn't know how we had cheated, or even *if* we had, but that didn't seem to matter. We were half a planet away from Las Vegas and our bondsman, for whom no counterpart seemed to exist in Macao.

Glen's cynicism was ordinarily a virtue all successful cross-roaders must possess, but he was terrible to be in prison with. "When do you think we'll get out?" I asked.

"Maybe never," he said.

"Can't you contact the people who wanted you to come here?"

"The deal is, we're on our own."

"We're just going to sit here?"

"Probably. Unless they kill us."

And cut off our hands first, I thought gloomily.

Three days in that medieval nightmare turned into three weeks. Rollie, Jackie, and Doug, we later learned, had despaired of accomplishing anything in Macao to secure our release and returned to the United States to use whatever influence they could muster with American authorities.

Three weeks became three months. Remarkably, Glen remained stoic and contemplative. He reminded me of a monk. The food was terrible, the living conditions (no air, cold stone floor to sleep on) were incredible, but what was worst was the thought of being buried in a grave (the cell was some four stories underground) from which we might never escape. It seemed altogether possible that we might simply be forgotten. If there were wheels of justice turning in Macao, they spun in super-slow motion.

One good thing: Glen lost sixty pounds, and he could well afford to shed the weight. I lost forty pounds and looked like a skeleton.

After eight months we were visited by a U.S. Embassy official. He said we would soon be released and would have twenty-four hours to leave the country.

"What are we going to do for money?" Glen asked him.

"The embassy will see that you have plane fare to Los Angeles."

Glen argued for money, mentioning the $25,000 that had been taken from us, and the embassy man got hot.

"Jesus," I said to Glen, "let's take the plane tickets and be satisfied!"

I took down the address of the Portuguese boy and told him I would send some money. Maybe he could buy his way out of that prison. Whether he was able to or not I can't say.

Rollie was waiting at Los Angeles International Airport when we arrived. He brought clothes and money for us. The FBI was also on hand and wanted to talk. We entertained them for two hours and they let us go. Both of us were starving.

"How about Chinese food?" I said to Glen, but he didn't get the joke.

We found out why we had been released from the prison. Doug Hinson and some Eastern bettors had used their influence, plus $100,000, to buy our way out. We would have to make good the amount. Worse — Doug, Jackie, and Rollie had left Macao without our winnings. They were afraid to be caught with so much money, and they stashed it in the hotel garbage dump.

So the entire Asian trip was a bust.

18

It sounded like a SWAT squad was attacking my door. It wasn't mere knocking: he was literally assaulting the door, threatening to tear it off its hinges. The entire house seemed to be vibrating. I groaned and looked at my nightstand clock — 6:30 a.m. — and decided to ignore the noise. It got louder, and the cursing would have made Joe Conforte blush.

"Glen," I said, when I reached the scene of the commotion, trying to focus through sleep-blurred eyes.

"Sit down, John. I've got the best plan yet."

"It's barely dawn. I'm tired."

"You're not tired. A young guy like you. I've spent the whole night getting here, and I'm not tired." He was already in the house and planted on the sofa.

"You're an old fire-horse, Glen. Always ready to answer the bell. Normal people need rest to function."

"I told you, this is the best yet. The biggest and the best." Glen wasn't usually given to superlatives, and because I never tired of listening to and profiting from his schemes, I knew I was hooked. I told him I'd make some coffee.

"No time for that. You're the first person I've talked to. I want to get in touch with the rest, and soon."

"Well, go ahead," I said.

"Know what was wrong with Rollie setting that dice down?"

"I never thought anything was wrong with it. We never got caught. We always got the money."

"We never got *enough* of it," Glen said. He leaned back on the sofa, a smile playing on his lips, waiting for me to reply.

I didn't know what he was talking about. Each of us had made what I considered a fortune. I was sure no other crossroaders had ever been so successful.

"Tell me what you have in mind," I said.

"Rollie could only set that dice down three, four times at the most. Jesus, that was risky enough. You throwin' one and palmin' one, and Jan walkin' that other dice around, and him bent over the table acting like some clumsy fool, just inviting attention."

"It took guts. We had them."

"Think bigger, John. What did we win? Eight, ten thousand dollars at a time. And then we'd have to get out. Shit, a blind man could see something was screwy with you whipping that dice like a Koufax fastball, and Rollie perpetually in a weird posture."

"I thought it looked pretty natural."

"Stone Age stuff in a modern world. We've got to stay on the cutting edge. This is the age of technology. We need to put technology to work for us."

"I thought we did that. Keys to open all the slots. Dice that match those the casinos have. Every conceivable way to doctor cards."

"And all primitive compared to this."

He reached into his pocket and handed me a pair of dice. They looked like any other set, which wasn't surprising (Glen wouldn't be handling anything that was crudely made and easily spotted), and I turned them over and over with my fingers, trying to discover what had been done to them. I couldn't see a thing.

The dice, Glen said, had been given to him by a Reno casino owner who wasn't above cheating other casinos. The dice were weighted down with a transparent substance so that when thrown they would favor certain numbers. One of the dice was coated on the side of the three, so its opposite end, the four, was most likely to appear. The other die was coated on the side of the two, so the five would most often come up. In short, the dice were weighted so "numbers" would appear, not a seven which spelled defeat for the player trying to make a point. The dream of every knowledgeable craps player is to roll a long series of numbers, uninterrupted by the streak-ending seven, betting every number but the seven. Glen figured that with his weighted dice the dream was about to become a regular reality for us.

I kept studying the dice he'd handed me. It was just impossible with the naked eye to tell they had been tampered with. Glen said the casino would have to bring out a caliper to know, and asked how many times I'd seen that happen.

"Not often," I said. "But I've seen it."

"And it wouldn't make any difference, would it?" His eyes had the mischievous gleam of a little boy's who has just found a foolproof way to burgle the cookie jar.

No, it wouldn't. In the unlikely event the casino did bring out the micrometer, how could it tell which player had switched the dice into the game? It could have been anyone at the table. And where previously we could only bet when I was throwing dice, now we could bet regardless of who held them. It was also obvious that this new weapon would permit us to play as long as we wanted. No longer would we have to leave after three or four rolls.

I tried to bore holes into those dice with my eyes. But it just wasn't possible to tell, not without putting a caliper to them. My mind began to race.

I wouldn't even have to be at the table. Nor would the other regular members of the crew, whose faces may by now have become familiar to certain casino employees. The only thing necessary was to get the dice into the game, and we'd have something akin to a printing press. I understood now why Glen had come to me first. Switching dice into the game was no problem at all for me.

"We'll let the guys from the East," Glen said, "start out betting $2,000 across the board." It seemed he could barely contain an eruption of laughter as he waited for me to ponder the amount of money he was talking about.

It was a lot. Much more than we'd ever won with Rollie setting down the six. Two thousand dollars across the board, as Glen envisioned, meant betting $300 on the four, $300 on the five, $400 on the six, $400 on the eight, $300 on the nine, and $300 on the ten. This is a good deal of money and would send up warning flares in the minds of casino bosses, which is why it was necessary to import high rollers from the East to make the bets for us. Their wagering a lot wouldn't attract that much attention.

"Who are we getting from the East?" I asked.

"Nothing but the best. Vinnie Carlyle, Morris and Dennis Katz."

I knew all three of them, and knew also why they were included in the play. Carlyle was a medium-sized bookmaker in Brooklyn. He was in a no-risk business, at least with the kind of volume he handled. He figured that so were we, and added to his profits from bookmaking by placing bets the way we told him. Actually, like many bookmakers, Vinnie himself was addicted to gambling and couldn't keep himself from placing his own bets, though he more than anyone should have known the futility of this course of action. But Vinnie's high-rolling was perfect for us. He was known for placing and losing big bets. No eyebrows would be raised when he came out wagering $2,000 across the board. And although a casino never likes to lose, it would figure in Vinnie's case that he would soon lose the money back.

The brothers, Morris and Dennis Katz, were in their early fifties. They lived in Short Hill, New Jersey, and had bet on us a number of times before. Both had very large amounts of money, acquired from lucrative gambling operations in Harlem plus the promotion of gambling cruises and gambling excursions to Nevada. Because of the junkets they promoted to Nevada, they were popular people with casino owners. They were never questioned when they began to bet and win large sums of money on the tables.

The Katz brothers had some remarkable qualities. They were very personable and outgoing, the type of men you like right away. But they were sharks where gambling was concerned, always looking for and finding an edge. Dennis could throw a pair of dice and tell you what number was going to show up while the cubes were still in the air. This move, while not particularly effective in Nevada because of the table design, was a killer in games played in New York City back rooms.

Vinnie Carlyle, and the Katz brothers especially, had been dealing with Glen for many years. They had put up the $100,000 which the good authorities in Macao had demanded in exchange for our release, money which we couldn't get our hands on because of our isolation in prison. This money had to be repaid, of course. The crew had what might seem an utterly odd code of ethics: we had no compunctions about grabbing whatever we could from the casinos, but we were honest to a fault with one another and anyone we brought in with us. Now it was payback time for Vinnie and the Katzes.

"So," I said to Glen, who was still watching me with that semi-amused look, "we're going to win the hundred thousand dollars."

"Better than dipping into our own pockets."

"I don't know."

"A hundred and thirty thousand dollars, actually. We can't expect them to be a part of this, expend their time and effort, just to be repaid what we already owe. I've promised them an added $10,000 each."

"Well, that's fair. I just don't like the timing. Things were hot before we went to Macao. The joints were already collecting pretty good picture files on some of us, and then the Macao caper made the newspapers. Seems to me we stand a good chance of being busted just stepping into one of the joints. And you want us to stay long enough to win $130,000?"

"A hundred and sixty thousand."

"What?"

"The crew should get something."

"Damn, Glen. That much money in one session. I don't think it's ever been done."

"Once. At the Dunes." His smile now seemed as wide as his Texas homeland. He genuinely enjoyed this life.

"Well," I said, "I don't like it. Too many of us can be recognized. We need time for things to cool off. I'll admit your dice look good, but we've never tried this play before. We need some shake-down sessions, with more modest aims first."

"Now you listen to me," Glen said. He wasn't smiling any more. This was all business.

In a voice devoid of emotion, his face expressionless, no hand gestures or body movement whatever, Glen outlined a casino raid so bold yet so carefully plotted that even I — and I was looking for a way out, Macao had reinforced a hundred times in my mind how desirable it was to avoid prison — could not find a flaw. Anything *might* go wrong — most likely the unexpected and unwelcome intervention of some third party or event — but barring this, what Glen outlined seemed foolproof.

Besides the three from the East, whose only jobs were to bet, we'd use key members of our regular crew. Jan Deerwood, looking her glamorous best, would stroll to the target table arm in arm with me. Jan's job was more than just to turn heads and distract attention. She also had to get the casino's dice out of the casino. If she was caught, everything would immediately deteriorate to disaster: the play would be blown and even our lives might be blown away.

Rollie's job was to create disorder. At the critical moment he was to cause confusion by fumbling money onto the table while asking for chips. Rollie was just naturally clumsy — a good deal of play-acting wouldn't be required of him — and he was so big and fat and conspicuous he could attract attention just by being himself.

Jackie Gillitzer's role in the drama would consist of one line. At the designated moment he would grab the stickman's arm (I was on one side of the stickie, Jackie on the other), hold out a twenty-dollar bill, and tell him to "bet ten dollars for me and ten dollars for the boys on eleven." The "boys," of course, referred to the stickman himself, plus the two dealers. Jackie would make the stickman reach for the twenty, which meant he was looking in the opposite direction from me.

Also part of the action would be a relatively new member of the crew whom we all called Skinny Minnie. In reality she was a gorgeous woman with dark brown hair and deep blue eyes and a body straight out of a *Playboy* centerfold. She would wear a low-cut dress which guaranteed that people wouldn't be looking at me when she leaned over the table to place a bet.

Skinny Minnie was Glen's latest wife, so she'd learned the ways of crossroaders from the master. The crew had attended their wedding and the big reception afterward at the Fireside Inn on the Tonapah Highway north of Las Vegas. The crew was paying for the bash. Glen despised the idea of any of his friends spending money out of their own pockets, and he suggested we all go to the Fremont Hotel and put on a jackpot. So forty minutes later, before he even bedded his bride on their wedding night, there was Skinny Minnie in her wedding dress, squealing like an excited child, collecting a pot the crew had put on just a few minutes before.

My role would be the briefest of all, requiring even less time than Jackie Gillitzer's one-liner or Skinny Minnie's revealing dip over the table. But it would also be the most crucial move of the play, the *sine qua non*, and by far the most dangerous. Glen told me I would have to switch *eight dice* into the game, all at once, with one move!

I'd never switched eight dice into a game all at once. I'd never heard of anyone ever doing it.

"Has this ever been done before?" I asked Glen.

"Not that I know of," he said.

And he would know.

"I don't think I can do it," I said.

"Well, you'll have to."

For a crossroader, switching eight dice simultaneously into a game was roughly comparable in degree of difficulty to scaling Everest for a mountain climber — before Tenzing Norgay and Edmund Hillary did it. It was like being the first to break the sound barrier in one of those cars they drive on the salt flats. The difficulty was there — think of palming *eight dice* right under the cold eagle eyes of a hardened casino boss — and so was the danger. Falling off a cliff or dying instantly in some spectacular fiery crash was likely to be more pleasant than what awaited me if I were caught.

"Count me out," I told Glen.

"You should consider this a challenge. One worthy of your skills."

"Forget it, Glen."

"Think of the glory. Crossroaders will talk about it forever."

"I'm not going to do it."

"Think of the money."

He had me there. If I could switch a whole bowl of dice with one move, it wouldn't be long before we'd own Nevada, I thought. Well, maybe not own it all. I didn't want to own it all, I told myself. At the least, though, we'd be living in a style that a Rockefeller would find familiar. My greed wrestled with my common sense, and I could feel the greed winning.

"I'll have to practice a lot," I said. "See if I can do it."

"The play will be set for three days from now."

"You're really pushing."

"You can either do it or you can't. An hour of practice and you'll know."

He was right about this. It wasn't like learning to deal cards, where there are no shortcuts if you're going to be good. But *eight dice*. It was tough enough getting two into a game.

"I'll give it a try," I said. I realized I was again acceding to his wishes. Never once in our many years together did I *not* accede to his wishes.

"Good," he said. "I've got to leave. I'll get in touch with the others."

"Shouldn't you wait for a report from me?"

"You can do it, John. I don't have to wait."

He could do whatever he wanted, I thought, but if the move couldn't be made as smooth as silk, I was going to back out. I leaned back, smiled at Glen, and he smiled back. A minute went by. Two. He'd said he was leaving, but there was no movement at all. We smiled at each other again, and I started to fidget. He would win this kind of game.

"I thought you were leaving," I said.

"You haven't asked the name of the casino."

"Does it matter? I figured you'd let me know."

"Harvey's Wagon Wheel."

I stared at him, not comprehending, and the smile on his face never changed. It had something to do with Harvey's Wagon Wheel, and he wanted me to figure it out. Well, that joint would be no hotter than any other for me — which meant it would be steaming, especially after the publicity about Macao.

I thought about Harvey's Wagon Wheel. It was clear Glen was prepared to sit in my house forever or until I got the point. Harvey's Wagon Wheel at Lake Tahoe, one of the biggest hotel/ casinos in the area . . . owned by Harvey Gross, an old-timer, a gambling pioneer in the mold of Harold Smith and Benny Binion . . . a place featuring big-name entertainment and catering to the ski crowd. All of this didn't amount to a hill of ferns to Glen. I thought harder; it was a challenge now to figure out why Harvey's Wagon Wheel should hold significance for me. When it finally dawned on me I almost told him to get out, screw you and your whole crazy scheme, you're aiming to win me a desolate desert grave with only jackrabbits and coyotes to visit the site and honor my memory.

Harvey's Wagon Wheel was significant because it used extra-large dice, the largest dice in Nevada, in fact. Whenever I'd held them they'd felt like golf balls. I just didn't see how a smooth transition from Harvey's dice to ours was possible. What would happen, I thought, Harvey's dice in my mind beginning to resemble boulders, was that all sixteen (ours and theirs) would drop thudding onto the table and I would be hustled out of the joint to a waiting helicopter.

Glen could tell I'd finally fastened on the critical point, but he just sat there smiling patiently, hands folded on his lap, waiting for the explosion. I decided to fool him. I'd discuss it with him calmly for a moment or two, cooly demonstrate the errant path of his thinking, and *then* I'd explode and throw him out.

"The dice at Harvey's are a bit large," I began.

"Like buzzard's eggs," he said.

"Clever of you to pick the casino with the world's largest dice."

"They're not the world's biggest. Once, in the Middle East, I . . ."

"I don't care about the Middle East! Dammit, Glen, what's the matter with you? Did you hit your head on a wall? Are you smoking some of that Hee-Haw?"

"Relax, kid. Have I ever gotten you in trouble?"

"What about Macao?" The memory made me shiver.

"That had nothing to do with hustling. They couldn't prove a thing. They were just sore losers."

"I'm supposed to take consolation from that? And this time I may not have it so easy. It would be time for that helicopter ride."

"Stop thinking morbid. I wouldn't ask you to do this if I didn't think you could. You're good, John. The best I've seen. Now before you do any more ranting, listen to what I'm saying. I just want you to practice the move. If you can do it, fine. If you can't, the deal is off. We can always go back to Rollie setting down that six. But give it a try. That's not too much to ask. I'll call you tomorrow and you can tell me if it's on or off."

"Why on earth did you choose the Wagon Wheel?"

"The casino owner who got me the dice has something against Harvey's. I don't know what, and I don't care. But this time it's got to be the Wagon Wheel. Later it can be just about any joint we want. It's later I'm mainly thinking of. With this move our horizons are unlimited. We can play as long as we want, win as much as we want. And our own risk is cut ninety percent. The crew only needs to be around the table just a few minutes. We leave and the bettors take over."

Try as I might, I couldn't find flaws in Glen's plan. It was true that he'd often sent us on daring escapades, deals that had seemed foolhardy at first, but he was always right about what we could and couldn't do, and we were able in every instance to work within our capabilities.

"Give me that call tomorrow," I said.

Glen didn't nod or change expression. He got up off the sofa and left. He'd obtained what he'd come for.

Glen hadn't had the duplicate Wagon Wheel dice yet, so I had to drive into Los Angeles to King's gaming supply house to get the right size. When I returned home I put the car in the garage and closed the doors, drew the drapes shut, and disconnected the telephone. I wanted absolutely no interruptions.

I'd purchased sixteen dice, and eight of these I scattered on my dining-room table, in a configuration similar to how they would be placed had a stickman emptied the bowl in front of me. The other eight dice I held in my right hand, palm down. With my left hand I raked all of the dice on the table together under the palm of my hand. I shook them until they felt comfortable and I was confident I had them all locked up, and then I picked them up off the table. One came out of my hand, and then they all came clattering down, like an avalanche or rock slide. If that happened in Harvey's, my life expectancy as a crossroader, and maybe as a human being, could be tabulated in microseconds.

Nevertheless, I knew right then I could do it. Had Glen burst into the house that instant, I would have told him everything was go. I *could* hold the dice in my right hand, and I'm left-handed. There wasn't a doubt in my mind, even after this first tentative run-through, that I'd be able to hold the dice with my left hand. It was just a matter of positioning them a certain way, so one die wouldn't fall out and precipitate the domino effect.

I practiced palming the eight dice off the table for what must have been an hour, and although those big dice Harvey's used felt like a handful and a half, I could do it, and I didn't think there was a pit boss in the world who could spot the move. Glen was right: when we started to work with regulation-sized dice, a sheet of paper signed by the government giving us authorization to steal wouldn't be any more valuable.

I positioned a paper sack on the edge of the table and went through the entire move, but I knew it would be okay. After I'd shaken the dice into position to pick them up with my left hand, I dropped my right hand — which held the *other* eight dice — down to the table next to the left. Both hands were cupped and I seemed to be shaking the dice the stickman had left in front of me with both hands. I was doing no such thing, of course, and then I came up with my left hand, bringing it across my body and under my right arm, depositing the purloined cubes in the paper sack, which at the Wagon Wheel would be Jan Deerwood's purse. The second my left hand left the table, I opened my right hand to reveal the eight new dice, the dice that would spell financial loss for Harvey's.

I practiced the move over and over through what remained of the afternoon and into the evening. I wanted it to become second nature to me, just as dealing cards had been when Ned Coleman was finished with me. Then I called a friend, a fairly sharp gambler, and asked him to come over for a demonstration. I told him to watch closely, but he couldn't tell a thing was amiss. His attention was one hundred percent riveted on the play, and he couldn't see it happen. What chance would the casino have? Jackie Gillitzer would be asking for change and promising to place a bet for the boys, Rollie would be spilling a drink, Skinny Minnie would be showing delicious cleavage. The casino would have no chance at all.

It was one thing to make the move in my dining room in front of a friend, another to do it under pressure in a casino, but I felt I'd manage just fine. I felt that in the past I'd done *better* under pressure, and it would be the same this time.

When Glen called the next day and I said it was go, he merely replied "Okay," as if the answer couldn't have been anything else, as if switching eight dice was as commonplace as breathing. Then in his best businesslike voice he launched into the logistics of the scam.

I was to fly to Reno Saturday afternoon, rent a car, and check into the Sands Motel, which was about ten blocks from Harvey's Wagon Wheel. Promptly at 10:00 p.m. I was to be at the crap table nearest the bar, positioned at the end of the table near the dealer on third base (the dealer to the left of the boxman), ready to switch our dice in when the bowl came around to me.

There would be no contact with any other crew members before or during the play. They would be in position, Glen assured me in a voice that left no doubt he had explained the importance of this item. I knew he was referring to Rollie. That free soul had a history of being late for engagements, whether because of smashing up a car, staying too long at a madam's house, or just forgetting, but this time it wouldn't be tolerated.

I visited my Hollywood makeup friend. I wanted my appearance changed enough so I wouldn't be recognized from photographs the casino might have, but not so much that the crew would do a double-take when they realized it was me. The plan called for me to be at the table only a few minutes, but I'd be inside the casino much longer. Once the dice were switched in, I was to find a place at the nearby bar and stay until the play was over. If anything went wrong, Glen wanted me present and ready to react however seemed appropriate.

Mainly I spent hour after hour practicing the move. The key was getting the dice *locked up* in my left hand. If one was just a fraction off line, all of them would come out. It was a matter of feel and dexterity — I couldn't see the dice, of course, they were hidden by my own hand — and some strength was involved also.

I practiced right up until Saturday at noon when it was time to leave to catch the flight.

Los Angeles was bright and sunny, but when I landed in Reno it was dark, cold, and threatening. Snow had fallen two days earlier and was still on the ground, but this was nothing compared to the storm forecast for that evening. It was going to be a blizzard, and people were being warned to stay at home.

The first snowflake fell when my rented car was less than a mile from the airport. These weren't dancing, delightful snowflakes, the kind you like to watch fall past street lamps on clear Christmas Eves. They seemed grey and sooty, more like hard little projectiles. There was nothing delicate about them. And they were blown by a hard wind capable of pushing the moving compact car sideways. A man standing out in that wind, I thought, could be knocked down and bowled over, a human snowball tumbling down the mountain.

The closer I came to Tahoe, the more diminished was the visibility. I was just creeping along, and despite having the car radio on loud I could hear the wind howl, feel the vehicle shudder and fight for purchase on a road now invisible beneath hard snow. A blizzard in northwest Nevada, with the wind thundering out of the Sierra Nevadas, is not what most people think of when they picture this popular resort area. It can be the most fearsome killer.

The trip from Reno to Tahoe up in the mountains would normally take fifty minutes, but I was on the road almost three hours. I checked into my room at the Sands Motel, which is several blocks from the Nevada state line inside California. In fact, if you step out of a side door at Harvey's Wagon Wheel and walk across the street, you're in California. For reasons that are readily apparent, the crew had often stayed at the Sands. If a hurried departure was necessary, what could be better than to flee across the street to California? The security guards weren't going to follow. California authorities didn't want Nevada's problems spilling over its own borders. In his earlier years just such an exit was required of Glen. He raced across the street and then stopped to jeer at his frustrated pursuers. This was before the widespread use of cameras, one of the crossroader's worst enemies, and the increasingly long memories of casino authorities.

I turned on the television to check for weather bulletins, then relaxed on the bed. The blizzard outside was predicted to continue all night and maybe through the next day. I thought there was a good chance our play would be off. I didn't think everyone would make it, and knew Glen wouldn't go ahead if we were even one person shorthanded. But that would be okay, I reasoned. There were worse things than spending a few days at the Sands, with its pleasant lounge and excellent food. I might even meet some young singles on a ski holiday.

Outside the window I could see what seemed to be blowing sheets of snow, and a white landscape so desolate it might have been locked in a Siberian permafrost. It made me shiver just looking out that window. I figured I could forget about Glen, and at 8:00 p.m. when there was pounding on my door, I wondered who it might be.

"Goddammit, open up!" bellowed the belligerent voice of my friend.

He looked like the Abominable Snowman. Certainly he was big enough to be. His topcoat was covered with icy snow, his shoes were caked with the stuff, and the skin on his face appeared frozen stiff.

"Jesus," I said. "Did you walk here from Reno?"

"From the parking lot."

"You could have called. I figured it was off."

"Off? Hell, no, it's not off. I brought you the dice."

"Rollie made it in this snowstorm?" Rollie could total a car on the clearest day on a road straight as a rifle shot.

"I anticipated this. Had him come early."

"Well," I said, "I'll be there if I don't freeze to death on the way."

When I left the room I planned on walking — the road seemed virtually impassable — but just a few moments in that storm made me reconsider and take my chances with the car. It was well below zero outside and the wind was a gale, steady, harsh, and brutal. I was afraid my hands would freeze and wouldn't thaw out soon enough to lift those dice off the table.

Driving at a snail's pace, skidding and buffeted by the cold wind, I made it to the state border and parked on the California side. It was fifteen minutes before I was due at tableside, and I thought of warming myself inside Harrah's, which is just across the street from the Wagon Wheel. This latter casino, perhaps twenty stories high, loomed almost directly in front of me. I'd been in its magnificent rooftop restaurant, with its breathtaking view of the entire area, including beautiful Lake Tahoe. But it was crazy even to think of plodding through the snowdrifts to Harrah's. I waited five minutes in the car, then stepped out into the arctic air and made my way as best I could to the Wagon Wheel.

Outside the casino was a scene from a Jack London novel, but inside it was warm and toasty and alive with the sounds of a gambling house going full blast. The place was just about packed and would be overflowing when the main show let out. Actually, the blizzard was probably good for business. Hotel guests weren't tempted to take time for recreational activities like skiing or boating. The casino had them all to itself.

I had a minute or so to warm my hands. I sneaked a glance at the target table to see which player held the dice, and they were not far away from the position next to the stickman which I intended to occupy. A moment later, catching me by surprise, a smiling, vivacious Jan Deerwood was in my face, kissing me and greeting me as if she'd been awaiting my arrival with great anticipation. I hugged her and imagined, if anyone was watching, that we seemed like a handsome, loving couple together for an exciting Tahoe weekend. While we continued to talk animatedly, I reached inside my jacket pocket and locked up the eight rigged dice I intended to palm into the game. Together, still talking happily, we strolled as casually as we could to the scene of the action. The dice in my right hand felt uncomfortable, unwieldy, but because they were so oversized it couldn't have been any other way.

My mouth was dry, not like sawdust or cotton but a healthy dryness that told me I was nervous and had reason to be. As far as I knew, switching eight dice into a game had never been done before under real conditions. To be overconfident, not to be nervous, *that* would have been cause for alarm.

I pretended to take stock of the action. It was what many players do before plunging into the fray. My arms were folded over my chest; the back of my right hand, inside which were the dice, lightly brushed against the inside of my left elbow. It was a perfectly normal posture for a dice thrower.

Everyone was in position. Rollie, looking as flaky as ever, appearing to be slightly inebriated, was betting five-dollar checks and acting like this made him Diamond Jim Brady. The furtive

Jackie Gillitzer was on the opposite side of the stickman from me. His Peter Lorre appearance made him look so much like a weasel, someone whose picture just had to be on a post office wall, that he couldn't be guilty of anything. Skinny Minnie already had caught the attention of every man at the table, and probably the women too, but for a different reason.

Now there was added commotion, a buzz of excitement, and I knew the show was letting out and scores of new bettors were pouring into the casino.

The timing, which we could take no credit for, at least as far as the positioning of the dice was concerned, couldn't have been more perfect. In fact, the stickman's emptying the bowl in front of me caught me a little by surprise. But there wasn't any time to think. I could either do it or I couldn't. My left hand started down for the dice and a mini-hell broke loose.

"Jesus Christ!" Rollie bellowed, as his drink, glass and all, came waterfalling onto the felt. I could sense the disgust in the faces of other players, some of whom had been spattered.

"Sir!" Jackie Gillitzer was saying at the same time, drawing the addled stickman's attention to him, telling him how he wanted change and intended to place a bet for the boys.

And leaning over the table in an X-rated pose was Skinny Minnie.

I could have dropped all sixteen dice on the table and no one would have noticed. They didn't know whether to be disgusted with Rollie or filled with lust for Skinny Minnie.

But I didn't drop any dice. I like to think I wouldn't have been noticed switching those dice even if there had not been the spectacular diversions. When I had the casino's dice locked up in my left hand, I lifted them up and to my right, depositing them in Jan's open purse, and at the same time releasing the eight new dice in my right hand onto the table. As it worked out, I probably could have made one or two more switches without drawing attention. Rollie had succeeded in spattering one of the dealers, and a floorman had made an appearance to suggest that my fat friend call it a night. This, of course, was greeted by loud objections from Rollie. Meanwhile, Jackie Gillitzer continued to annoy the stickman for change. Skinny Minnie, after what seemed like an eternity bent over the table, remained an attraction just standing there. As soon as the dice were switched, Jan whispered some nonsense in my ear, and left. Had people been watching, and I don't think they were, they'd have thought she'd gone up to our love nest to wait for me.

It was crucial for Jan to get out. This made it impossible to find the purloined dice. And it made it impossible to pin the switch on anyone, in the unlikely event the house discovered the crooked cubes we'd introduced into the game.

Order restored (Rollie had left in a huff), I bet five dollars on the come line and hoped for a quick loss. I won five times before it occurred, a welcome sign that the dice were indeed weighted to favor numbers, but a tense time for me. Even wearing makeup, there was a danger of being spotted any time I came near a table.

I held the dice for so long I became afraid the bettors might arrive at the table before I could get away. Skinny Minnie and Jackie had already left, and I knew Glen must have telephoned our high rollers from the East, who had taken rooms in the Wagon Wheel, to tell them it was time to come downstairs and win the money. Glen had been waiting across the California state line in his car to receive news from the first crew member out of the casino that the dice had been switched.

I was at the bar drinking a Coke and trying to look casual when the bettors made an appearance. They were familiar faces in the Wagon Wheel. Various casino employees nodded at them to acknowledge their presence. The Katz brothers wore sport shirts and khaki pants, serious gambling attire for them, and Vinnie Carlyle sported an atrociously mismatched orange jacket and fire-engine red slacks. Even if I hadn't known his occupation, I'd have guessed bookmaker.

It wasn't necessary to be close enough to the table to follow every roll to know they were embarked on a blistering "hot streak" right away. When the numbers are appearing and big money is on the table, the entire casino somehow is aware of it, and an excitement pervades the air which is unique to the game of craps. It is something palpable, as if the air has grown more heavy, and cries of delight can be heard each time another number is thrown. People even in distant corners of the casino get word of what is going on, and gravitate toward the action. There are even books that say when the numbers are running you should run — not walk — to the site to attempt to catch part of the action. I think many gamblers have high hopes based on mostly fictionalized accounts of "breaking the bank," and even a relatively short run of numbers sets their blood racing and their imaginations on fire.

There wasn't any specific duty left for me to perform. My job was just to be there in case an emergency arose. I didn't think one would. Every casino knows there are occasions when the dice will wax hot, and all they can do is to suck it up and ride it out, wait until the immutable laws of averages restore sanity to what in the long run is a no-lose world for the house. The casinos hate these hot streaks — they really don't want anyone to win ever. But they have learned to live with them.

An hour went by. And hour and a half. I knew the bettors had well over $100,000 in winnings, and wondered how much longer they would go on. It wasn't of particular concern to me. Vinnie Carlyle, and especially the Katz brothers, had good feel for how far they could push. They wouldn't lose control in a paroxysm of greed.

Louis Armstrong was appearing in the Wagon Wheel lounge, and I could hear the strains of "Old Man Mose." Through the windows I could tell the blizzard was continuing unabated. On the rare occasions when an intrepid customer came in from the outside, a blast of cold air would enter with him. I was wondering how I'd be able to get back to the Sands Motel, when the lights went out.

They just died all at once. There wasn't even a warning stutter, and all of a sudden the Wagon Wheel was pitch black. There were a few howls of fear and surprise, and for an instant I feared the danger of a blind stampede. That thought was immediately replaced by wonder over whether this had anything to do with our play. My mind raced. Were we going to be grabbed in the darkness and hurried to a back room, to be beaten or perhaps even killed? Or would we be shot or knifed right there in the casino, a thousand witnesses nearby but none able to see?

The answer, of course, was more prosaic. The blizzard had knocked out electrical lines, plunging the Wagon Wheel and probably most of Tahoe into darkness.

The casino's emergency generating system sputtered to life about fifteen seconds after the blackout, but it would be a few more minutes before life returned to what the Wagon Wheel considered normal. I knew before I saw them that our play was over. But there they were, bosses all, big men dressed in dark suits, some of them tough guys, all of them thinking they were, walking between the crap tables and picking up all the craps. At the blackjack tables the same kind of men would be gathering up the cards. They thought they were clever, guarding against the possibility that during those fifteen seconds of darkness some sharpster had pulled a switch on them.

I laughed to myself. Did they really think someone would arrange a power failure just to cheat them? Or hang around in the hope a blackout would occur? But those men in the dark suits thought they were being very alert. After all the years we, and other crews, had beaten them, they were still cocky and arrogant about their methods, which in this instance amounted to locking the door after the horse was stolen. I guess the vast sums of money they won on the "up-and-up" provided them confidence, that and their fearsome images. Maybe they would never accept — for the sakes of their public image could not accept — that people shrewder than they were could beat them. Well, I thought, we didn't need a massive power failure to work our little number. We'd done it right under their noses.

With the dice now gone from the table, there was no reason to stay any longer. I'd get word to Glen, who by now had probably burned a whole tank of gas out there in his car, and then join my friends at the Sands. Glen would meet the bettors and split up the take.

I didn't have to wait for Vinnie Carlyle and the Katz brothers to leave. They were pros, unlike some bettors we had worked with, and could be counted on to get out without my urging.

Jackie, Jan, Rollie, and Skinny Minnie were in the Sands' comfortable Twilight lounge when I arrived, and I had to answer a flurry of questions about how it had gone. We got the money, I told them. A good amount, but I didn't know how much.

It came to $148,000. With the money we owed the bettors — $100,000 plus $30,000 more — it left us with $3,000 apiece. This was hardly a stunning amount; an hour's work opening slot machines would net us more. But Glen was just ecstatic. And I thought he had reason to be.

Glen beat out a rhythm on the table with his hands. He practically got up and did a tap dance. All the time he talked about our bright future, how with our new play our earning potential was limitless. All of us caught the exuberance of his spirit. We were dreaming big dreams.

A waitress came over and asked if we wanted to eat.

"Sure," said Glen, waving at the rest of us. "Five chilis." Then he pointed to himself. "And one T-bone."

It was just a joke with him. He was the boss, and ordering that way, as he always did when we were together, was what he imagined was a humorous way to emphasize the fact.

"No," he added, when the waitress seemed to be taken aback, "they've been good kids today. Make it six T-bones."

Glen was a master storyteller when he wanted to be, and he reached deep into his bag of experience this night to keep us entertained. Between stories he kept raving about our future, about all the plans he'd cook up, the adventures we'd have, the money we'd make.

It was good to see him so happy. It's how I want to remember him.

EPILOGUE

After the Macao caper, I went into a huddle with my accountant and learned the restaurant was a disaster. I had lost enormous amounts of money during the time I'd languished in jail. The accountant said business simply had tailed off after an initial success.

My friends told a different story. They said the restaurant was the most popular place on the boulevard, always packed.

I fired the accountant, hired a new one, and together we discovered the cause of my problem. The accountant had stolen from me, and so had the chef, the waiters, and the bartenders. I was lucky, I believed, that our new method at the crap tables had surfaced just at the right time.

I declared bankruptcy, dissolved the business, and went to Newport Beach to wait for Glen to call.

But he never did.

Glen was flying his Cessna from his ranch to Nevada to pick up Jackie. Glen said he was onto something big, and with our new play I'm sure it would have been.

Glen always enjoyed flying over his favorite whorehouse in Virginia City whenever he was in the area. He would buzz the house and the madam would come out and wave a white towel at him. This time something went terribly wrong and the plane crashed into a pile of boulders.

I attended the funeral in Virginia City, and it was a memorable one. The floral shops had never done such a business, and people came from everywhere. The crew bought two gigantic wreaths with four "7"s across each one of them to symbolize the jackpot. Several FBI agents were on hand filming everyone who attended the service, but no one paid any attention to them.

After the funeral I drove back to Newport Beach to sort everything out in my head. I thought about my talent, about the big money I could make on the crap tables and "21" tables and slots, about our new Space Age move, and, naturally, about organizing a crew of my own. But my heart wasn't in it. Besides, finding people as honest and loyal to one another as our crew had been might take a lifetime.

My ex-wife Peggy called one afternoon.

"What are you going to do now?" she asked.

"I don't know. The restaurant went under, and I'm through as a crossroader."

"Well," she said, "you had quite a ride."

There was a long silence at the other end of the telephone.

"Have you ever thought of opening a donut shop in Visalia?" Peggy asked.

We both laughed like hell.

AFTERWORD

by George Joseph
Casino Surveillance Expert
and Former Crossroader

"LAYING DOWN SIXES"

The crap scam that John Soares relates in this book is considerably different from the scam as I know it today. I frankly do not see how they could have successfully pulled it off consistently, as I have witnessed variations on this scam several times under close surveillance. It may well be that the surprise element, their nerve, and the particular setting in the casinos of the 1960s enabled them to accomplish it, but as I see it (perhaps because I expect it) the scam is realistically a one-roll proposition. Basically, the scam today works as follows: One player throws one die instead of two and another player on the opposite end of the table is placing a small late bet in the field at the same time leaving one die exposed on the layout with the 6 up. Several other players are doing the actual big betting and will bet as follows: (Bets will reflect the limits in standard casino play during the early and middle sixties.)

$500	Field Bet (Pays even money, double on 12)	
$300	Place bet on 10 (Pays 9 to 5 = $540)	
$300	Place bet on 9 (Pays 7 to 5 = $420)	
$100	12 "On the Hop" (Pays 30 for 1 = $3,000 - 1 roll bet)	
$200	11 "On the Hop" (Pays 15 for 1 = $3,000 - 1 roll bet)	
$300	Any 7 (Pays 5 for 1 = $1,500 - 1 roll bet)	
$1,700	Total Wager per Player	

("On the Hop" is a term which means the next roll of the dice. The proposition bets, 11, 12, 2, 3, any 7, any craps, C & E, are all one roll bets.)

OUTCOME PER ROLL BY NUMBER

# Thrown	Win	Loss	Net Win /Loss
If 7	$1,500	$500 - field $100 - 12 $200 - 11 $300 - 9 $300 - 10 $1,400.00	$100.00
If 8	0	$500 - field $100 - 12 $200 - 11 $300 - Any 7 $1,100.00	-$1,100.00
If 9	$500 field $420 place $920	$100 - 12 $200 - 11 $300 - 7 $600.00	$320.00
If 10	$500 field $540 place $1,040.00	$100 - 12 $200 - 11 $300 - 7 $600.00	$440.00
If 11	$500 field $3,000 On the Hop $3,500	$100 - 12 $300 - 7 $400	$3,100.00
If 12	$1000 field $3000 "Hop" $4000	$200 - 11 $300 - 7 $500	$3,500

Examining the Win/Loss figures, it becomes apparent that when this scam of throwing one die and killing the 6 on the other is employed, the cheats are hoping for a 5 or 6 on the fair die. Only 1 roll in 6 (the 8) loses money, 3 rolls win small amounts, and 2 rolls obviously make big money. Remember, the amount won is for a single roll of the dice per player. So, with several player accomplices and a little luck (2 rolls out of 6), big money can be made on 1 or 2 rolls.

If Soares and crew indeed laid down sixes for up to twenty rolls, which I think is next to impossible in today's casinos, they should indeed be ranked as the best crew of crossroaders in Las Vegas history. If I had to bet, I'd put my money on Soares.

4, 5, 6, "TOPS"

"TOPS" are mis-spotted dice. The same number appears on opposite sides of the cube. "TOPS" are based on the premise that you can't see more than three sides of a cube from one vantage point. When using 4, 5, 6 "TOPS" for casino play (very gutsy) the #7 cannot be thrown, nor can any number below 8.

With any six sided cube there are 36 possible combinations or ways they can land.

Fair Dice		*4, 5, 6, TOPS*
#2	1 way	1-1	#8	4 ways	4-4,4-4,4-4,4-4
#3	2 ways	1-2,2-1			all hardways
#4	3 ways	1-3,3-1,2-2	#9	4 ways	4-5,5-4,4-5,5-4
#5	4 ways	1-4,4-2,2-3,3-2	#10	8 ways	4-6,6-4,4-6,6-4
#6	5 ways	1-5,5-1,2-4,4-2,3-3			easy ways
#7	6 ways	1-6,6-1,2-5,5-2,3-4,4-3			5-5,5-5,5-5,5-5
#8	5 ways	2-6,6-2,3-5,5-3,4-4			hardways
#9	4 ways	3-6,6-3,4-5,5-4	#11	4 ways	6-5,5-6,6-5,5-6
#10	3 ways	4-6,6-4,5-5	#12	4 ways	6-6,6-6,6-6,6-6
#11	2 ways	5-6,6-5			
#12	1 way	6-6			

_____   _____
36 ways   36 ways

The betting strategy is as follows. Place all the numbers to the limit. (In the 60's 300 across the board on the numbers 4, 5, 6, 8, 9, 10. Even though the 4, 5, 6 points cannot be thrown with 4, 5, 6, TOPS the bets are made to simulate fair play as they cannot lose.) $300 on each of the "Hardways", 4, 6, 8, 10. The Hard 4 and Hard 6 cannot be thrown as there are no 2's or 3's on the cubes, but the bets are made to simulate fair play as they cannot lose.

OUTCOME PER ROLL BY NUMBER
4, 5, 6, "TOPS"

# *Thrown*	*Win*	*Loss*	*Net Win* */Loss*
8	$350 place bet $3,000 hardway $3,350	$500 field -$500	$2,850
9	$420 place bet $500 field $920	-0-	
10 easy	$540 place bet $500 field $1,040	$300 hard 10 -$300	$740
10 hard	$540 place bet $500 field $2,400 hardway $3,440	-0-	$3,500
12	$1,000 field $3,000 on the hop $4,000	-0-	$4,000

Remember the amount you won on the number above is per roll (if it hits) per player, and you can't lose! With three or four players on the game it's easy to see how much can be won in a few rolls.

(Note: The hardway proposition bets are not one roll bets. A hardway bet stays up unless the number is made "easy" or a 7 is thrown.)

"FLATS"

Flats are mis-shaped dice. Certain sides of the dice are slightly larger (Flat) 1/5000th to 1/10,000th of an inch. The laws of physics dictate that the cube will land on that side with the greater surface area more often than probability calls for. Betting the numbers which the flatted sides favor gives you a big advantage, but not a lock, for the dice will still lose, just not as often.

Although I may question a few technical matters regarding the cheating methods of Soares and crew, all in all, in my professional capacity as a surveillance expert (and a former crossroader), I have reason to believe that Soares and his crew are indeed among the best cheats to hit the Nevada casinos.

George Joseph
June, 1985